The SCIENCE Teacher's Activity-a-Day

Over 180 Reproducible Pages of Quick, Fun Projects that Illustrate Basic Concepts

Pam Walker • Elaine Wood

JOSSEY-BASS
A Wiley Imprint
www.josseybass.com

Published by Jossey-Bass
A Wiley Imprint
989 Market Street, San Francisco, CA 94103-1741—www.josseybass.com

Jossey-Bass books and products are available through most bookstores. To contact Jossey-Bass directly call our Customer Care Department within the U.S. at 800-956-7739, outside the U.S. at 317-572-3986, or fax 317-572-4002.

Jossey-Bass also publishes its books in a variety of electronic formats. Some content that appears in print may not be available in electronic books.

ISBN 978-0-470-40881-0 (pbk.)
ISBN 978-0-470-77061-0 (ebk.)
ISBN 978-0-470-87244-4 (ebk.)
ISBN 978-0-470-87245-1 (ebk.)

Printed in the United States of America
FIRST EDITION
PB Printing   10 9 8 7 6 5 4 3 2 1

ABOUT THIS BOOK

The Science Teacher's Activity-a-Day, by Pam Walker and Elaine Wood, is a book of 180 easy five-minute hook or sponge activities to captivate learners' attention. Hook activities are valuable for both the students and the teacher. Research shows that students are most active mentally at the beginning of the lesson. The activities in this book will interest and engage students in the lesson. Students who are interested are more likely to take in and retain information. In addition, hook activities enable students to link prior knowledge to the new topic as well as set goals for learning. For teachers, sponge activities can help reveal any misconceptions that students have on the topic. Through student participation in the hook, teachers find out what students already know on the topic, enabling them to fine-tune the lesson.

This one-of-a-kind book contains hands-on hook activities that are specifically designed for science classes. Starting science class with a fun activity puts the students in a receptive state of mind. Students begin to look forward to the first five minutes of class because they know that something new and interesting is coming their way. The hands-on activities are especially stimulating for kinesthetic learners. Research shows that the majority of students are kinesthetic learners, who learn best by becoming physically involved in the learning experience.

This volume is divided into three units, each of which focuses on one group of National Science Education Standards: physical science, life science, and earth science. In the physical science unit, concepts covered include organization of matter; interactions of matter; energy of motion; heat, light, and sound waves; and magnetism and electricity. Activities in the life science unit cover cells, genetics, evolution, diversity of life, ecology, and body systems. The final unit, on earth science, is composed of activities that focus on the structure of Earth systems, Earth's history, meteorology, the universe, and the solar system.

The authors have included activities in this volume that have high interest value, are easy to present to a class, and can be done with inexpensive, easy-to-find materials, such as string, clay, scissors, chalk, and plastic bottles. Most activities can be prepped and ready for class in about five minutes. All activities should be supervised by an adult and students should follow the standard safety rules of science classrooms. *The Science Teacher's Activity-a-Day* can help every science teacher get the lesson off to a dynamic start.

ABOUT THE AUTHORS

Pam Walker and Elaine Wood together have more than forty-five years of science teaching experience. Pam was the 2007 Georgia Teacher of the Year and as such served as a leader in developing science curricula in the state. Both are master teachers in Georgia and hold specialist degrees in science and science education. They are the authors of dozens of books for middle and high school science teachers and students. Their publications include *Crime Scene Investigations: Real-Life Science Labs for Grades 6–12* and *Hands-on General Science Activities with Real-Life Applications*.

CONTENTS

About This Book • *iii*

About the Authors • *iv*

*Correlations of Activities to the
National Science Content Standards* • *xii*

UNIT I. PHYSICAL SCIENCE

Section 1: Organization of Matter

1.1 Boyle's Gas Law: Marshmallow Under Pressure • 3

1.2 Buoyancy: Ketchup Packet Cartesian Divers • 4

1.3 Counting Molecules and Atoms:
   Number of Molecules of Chalk in Your Signature • 5

1.4 Identifying and Naming Isotopes: "EggCeptional" Isotopes • 6

1.5 Chemical and Physical Changes: Examining Paper for Change • 7

1.6 Physical Properties of Matter: Tootsie Roll Properties • 8

1.7 Density: Can't Hold a Good Ping-Pong Ball Down • 9

1.8 Atomic Size in Picometers: Cutting Paper to Atom Size • 10

1.9 Surface Tension: Why Some Insects Can Walk on Water • 11

1.10 Birds in Flight: How Birds' Wings Enable Them to Fly • 12

1.11 Mendeleev's Periodic Table: It Was All in the Cards • 13

1.12 Volume of a Cylinder: The Long and Short of Volume • 14

Section 2: Interactions of Matter

2.1 Acids and Bases: Cabbage Juice Indicators • 16

2.2 Polymers: Water-Loving Chemicals in Diapers • 17

2.3 Freezing Point: Why We Sprinkle Salt on Icy Roads • 18

2.4 Exothermic and Endothermic Reactions: Hot Packs and Cold Packs • 19

2.5 Chemical Reactions: Alka-Seltzer and Water Temperature • 20

2.6 Balancing Chemical Equations: Rearranging Atomic Dots • 21

2.7 Limiting Reactants: Putting a Halt to the Reaction • 23

2.8 Writing Ionic Formulas: Equating the Ions • 24

2.9 Single Replacement Reactions: Turning Iron into Copper • 25

2.10 Double Replacement Reactions: Trading Partners • 26

2.11 Polarity and Solubility: Breaking Bonds of Packing Peanuts • 27

2.12 Surface Area and Solubility: Sweet Solutions • 29

Section 3: Energy of Motion

3.1 Potential Energy and Kinetic Energy: Bouncing Golf Balls • 31

3.2 Potential Energy: The Energy of Falling Objects • 32

3.3 Friction Through a Fluid: Fluids and Falling • 33

3.4 Newton's First Law of Motion: Inertia—the Magician's Friend • 34

3.5 Law of Conservation of Momentum: Marble Collisions • 35

3.6 Static Friction: Going Against the Grain • 36

3.7 Newton's Second Law of Motion: Acceleration of the Coffee Mug • 37

3.8 Using the Speed Formula: Speedy Manipulations • 38

3.9 Newton's Third Law of Motion: What Is a Reaction? • 39

3.10 Inclined Planes: Making Lifting Easier • 41

3.11 Levers: First-Class Machines • 42

3.12 The Three Classes of Levers: Lots of Levers and Lots of Class • 43

Section 4: Heat, Light, and Sound Waves

4.1 Thermal Energy: What Does Temperature Really Measure? • 46

4.2 Measuring Temperature: Human Thermometers • 47

4.3 Refraction: A Real Light Bender • 48

4.4 Concave and Convex Mirrors: An Up-Close Look at the Spoon • 49

4.5 Magnifying Lens: Water Drop Microscopes • 51

4.6 Mechanical Waves: The Stadium Wave • 52

4.7 Transverse Waves: Anatomy of a String Wave • 53

4.8 Compressional Waves: Making Waves with a Slinky • 54

4.9 Sound and Its Mediums: Sound Matters • 55

4.10 Sound Vibrations: Rubber Band Music • 56

4.11 Sound and Water: Tuning Forks and Water • 57

4.12 Energy Conductors and Insulators: The Cook's Choice • 58

Section 5: Magnetism and Electricity

5.1 Charging by Friction: Balloons and Dancing Salt Grains • 60

5.2 Closed Circuits: A Battery, a Bulb, and a Paper Clip • 61

5.3 Electrochemical Cell: Nine-Volt Battery Electrolysis • 62

5.4 Resistance: Series and Parallel Circuits • 63

5.5 Making Electricity: A Shocking Activity • 64

5.6 Schematic Circuit Diagrams: Seeing the Circuit • 65

5.7 Electromagnets: The Art of Magnetizing a Nail • 67

5.8 Magnetic Field: Long-Distance Attraction • 69

5.9 Magnets: What's in a Refrigerator Magnet? • 70

5.10 Magnetizing Metals: The Magnetic Nail • 71

5.11 Magnets and Compasses: Which Way Is North? • 72

5.12 Magnetic Forces: Force Blockers • 74

UNIT II. LIFE SCIENCE

Section 6: The Cell

6.1 Characteristics of Life: Is It Alive? • 77

6.2 Energy Molecules: ATP and ADP • 78

6.3 ATP and Lactic Acid: Muscle Fatigue • 79

6.4 The Cell Cycle, Part One: Getting Started • 80

6.5 The Cell Cycle, Part Two: The Process • 81

6.6 Cell Transport: When It Comes to Cells, Small Is Good • 82

6.7 Proteins as Enzymes: Saltine Crackers and Amylase • 83

6.8 Plant Cell or Animal Cell: Shoestring Venn Diagram • 84

6.9 Enzymes: Temperature and Paperase • 86

6.10 The Mitochondria: Surface Area and the Folded Membrane • 87

6.11 Photosynthesis and Respiration: Formula Scramble • 88

Section 7: Genetics

7.1 DNA: Candy Nucleotides • 90

7.2 Chromosomes: Learning to Speak "Chromosome" • 92

7.3 Genetic Diversity: Crossing Over During Meiosis • 93

7.4 Genetic Combinations: Tall and Short Pea Plants • 95

7.5 Mendel's Law of Segregation: Cystic Fibrosis • 96

7.6 Dominant and Recessive Genes in Cat Breeding: Curly-Eared Cats • 97

7.7 Pedigrees: The Higgenbothum Hairline • 98

7.8 Sex-Linked Traits: Flipping Over Color Blindness • 99

7.9 Gene Splicing: Human Growth Hormone and Recombinant DNA • 100

7.10 Protein Synthesis: Modeling Transcription • 101

Section 8: Evolution

8.1 Natural Selection: Life as a Peppered Moth • 103

8.2 Advantageous Traits: Which Creature Is the Fittest? • 105

8.3 Primate Adaptations: The Importance of the Opposable Thumb • 106

8.4 Steps of Natural Selection: Natural Selection Sequencing • 107

8.5 Plant Adaptations: Features for Survival in the Rain Forest • 108

8.6 Adaptive Radiation: The Beaks of Darwin's Finches • 109

8.7 Variations and Survival: Pine Needle Variation • 110

8.8 Horse Evolution: Horse Height Over Time • 111

8.9 Fossil Dating: Stacking Up Rock Layers • 112

8.10 Antibiotic Resistance: Present-Day Evolution • 115

Section 9: Diversity of Life

9.1 The Six Kingdoms: Kingdom Match Game • 117

9.2 Vascular Plants: Checking Out a Fern Frond • 119

9.3 Flower Parts: Dissecting the Flower • 120

9.4 Food Storage in Seeds: Dissecting a Dicot • 122

9.5 Seed Dispersal: Where Plants Come From • 123

9.6 Animal Symmetry: What Symmetry Is This? • 124

9.7 Viruses: Nuts and Bolts of a Bacteriophage • 125

9.8 Bird Digestion: Why Birds Don't Need Teeth • 126

9.9 Examining a Fungus: Close-Up Look at a Mushroom • 127

9.10 Taxonomic Categories: Addressing Classification • 129

Section 10: Ecology

10.1 Energy Flow Through the Food Chain: The 10 Percent Rule of Energy Flow • 131

10.2 Population Growth Rate: Growing Exponentially • 132

10.3 Food Web: Piecing Together a Food Web Puzzle • 133

10.4 Population Estimations: Mark and Recapture of Wildlife • 134

10.5 The Importance of Niches: Extinction and the Paper Clip Niche • 135

10.6 Symbiosis: Want Ads for Mutualism • 136

10.7 Human Pollution: Plastic Killers • 137

10.8 Plant Growth Requirements: When Seeds Get Too Crowded • 138

10.9 Packaging and the Environment: Convenience or Conservation? • 139

10.10 Arthropod Behavior: Response of the Pill Bugs • 140

Section 11: Body Systems

11.1 The Role of Bile in Digestion: Emulsifying Fat • 143

11.2 Tendons: Visualizing How the Fingers Work • 144

11.3 The Heart: The Strongest Muscle of the Body • 145

11.4 Partnering of the Brain and Eyes: Putting the Fish in the Bowl • 146

11.5 Lung Capacity During Exercise: Balloons and Vital Capacity • 148

11.6 Blood Vessels: Arteries or Veins? • 149

11.7 Muscle Interactions: Pairing of the Biceps and Triceps • 150

11.8 Mechanical Digestion: The Initial Breakdown of Digestion • 152

11.9 Peristalsis During Digestion: Moving Food Through the Esophagus • 153

11.10 Why We Sweat: Staying Cool with the Sweat Glands • 155

UNIT III. EARTH SCIENCE

Section 12: Structure of Earth Systems

12.1 Core Sampling: Seeing Inside the Cupcake • 158

12.2 Metamorphic Rocks: Pressure and the Candy Bar • 159

12.3 Sedimentation: Making Sedimentary Rocks • 160

12.4 Soil Conservation: How Much of the Earth Is Usable Soil? • 161

12.5 Physical Weathering of Rocks: Sugar Cube Breakdown • 162

12.6 Mineral Hardness: Mineral Ranks • 163

12.7 Cross Section of the Earth: Egg Modeling • 165

12.8 Porosity of Soil Samples: Soil's Holding Power • 166

12.9 Groundwater and Permeability: Just Passing Through • 167

12.10 Water in the Ocean: Sink or Float? • 168

12.11 Ocean Currents: Temperatures Start the Motion • 169

12.12 Bottle Eruption: Volcanic Activity • 170

Section 13: Earth's History

13.1 Inferences from Fossils: Who Was Here? • 172

13.2 Magnetic Rocks: Lodestones • 173

13.3 Radioactive Rocks: The Age of Rocks • 174

13.4 Continental Drift: Puzzling Over the Continents • 175

13.5 Strength of Earthquakes: It's the Cracker's Fault • 176

13.6 Fossil Molds and Casts: Making Fossils • 177

13.7 Glaciers: Ice in Motion • 178

13.8 Deformation of Rocks: Rocks Under Stress • 179

13.9 Geologic Time Scale Model: Earth's History on a Football Field • 181

13.10 Graded Bedding: Breaking the Law • 182

13.11 Seismic Waves: Human Wave Form • 183

13.12 Mountain Building: Paper Peaks • 184

Section 14: Meteorology

14.1 Temperature Inversions: Weather Patterns and Pollution • 186

14.2 Cloud Formation: The Cloudy Bottle • 187

14.3 Warm Air Rises: Refrigerated Balloons • 188

14.4 Water Vapor: Dew on the Beaker • 189

14.5 Rain Gauge: Let It Pour • 190

14.6 The Loss of Ozone: Oxygen Is Not Just for Breathing • 191

14.7 Temperature: Do You Want That in Celsius or Fahrenheit? • 192

14.8 Heat Transfer: Spiraling Upward • 194

14.9 Read a Climatogram: Quick Take on Climate • 195

14.10 Air Has Weight: Living Under Pressure • 197

14.11 Make It Rain: Bottle Rainstorm • 198

14.12 Winds: Air Masses in Motion • 199

Section 15: The Universe

15.1 Telescopes: An Eye on the Universe • 201

15.2 Light-Years: Universal Time • 202

15.3 Star Constellations: How Many Do You Know? • 203

15.4 Viewing Constellations: Moving Patterns in the Sky • 204

15.5 The Gyroscopic Effect: Spacecraft Navigation • 206

15.6 Space Shuttle Orbits: Holding Onto Your Marbles • 207

15.7 Gravity and Space Instruments: Writing in Space • 209

15.8 Visible Light: A Blend of Colors • 210

15.9 Infrared Light: Feel the Heat • 211

15.10 Star Magnitude: The Brightness of Stars • 212

15.11 Inertia in Space: Objects Keep Moving • 213

15.12 The Parallax Effect: A Different Perspective • 214

Section 16: The Solar System

16.1 Planetary Revolutions: Birthdays on Mercury and Jupiter • 216

16.2 Jupiter's Atmosphere: A Stormy Planet • 217

16.3 Orbiting the Sun: Earth's Trip Around the Sun • 218

16.4 Planet Formations: How the Planets Were Made • 220

16.5 Surviving on the Moon: Lunar Trek • 221

16.6 Solar Eclipse: Blocking the Sun • 222

16.7 Astrolabe: Medieval Measurements • 223

16.8 Precession of Earth: Spinning on the Axis • 225

16.9 Lunar Surface Regolith: After the Meteorites Hit the Moon • 227

16.10 Weight and Gravity: Weighing In on the Earth, Moon, and Sun • 228

16.11 Auroras: Party Lights in the Sky • 229

16.12 Moon Face: The Moon's Revolution and Rotation • 231

Teacher's Notes • 232

Answer Key • 239

CORRELATIONS OF ACTIVITIES TO THE NATIONAL SCIENCE CONTENT STANDARDS

Standard Grades 5–12	Activity
Physical Science	
Properties and changes of properties in matter	1.1 Boyle's Gas Law: Marshmallow Under Pressure
	1.2 Buoyancy: Ketchup Packet Cartesian Diver
	1.3 Counting Molecules and Atoms: Number of Molecules of Chalk in Your Signature
	1.5 Chemical and Physical Changes: Examining Paper for Change
	1.6 Physical Properties of Matter: Tootsie Roll Properties
	1.7 Density: Can't Hold a Good Ping-Pong Ball Down
	1.8 Atomic Size in Picometers: Cutting Paper to Atom Size
	1.9 Surface Tension: Why Some Insects Can Walk on Water
	1.10 Birds in Flight: How Birds' Wings Enable Them to Fly
	1.12 Volume of a Cylinder: The Long and Short of Volume
Chemical reactions	1.5 Chemical and Physical Changes: Examining Paper for Change
	1.11 Mendeleev's Periodic Table: It Was All in the Cards
	2.1 Acids and Bases: Cabbage Juice Indicators
	2.2 Polymers: Water-Loving Chemicals in Diapers

	2.3	Freezing Point: Why We Sprinkle Salt on Icy Roads
	2.4	Exothermic and Endothermic Reactions: Hot Packs and Cold Packs
	2.5	Chemical Reactions: Alka-Seltzer and Water Temperature
	2.6	Balancing Chemical Equations: Rearranging Atomic Dots
	2.7	Limiting Reactants: Putting a Halt to the Reaction
	2.8	Writing Ionic Formulas: Equating the Ions
	2.9	Single Replacement Reactions: Turning Iron into Copper
	2.10	Double Replacement Reactions: Trading Partners
	2.11	Polarity and Solubility: Breaking Bonds of Packing Peanuts
	2.12	Surface Area and Solubility: Sweet Solutions
Motions and forces	3.1	Potential Energy and Kinetic Energy: Bouncing Golf Balls
	3.2	Potential Energy: The Energy of Falling Objects
	3.3	Friction Through a Fluid: Fluids and Falling
	3.4	Newton's First Law of Motion: Inertia—the Magician's Friend
	3.5	Law of Conservation of Momentum: Marble Collisions
	3.6	Static Friction: Going Against the Grain
	3.7	Newton's Second Law of Motion: Acceleration of the Coffee Mug
	3.8	Using the Speed Formula: Speedy Manipulations
	3.9	Newton's Third Law of Motion: What Is a Reaction?
	3.10	Inclined Planes: Making Lifting Easier
	3.11	Levers: First-Class Machines
	3.12	The Three Classes of Levers: Lots of Levers and Lots of Class
Transfer of energy and interactions of energy and matter	1.4	Identifying and Naming Isotopes: "EggCeptional" Isotopes

	4.1 Thermal Energy: What Does Temperature Really Measure?
	4.2 Measuring Temperature: Human Thermometers
	4.3 Refraction: A Real Light Bender
	4.4 Concave and Convex Mirrors: An Up-Close Look at the Spoon
	4.5 Magnifying Lens: Water Drop Microscopes
	4.6 Mechanical Waves: The Stadium Wave
	4.7 Transverse Waves: Anatomy of a String
	4.8 Compressional Waves: Making Waves with a Slinky
	4.9 Sound and Its Mediums: Sound Matters
	4.10 Sound Vibrations: Rubber Band Music
	4.11 Sound and Water: Tuning Forks and Water
	4.12 Energy Conductors and Insulators: The Cook's Choice
	5.1 Charging by Friction: Balloons and Dancing Salt Grains
	5.2 Closed Circuits: A Battery, a Bulb, and a Paper Clip
	5.3 Electrochemical Cell: Nine-Volt Battery Electrolysis
	5.4 Resistance: Series and Parallel Circuits
	5.5 Making Electricity: A Shocking Activity
	5.6 Schematic Circuit Diagrams: Seeing the Circuit
	5.7 Electromagnets: The Art of Magnetizing a Nail
	5.8 Magnetic Field: Long-Distance Attraction
	5.9 Magnets: What's in a Refrigerator Magnet?
	5.10 Magnetizing Metals: The Magnetic Nail
	5.11 Magnets and Compasses: Which Way Is North?
	5.12 Magnetic Forces: Force Blockers
Life Science	
Cells and their structure and function in living systems	6.1 Characteristics of Life: Is It Alive?
	6.2 Energy Molecules: ATP and ADP
	6.3 ATP and Lactic Acid: Muscle Fatigue
	6.4 The Cell Cycle, Part One: Getting Started

	6.5 The Cell Cycle Part Two: The Process
	6.6 Cell Transport: When It Come to Cells, Small Is Good
	6.7 Proteins as Enzymes: Saltine Crackers and Amylase
	6.8 Plant Cell or Animal Cell: Shoestring Venn Diagram
	6.9 Enzymes: Temperature and Paperase
	6.10 The Mitochondria: Surface Area and the Folded Membrane
	6.11 Photosynthesis and Respiration: Formula Scramble
Reproduction and heredity	7.1 DNA: Candy Nucleotides
	7.2 Chromosomes: Learning to Speak "Chromosome"
	7.3 Genetic Diversity: Crossing Over During Meiosis
	7.4 Genetic Combinations: Tall and Short Pea Plants
	7.5 Mendel's Law of Segregation: Cystic Fibrosis
	7.6 Dominant and Recessive Genes in Cat Breeding: Curly-Eared Cats
	7.7 Pedigrees: The Higgenbothum Hair Line
	7.8 Sex-Linked Traits: Flipping Over Color Blindness
	7.9 Gene Splicing: Human Growth Hormone and Recombinant DNA
	7.10 Protein Synthesis: Modeling Transcription
Regulation and behavior	11.1 The Role of Bile in Digestion: Emulsifying Fat
	11.2 Tendons: Visualizing How the Fingers Work
	11.3 The Heart: The Strongest Muscle of the Body
	11.4 Partnering of the Brain and Eyes: Putting the Fish in the Bowl
	11.5 Lung Capacity During Exercise: Balloons and Tidal Capacity
	11.6 Blood Vessels: Arteries or Veins?

	11.7 Muscle Interactions: Pairing of the Biceps and Triceps
	11.8 Mechanical Digestion: The Initial Breakdown of Digestion
	11.9 Peristalsis During Digestion: Moving Food Through the Esophagus
	11.10 The Reason We Sweat: Staying Cool with the Sweat Glands
Populations and ecosystems	10.1 Energy Flow Through the Food Chain: The 10 Percent Rule of Energy Flow
	10.2 Population Growth Rate: Growing Exponentially
	10.3 Food Web: Piecing Together a Food Web Puzzle
	10.4 Population Estimations: Mark and Recapture of Wildlife
	10.5 The Importance of Niches: Extinction and the Paper Clip Niche
	10.6 Symbiosis: Want Ads for Mutualism
	10.7 Human Pollution: Plastic Killers
	10.8 Plant Growth Requirements: When Seeds Get Too Crowded
	10.9 Packaging and the Environment: Convenience or Conservation?
	10.10 Arthropod Behavior: Response of the Pill Bugs
Diversity and adaptations of organisms	7.5 Mendel's Law of Segregation: Cystic Fibrosis
	8.10 Antibiotic Resistance: Present-Day Evolution
	9.1 The Six Kingdoms: Kingdom Match Game
	9.2 Vascular Plants: Checking Out a Fern Frond
	9.3 Flower Parts: Dissecting the Flower
	9.4 Food Storage in Seeds: Dissecting a Dicot
	9.5 Seed Dispersal: Where Plants Come From
	9.6 Animal Symmetry: What Symmetry Is This?
	9.7 Viruses: Nuts and Bolts of a Bacteriophage
	9.8 Bird Digestion: Why Birds Don't Need Teeth
	9.9 Examining a Fungus: Close-Up Look at a Mushroom

	9.10 Taxonomic Categories: Addressing Classification
Interdependence of organisms	6.11 Photosynthesis and Respiration: Formula Scramble 8.1 Natural Selection: Life as a Peppered Moth 8.2 Natural Selection: What Creature Is the Fittest? 8.3 Primate Adaptations: The Importance of the Opposable Thumb 8.4 Steps of Natural Selection: Natural Selection Sequencing 8.5 Plant Adaptations: Features Plants Use for Survival in the Rain Forest 8.6 Adaptive Radiation: The Beaks on Darwin's Finches 8.7 Variations and Survival: Pine Needle Variation
Matter, energy, and organization in living systems	6.2 Energy Molecules: ATP and ADP 6.3 ATP and Lactic Acid: Muscle Fatigue 6.11 Photosynthesis and Respiration: Formula Scramble
Biological evolution	8.1 Natural Selection: Life as a Peppered Moth 8.2 Natural Selection: What Creature is the Fittest? 8.3 Primate Adaptations: The Importance of the Opposable Thumb 8.4 Steps of Natural Selection: Natural Selection Sequencing 8.5 Plant Adaptations: Features Plants Use for Survival in the Rain Forest 8.6 Adaptive Radiation: The Beaks on Darwin's Finches 8.7 Variations and Survival: Pine Needle Variation 8.8 Horse Evolution: Horse Height Over Time 8.9 Fossil Dating: Stacking Up Rock Layers 8.10 Antibiotic Resistance: Present-Day Evolution

Earth Science	
Structure and energy in the earth system	12.1 Core Sampling: Seeing Inside the Cupcake
	12.2 Metamorphic Rocks: Pressure and the Candy Bar
	12.3 Sedimentation: Making Sedimentary Rocks
	12.4 Soil Conservation: How Much of the Earth Is Usable Soil?
	12.5 Physical Weathering of Rocks: Sugar Cube Breakdown
	12.6 Mineral Hardness: Mineral Ranks
	12.7 Cross Section of the Earth: Egg Modeling
	12.8 Porosity of Soil Samples: Soil's Holding Power
	12.9 Groundwater and Permeability: Just Passing Through
	12.10 Water in the Ocean: Sink or Float?
	12.11 Ocean Currents: Temperatures Start the Motion
	12.12 Bottle Eruption: Volcanic Activity
	14.1 Temperature Inversions: Weather Patterns and Pollution
	14.2 Cloud Formation: The Cloudy Bottle
	14.3 Warm Air Rises: Refrigerated Balloons
	14.4 Water Vapor: Dew on the Beaker
	14.5 Rain Gauge: Let It Pour
	14.6 The Loss of Ozone: Oxygen Is Not Just for Breathing
	14.7 Temperature: Do You Want That in Celsius or Fahrenheit?
	14.8 Heat Transfer: Spiraling Upward
	14.9 Read a Climatogram: Quick Take on Climate
	14.10 Air Has Weight: Living Under Pressure
	14.11 Make It Rain: Bottle Rainstorm
	14.12 Winds: Air Masses in Motion
Geochemical cycles	12.2 Metamorphic Rocks: Pressure and the Candy Bar
	12.3 Sedimentation: Making Sedimentary Rocks
	12.4 Soil Conservation: How Much of the Earth Is Usable Soil?

	12.5	Physical Weathering of Rocks: Sugar Cube Breakdown
	12.6	Mineral Hardness: Mineral Ranks
	13.8	Deformation of Rocks: Rocks Under Stress
Origin and evolution of the earth system	13.1	Inferences From Fossils: Who Was Here?
	13.2	Magnetic Rocks: Lodestones
	13.3	Radioactive Rocks: The Age of Rocks
	13.4	Continental Drift: Puzzling Over the Continents
	13.5	Strength of Earthquakes: It's the Cracker's Fault
	13.6	Fossil Molds and Casts: Making Fossils
	13.7	Glaciers: Ice in Motion
	13.8	Deformation of Rocks: Rocks Under Stress
	13.9	Geologic Time Scale Model: Earth's History on a Football Field
	13.10	Graded Bedding: Breaking the Law
	13.11	Seismic Waves: Human Wave Form
	13.12	Mountain Building: Paper Peaks
Origin and evolution of the universe	15.1	Telescopes: An Eye on the Universe
	15.2	Light-Years: Universal Time
	15.3	Star Constellations: How Many Do You Know?
	15.4	Viewing Constellations: Moving Patterns in the Sky
	15.5	The Gyroscopic Effect: Spacecraft Navigation
	15.6	Space Shuttle Orbits: Holding Onto Your Marbles
	15.7	Gravity and Space Instruments: Writing in Space
	15.8	Visible Light: A Blend of Colors
	15.9	Infrared Red Light: Feel the Heat
	15.10	Star Magnitude: The Brightness of Stars
	15.11	Inertia in Space: Objects Keep Moving
	15.12	The Parallax Effect
Earth in the solar system	16.1	Planetary Revolutions: Birthdays on Mercury and Jupiter
	16.2	Jupiter's Atmosphere: A Stormy Planet

	16.3 Orbiting the Earth: Earth's Trip Around the Sun
	16.4 Planet Formations: How the Planets Were Made
	16.5 Surviving on the Moon: Lunar Trek
	16.6 Solar Eclipse: Blocking the Sun
	16.7 Astrolabe: Medieval Measurements
	16.8 Precession of Earth: Spinning on the Axis
	16.9 Lunar Surface Regolith: After the Meteorites Hit the Moon
	16.10 Weight and Gravity: Weighing In on the Earth, Moon, and Sun
	16.11 Auroras: Party Lights in the Sky
	16.12 Moon Face: The Moon's Revolution and Rotation
Nature of Science	
Science in history	3.4 Newton's First Law of Motion: Inertia—the Magician's Friend
	3.5 Law of Conservation of Momentum: Marble Collisions
	3.7 Newton's Second Law of Motion: Acceleration and the Coffee Mug
	3.9 Newton's Third Law of Motion: What Is a Reaction?
	7.5 Mendel's Law of Segregation: Cystic Fibrosis
	8.1 Natural Selection: Life as a Peppered Moth
	8.6 Adaptive Radiation: The Beaks on Darwin's Finches
	13.4 Continental Drift: Puzzling Over the Continents
	15.4 Viewing Constellations: Moving Patterns in the Sky
	15.11 Inertia in Space: Objects Keep Moving
	16.7 Astrolabe: Medieval Measurements
Science as an endeavor	All

UNIT I
Physical Science

SECTION ONE

Organization of Matter

The physical sciences focus on the nature and structure of matter and energy. In this section we offer students activities that help them investigate and understand key concepts related to matter. All matter is made up of smaller particles. Materials, or particular types of matter, may be pure substances, such as elements or compounds, or mixtures. On the simplest level, everything on Earth, from the human body to the entire biosphere, is made up of elements. The particles of matter have physical and chemical properties that help us characterize them. Physical properties include hardness, strength, density, and melting point. Chemical properties of matter refer to the way matter interacts with other substances. Particles may exist as solids, liquids, or gases. Experiments in this section examine gas laws, buoyancy, density, volume, chemical changes, and the periodic table of elements.

1.1. BOYLE'S GAS LAW
Marshmallow Under Pressure

Boyle's Law states that when temperature is held constant, the *volume*—the amount of space occupied by matter—of a gas is inversely proportional to its *pressure*, the force per unit area. This simply means that if the pressure increases and temperature remains the same, the volume decreases. The opposite is also true (if the pressure decreases and the temperature remains the same, the volume increases). This activity will demonstrate Boyle's Law using a marshmallow and a syringe.

 **Materials**

Large plastic syringe (without a needle); Large marshmallow; Felt-tip pen

Activity

1. Draw a face on one side of the marshmallow and place it in the plastic syringe so the face can be seen from the side.
2. Place your thumb over the end of the syringe where the needle is usually located. Holding your thumb in place, push in the plunger. Observe what happens to the marshmallow as you do so.

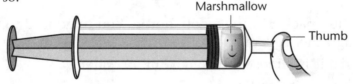

FIGURE 1.1. Boyle's Gas Law: Plunger In

3. With your thumb still in place, pull the plunger out and observe what happens.

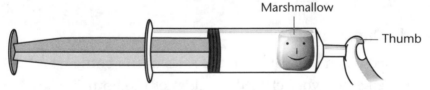

FIGURE 1.2. Boyle's Gas Law: Plunger Out

Follow-Up Questions

1. Marshmallows have bubbles of air trapped inside. What happened to the marshmallow when you pushed in the plunger? What happened when the plunger was pulled out?
2. Relate this demonstration to the definition of Boyle's Law. How did this demonstration verify the accuracy of that law?

Extension: Try to think of a real-life example of Boyle's Law in action.

1.2. BUOYANCY
Ketchup Packet Cartesian Divers

Objects either float or sink in water because of their *buoyancy*. An object placed in water pushes aside, or *displaces*, some of the water. If the weight of water displaced exceeds the weight of the object in the water, the object floats. A ketchup packet in a bottle of water can act as a Cartesian diver (named for René Descartes), floating or sinking as the outside of the bottle is squeezed. Changes in pressure on the bottle affect the sizes of the air bubbles inside the packet, changing the amount of water the packet displaces. As a result, the ketchup packet moves up and down in the bottle.

✓ Materials

Empty two-liter clear plastic bottle and cap (all outside labels removed)
Small packet of ketchup
Water

Activity

1. Place the ketchup packet in the empty bottle. You may need to bend the packet to get it through the neck of the bottle.
2. Fill the bottle so it is almost completely full of water.
3. Tighten the cap on the bottle.
4. Squeeze the sides of the bottle and see what happens to the packet.
5. Release the sides of the bottle and watch what happens.

❓ Follow-Up Questions

1. What happened when you squeezed the sides of the bottle?
2. What happened when you released the sides of the bottle?
3. Explain in your own words how buoyancy caused the ketchup packet to act as it did.

➕ Extension

Try using other condiment packets as divers. Also try a clear soy sauce packet. Watch carefully and see if you can actually see the change in the size of the air bubble within this packet as you squeeze the outside of the bottle.

1.3. COUNTING MOLECULES AND ATOMS
Number of Molecules of Chalk in Your Signature

Chemists often work with large numbers of small particles. To make counting easier, they use a unit called a *mole*. One mole of anything is equal to 6.02×10^{23}. Chalk is calcium carbonate: $CaCO_3$. One mole of calcium carbonate has a molar mass of 100 grams. Using this information, you can mathematically calculate how many molecules of chalk you use when signing your name on the board.

✔ Materials

Triple beam or electronic balance; Access to a chalkboard; Piece of chalk; Calculator

Activity

1. Use the balance to weigh and record the mass of the piece of chalk.
2. Sign your full name on the chalkboard.
3. Reweigh the piece of chalk and record the mass.
4. Subtract the new mass from the original mass to get the number of grams of calcium carbonate you used to write your name.
5. Convert the grams of chalk to moles of chalk by dividing the grams of chalk used by 100 grams, the molar mass of calcium carbonate.
6. Convert the number of moles of chalk used to the number of molecules of chalk used by multiplying the number of moles by 6.02×10^{23}. This tells you the number of molecules of calcium carbonate required to write your name.
7. If time allows, compare your calculations with your classmates' results.

❓ Follow-Up Questions

1. How many moles of calcium carbonate did you use to sign your name?
2. How many molecules of calcium carbonate did you use to sign your name?

➕ Extension

If you want to determine the number of atoms of calcium carbonate you used when signing your name, multiply the number of molecules by 5. What number did you get? Why do you think you had to multiply by 5 to get this?

1.4. IDENTIFYING AND NAMING ISOTOPES
"EggCeptional" Isotopes

The *nucleus* (central core) of an atom consists of *protons* (positively charged particles) and *neutrons* (particles that don't have any electrical charge). *Electrons* (negatively charged particles) are found in levels, or *orbitals,* outside the nucleus. An electrically neutral atom has an equal number of protons and electrons. Some atoms occur as *isotopes*—two or more atoms with the same atomic number but different numbers of neutrons. When writing the name of an isotope, you write the name of the element, a hyphen, and the sum of the number of protons and neutrons found in the nucleus of that atom. For example, bromine-80 is an isotope with 35 protons, 35 electrons, and 45 neutrons.

✔ Materials

Plastic egg isotope (prepared by the teacher; see Teacher's Notes); Periodic table

Activity

1. Obtain an egg isotope from your teacher. This represents one of the isotopes of an element on the periodic table.
2. Examine the egg carefully and identify which structures inside the egg represent protons, neutrons, and electrons. The egg itself is the nucleus of the atom.
3. Use the periodic table to identify the element your egg represents.
4. Determine the specific isotope of the element.

❓ Follow-Up Questions

1. Which part of the egg represented each of the following? How many of each did you find?

   a. Protons   **b.** Neutrons   **c.** Electrons

2. Which element did your egg represent?
3. Write the correct isotope name.

➕ Extension

Obtain the eggs of five of your classmates. Write down the names of the isotopes of those five eggs. Compare your answer with your classmates' answers. Did you agree or disagree with their determinations?

1.5. CHEMICAL AND PHYSICAL CHANGES
Examining Paper for Change

Substances can undergo changes that do not always involve chemical reactions. When ice melts and changes to water, the appearance of the substance changes but its chemical composition remains the same. As ice or water, the substance is still H_2O. Melting is an example of a *physical change*. During a *chemical change*, such as the formation of rust (iron oxide) from iron, a new substance is formed. The following activity will test your ability to differentiate between chemical and physical changes that might occur in a piece of paper.

✔ Materials

Envelope prepared by the teacher (see Teacher's Notes) that contains the following four pieces of paper (all the pieces were originally of equal size):

Burned paper

Paper that has a circle cut out of the middle

Paper folded over three times into a square

Paper that has been soaked in water and dried

Activity

1. Remove the four papers from the envelope and examine each one. All four papers were the same size before they experienced the changes you now see.

2. Examine each paper closely and consider what you know about physical and chemical changes.

❓ Follow-Up Questions

1. Which of the pieces of the paper do you think experienced chemical changes? Explain your answer.

2. Which of the pieces of paper do you think experienced physical changes? Explain your answer.

3. In your own words, write a sentence that differentiates chemical from physical change.

➕ Extension

If you were asked to prepare an envelope of items for another student so he could identify physical and chemical changes, what items would you select, and how could you modify each one to show these types of changes?

1.6. PHYSICAL PROPERTIES OF MATTER
Tootsie Roll Properties

Matter is anything that has mass and occupies space. Different types of matter are characterized by unique chemical and physical properties. We can observe the physical properties of a substance without knowing anything about its composition. One physical property of water is that it has a *density* of 1 g/ml. Density is a property of matter equal to its mass per unit volume. An object with a density less than 1 g/ml will float on water, but an object with a density greater than 1 g/ml will sink. In this activity you will calculate the density of a Tootsie Roll to see whether it will sink or float in water.

✅ Materials

Snack-size Tootsie Roll; Cup of water; Ruler

Activity

1. To calculate the density of a Tootsie Roll, use the formula D = m/v, where D represents density, m is mass, and v is volume.

   a. Find the volume of a Tootsie Roll. Since the candy is cylindrical in shape, use the formula V = 3.14 × r^2h. Unwrap the Tootsie Roll and measure its height (h) and radius (r) in centimeters. Use this information and the formula to find the volume of the Tootsie Roll.

   b. Most Tootsie Rolls this size have a mass of about 7 grams. Use the density formula to calculate the density of the Tootsie Roll. Remember that 1 cm^3 is equal to 1 ml.

2. Judging by your calculations, do you expect the Tootsie Roll to sink or float in water?

3. Place the Tootsie Roll in the cup of water to see whether your calculations were correct.

❓ Follow-Up Questions

1. According to your calculations, what was the density of the Tootsie Roll?
2. Did you expect it to sink or float in water? Were you right?

➕ Extension

Density is one physical property of a Tootsie Roll. Look at the Tootsie Roll and list three other physical properties it has. List three physical properties of water. How do they compare?

1.7. DENSITY
Can't Hold a Good Ping-Pong Ball Down

Density is a property of matter measured by its mass per unit volume.
The density of a substance can be calculated using the formula D = m/v, in which
D is density, m is mass, and v is volume. Two objects of equal size may have different
densities depending on their masses. A very dense object tends to fall down through
less dense particles. This activity will demonstrate how two objects of the same size
but very different densities act when placed in a medium that has an intermediate
density.

✅ Materials

Large beaker or glass jar
Bag of dried pinto beans
Ping-Pong ball
Metal ball (same size as Ping-Pong ball)

Activity

1. Place the Ping-Pong ball in the bottom of the beaker or glass jar.
2. Pour the pinto beans into the beaker with the Ping-Pong ball so the ball is completely covered.
3. Place the metal ball on the top of the pinto beans.
4. Gently shake the beaker or jar from side to side and watch what happens.

❓ Follow-Up Questions

1. What happened to the Ping-Pong ball after you shook it? What happened to the metal ball after you shook it?
2. What does this demonstration suggest about the density of the pinto beans?

➕ Extension

Find the actual density of the two balls by dividing the mass of each by its volume.
You will need a triple beam or electronic balance, a tape measure, and the formula
$V = 4/3\pi r^2$ (where π is 3.14 and r is the radius) to complete this task.

1.8. ATOMIC SIZE IN PICOMETERS
Cutting Paper to Atom Size

Atoms are extremely small. The specific size of an atom is shown by its location on the periodic table. However, all atoms range in size from 32 picometers to 225 picometers. A *picometer* is one-trillionth of a meter, or 1×10^{-12} m. To put this in perspective, the width of an atom is about one-millionth the width of a human hair. The width of a human hair is one-tenth of a millimeter. In this activity you will visualize atomic dimensions by cutting a strip of paper in half as many times as possible.

✔ Materials

28 cm × 2.5 cm strip of paper (prepared by the teacher)

Scissors

Activity

1. Use your scissors and cut the strip of paper in half.
2. Keep one half and throw the other half away.
3. Cut this strip of paper in half again. Discard one half and retain one half.
4. Continue this process, keeping count of the number of cuts you have made, until you can no longer make any additional cuts in the paper.

❓ Follow-Up Questions

1. How many cuts were you able to make in the paper?
2. How many cuts do you think you would have to make to get a piece of paper the exact width of an atom?
3. Do you think you can see an atom with the naked eye?

➕ Extension

How many cuts would you have to make to get the paper to the size that is equal to the width of a human hair? Pluck out a piece of hair and devise a technique that would allow you to figure this out.

1.9. SURFACE TENSION
Why Some Insects Can Walk on Water

Water tends to form beads or drops. This ability of water molecules to stick together, a property known as *surface tension*, is due to the mutual attraction of water molecules. One side of each water molecule has a slight positive charge; the other side has a slight negative charge. The attraction of two molecules is maintained by a hydrogen bond. The high surface tension of water forms a kind of "skin" on the top of water. Lightweight insects such as water striders can scoot across the water's surface without sinking. In the following activity, you will examine the property of surface tension.

✅ Materials

Penny; Medicine dropper; Cup of water; Paper towel

1. Place the penny on a paper towel so the head side of the penny faces up.
2. Using the medicine dropper, slowly add small drops of water to the penny. Count the number of drops as you add them.
3. Notice what happens to the water as more and more drops pile up on top of the penny.
4. Continue this process until water finally spills over the side of the penny.

❓ Follow-Up Questions

1. How many drops of water were you able to place on the penny before it ran over the side?
2. Describe the appearance of the water on top of the penny just before it spilled over the side.
3. What finally caused the water to break through the "skin"?

➕ Extension

Stir a small amount of hand soap into the cup of water. Dry the penny and repeat this activity using the soapy water. Count the number of drops the penny can hold. Write a statement about how soap affects the surface tension of water. How would it affect the water strider's ability to walk on water?

1.10. BIRDS IN FLIGHT
How Birds' Wings Enable Them to Fly

Birds' wings, like airplane wings, have a specific shape that makes them perfect for flight. Air travels faster around the upper curved surface of the wing than it does around the lower flat surface. This reduces the air pressure on top of the wing. The greater air pressure below the wing lifts the bird upward in flight. The differences in air pressure above and below a wing are explained by Bernoulli's Principle, which states that as air speed increases, air pressure decreases. This activity will demonstrate how Bernoulli's Principle allows birds to fly.

 **Materials**

Two empty soda cans

 **Activity**

FIGURE 1.3. Bernouilli's Principle

1. Place two empty soda cans on their sides on a table so that the bottoms of the cans are facing you. Position both cans with only a small space between them.
2. Predict what will happen if you blow in the space between the cans.
3. Blow in the space between the cans so the stream of air travels along the length of the cans. Notice what happens to the cans.

❓ Follow-Up Questions

1. What did you predict would happen if you blew in the space between the cans?
2. What actually happened when you blew between the cans?
3. How does this activity demonstrate what happens to air that travels around the bird's wings when it is in flight?
4. What are the similarities between an airplane's wings and a bird's wings?

➕ Extension

Not all birds are able to fly. Do some research and find out why some birds can fly, but other birds cannot. Base your explanation on Bernoulli's principle.

1.11. MENDELEEV'S PERIODIC TABLE
It Was All in the Cards

The modern periodic table of elements, which is based on chemical properties and increasing number of protons, or *atomic number,* is different from the first periodic table developed by Dmitri Mendeleev in 1869. Mendeleev wrote the names, atomic weights, and physical and chemical properties of each element on a separate card, then arranged the cards to show trends or patterns. He discovered that the elements, when arranged in order of atomic number and by similar properties, formed a repeating periodic pattern. The patterns were so clear that Mendeleev predicted the locations on the table of undiscovered elements. In this activity you will simulate Mendeleev's technique of arranging cards into patterns.

✔ Materials

Nine element cards (prepared by the teacher; see Teacher's Notes)
Scissors

1. Cut out the nine cards and shuffle them.
2. Pretend these are nine of the elements Mendeleev was attempting to arrange into a pattern.
3. Based on the information on the cards, place the cards so that they form a pattern that makes sense.

❓ Follow-Up Questions

1. How did your group or arrange the cards?
2. Based on your arrangement, where would you put a card for an element that is a liquid with an atomic mass between 9 and 13? What would its atomic mass actually be?

➕ Extension

Look at the modern periodic table and find the elements that would not have fit correctly in Mendeleev's periodic table of increasing atomic mass. Explain why they do fit correctly in the modern periodic table.

1.12. VOLUME OF A CYLINDER
The Long and Short of Volume

Volume is the amount of space occupied by an object. You can calculate the volume of a cylinder by using the formula $V = \pi r^2 h$. In the formula, π is 3.14, r stands for the *radius* (one half of the diameter of a cylinder), and h for the height of the cylinder. Volume is measured in cubic centimeters or milliliters ($1\ cm^3 = 1\ ml$). In this activity you will examine two cylinders of different sizes made from overhead transparencies. You will predict the volume of the cylinders, then test your prediction to see if you were correct.

✅ Materials

Two overhead transparencies ($8\,1/2'' \times 11''$);
Packing tape; Aluminum pie plate; Sand

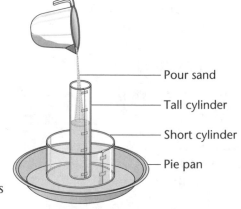

Pour sand

Tall cylinder

Short cylinder

Pie pan

FIGURE 1.4. Volume of a Cylinder

1. Make a cylinder from one of the transparencies by rolling it, starting at one long end so it stands at the tallest height possible. Do not overlap the ends of the transparency. Use tape to hold the cylinder in place.

2. Make a cylinder from the second transparency in the same way, but this time roll the cylinder from one of the short ends so it is shorter and fatter than the first one you made.

3. Look at the two cylinders and predict which one has the greater volume.

4. Set the short cylinder in the center of the pie pan. Now set the tall cylinder in the pie pan so it stands inside the shorter one. Pour sand into the tall cylinder until it is completely full.

5. Carefully lift the tall cylinder out of the pan, allowing the sand to fill the short cylinder.

6. Note how much sand filled the short cylinder.

❓ Follow-Up Questions

1. Which cylinder did you predict would have the greater volume?

2. After the sand experiment, which cylinder actually had the greater volume? Look back at the volume formula and explain why you think this was so.

➕ Extension: Use a metric ruler and calculate the actual volume of both the tall and short cylinders. Did your calculations match the results you saw from the activity?

SECTION TWO

Interactions of Matter

The atoms that make up matter undergo chemical reactions. In this section, students carry out activities to help them understand two important laws: the law of conservation of mass and the law of conservation of energy. The wide variety of chemical reactions is best understood by classifying them. Students examine chemical equations and use them to group reactions as single replacements or double replacements. During every chemical reaction, energy is either absorbed or released. Reactions that absorb energy are described as endothermic, and their products feel cool to the touch. Those that release energy, the exothermic reactions, feel warm. Students also explore factors that affect the rate of chemical reactions such as temperature, surface area, agitation, and concentration.

This section also includes activities on properties of acids and bases, bonding, freezing point depression, limiting reactants, formula writing, balancing equations, the relationship between polarity and solubility, and the relationship between surface area and solubility.

2.1. ACIDS AND BASES
Cabbage Juice Indicators

The term *pH* refers to the acidity or alkalinity of a solution. Substances that release hydrogen ions when dissolved in water are *acids*. The more hydrogen ions they release, the more acidic they are. Substances that release hydroxide ions when dissolved in water are *bases*. Alkalinity increases with the concentration of hydrogen ions. *Indicators* are chemicals that change colors when mixed with an acid or base. Cabbage juice is one type of indicator; it turns reddish-blue to red in acids and yellow to green in bases. In this activity you will test five solutions with cabbage juice to see whether they are acids or bases.

✅ Materials

Safety goggles

Piece of white unlined paper

About ten drops of red cabbage juice (prepared by the teacher; see Teacher's Notes)

Medicine dropper or pipette

Well plate or five small clear dishes (labeled as A1, A2, A3, A4, and A5)

Solutions partially filling wells (prepared by the teacher; see Teacher's Notes):

> A1: vinegar; A2: ammonia solution; A3: lemon juice; A4: baking soda solution; A5: Alka-Seltzer solution

Activity

1. Put on your safety goggles.
2. Place the piece of paper under your well plate so you can see the color changes clearly.
3. Place two drops of cabbage juice into each of wells A1 through A5.
4. Record the colors you see for each of the five substances you tested.

❓ Follow-Up Questions

1. Which of the substances in the well plate are acids?
2. Which of the substances in the well plate are bases?

➕ Extension

Cabbage juice is just one indicator of acids and bases. Litmus paper is another indicator used in science labs. Use litmus paper to check your results. What color do you think litmus paper turns in acids? What color do you think it turns in bases?

2.2. POLYMERS
Water-Loving Chemicals in Diapers

Baby diapers can hold lots and lots of water. Diapers are filled with a synthetic *polymer,* a large organic molecule made of repeating smaller bonded parts. Most synthetic polymers, such as those in plastic cups, are *hydrophobic,* or water fearing, and do not interact with water. But the polymer in baby diapers is *hydrophilic,* or water loving. Hydrophilic materials can interact with watery substances. In this activity you will see what actually happens inside the diaper when it comes in contact with water.

✅ Materials

Safety glasses; Diaper; Large piece of black construction paper; Resealable plastic bag; Four ounces of warm water; Scissors

1. Place the black paper on the desk top. Put the diaper on top of the black paper.
2. Put on your safety glasses. Use the scissors to carefully cut open the diaper.
3. Remove all of the polymer particles from inside of the diaper and place them in the plastic bag. The polymer looks like large grains of sand and will be trapped in some of the cotton stuffing. It's OK if some of the stuffing gets in the bag.
4. Blow a little air into the plastic bag and seal it so the bag is puffed up like a balloon. Shake the bag from side to side so the cotton will separate from the polymer powder. The polymer will be in the bottom of the bag.
5. Remove all the pieces of cotton stuck to the sides of the bag.
6. Add four ounces of warm water to the polymer in the bag. Watch what happens.

❓ Follow-Up Questions

1. What color was the polymer?
2. What happened when you combined the polymer with water?
3. Why do you think that babies in diapers are not allowed in swimming pools?

➕ Extension

Make some simulated baby urine by dissolving table salt in water. Obtain two baby diapers and see if a diaper can hold more tap water or "simulated urine." Try to find out the reason for this.

2.3. FREEZING POINT
Why We Sprinkle Salt on Icy Roads

If you live where there is lots of ice and snow in the winter, you may have noticed that the highway department spreads salt on the roads to prevent automobile accidents. Salt lowers the *freezing point* of water, the temperature at which water changes from a liquid to a solid, causing ice to melt. This activity will illustrate the effect of salt on ice.

✅ Materials

Large ice cube; Small bowl; Table salt; Small cup of water; Piece of thin string about eight inches long

FIGURE 2.1. Freezing Point Depression

1. Place the ice cube in the bowl and put the bowl on a table in front of you.
2. Dip one or two inches of the piece of string in the water to get that end of the string thoroughly wet.
3. Gently place the wet part of the string on top of the ice cube and sprinkle salt over the wet string until the salt completely covers the part of the string that's lying on the ice cube.
4. Wait about thirty seconds and lift the dry end of the string. What happens to the ice cube?

❓ Follow-Up Questions

1. What happened to the ice cube when you pulled upward on the string?
2. What do you think salt had to do with the success of this activity?
3. When making homemade ice cream, you add salt to the ice in the churn. Why is salt needed? What does the salt in an ice cream churn have to do with this activity?

➕ Extension

Repeat the activity using different types of salt. In this activity, you used table salt. Try using rock salt, "No Salt" (potassium chloride), and calcium chloride. Do they all work the same as the table salt?

2.4. EXOTHERMIC AND ENDOTHERMIC REACTIONS
Hot Packs and Cold Packs

All reactions, whether chemical or physical, involve energy. *Exothermic* reactions release more energy than they absorb. These reactions can often be identified because they cause an increase in temperature. *Endothermic* reactions absorb more energy than they release, so they cause temperatures to drop. In this activity you will compare an endothermic reaction to an exothermic reaction.

✔ Materials

Safety goggles; Resealable plastic bag of calcium chloride (prepared by the teacher; see Teacher's Notes); Resealable plastic bag of ammonium nitrate (prepared by the teacher; see Teacher's Notes); Water; Graduated cylinder

Activity

1. Put on your safety goggles.
2. Open the bag containing powdered calcium chloride. Using the graduated cylinder, carefully add 65 ml of water to the bag.
3. Seal the bag. Use your hands to knead the water and calcium chloride until all of the solid dissolves.
4. Can you feel any difference in temperature on the outside of the bag as the dissolving takes place? Set this bag to the side.
5. Open the bag containing solid ammonium nitrate. Carefully add 65 ml of water to the bag.
6. Repeat steps 3 and 4 with this bag.

❓ Follow-Up Questions

1. Which bag would make the better hot pack? Which bag would make the better cold pack?
2. In which bag did an endothermic reaction occur? In which bag did an exothermic reaction occur?
3. Do you know for sure whether these reactions were physical or chemical? Why?

➕ Extension

Repeat steps 1 through 3 substituting three tablespoons of potassium bromide for the calcium chloride. Would this bag make a hot pack or a cold pack? Was the reaction of potassium bromide with water endothermic or exothermic?

2.5. CHEMICAL REACTIONS
Alka-Seltzer and Water Temperature

A chemical reaction takes place when molecules collide with sufficient energy to break old chemical bonds and form new ones. Some reactions occur quickly, while others take place slowly. Temperature is one of the factors that can influence the speed of a chemical reaction. In this activity you will see how temperature affects the speed at which Alka-Seltzer reacts with water. Alka-Seltzer contains dried citric acid and sodium bicarbonate, or baking soda. When these chemicals are dissolved in water, they react, producing a fizz.

✔ Materials

Safety goggles

One small paper cup half-filled with room-temperature water

One small paper cup half-filled with very warm (but not scalding) water

One small paper cup half-filled with cold water

Three equal-sized pieces of Alka-Seltzer

1. Line up the cups of water in order from warmest to coolest.

2. Put on your safety goggles. Simultaneously, drop a piece of Alka-Seltzer tablet into each of the cups.

3. Compare the amount of fizz produced in each cup over the next few minutes. The fizz represents a chemical reaction occurring between the Alka-Seltzer and water.

❓ Follow-Up Questions

1. In which cup was there the most fizzing?

2. Write a statement that explains how water temperature affects the speed of this chemical reaction.

➕ Extension

See how surface area affects the speed of a chemical reaction. Use room-temperature water and two cups. In one cup place an intact Alka-Seltzer. In the other cup place an Alka-Seltzer that has been crushed into a powder. How do reactions in the two cups compare?

2.6. BALANCING CHEMICAL EQUATIONS

Rearranging Atomic Dots

In a chemical equation, symbols represent the *reactants* (starting materials) and the *products* (ending materials) of a reaction and the relationship between them. Chemical equations must be balanced by showing the same number of atoms of each element on both the reactant and product side. Coefficients can be used to balance an equation. A *coefficient* is a number written in front of a formula to show the relative amount of a compound in a reaction. In this activity you will learn to balance equations by using colored dots to represent atoms.

 **Materials**

Two index cards

Single hole puncher

Construction paper (blue, red, and green)

Clear tape

Activity

1. Work through the example to learn how to balance an equation:

   a. Write the equation ____ Mg + ____ O_2 → ____ MgO across the top of an index card.

   b. Use colored paper dots to represent atoms in the equation. To do so:

   i. Punch out one blue dot and tape it below the Mg.

   ii. Punch out two green dots and tape them together so they touch below the O_2.

   iii. Punch out a blue dot and a green dot and tape them together so they touch beneath the MgO.

   c. This equation tells us that 1 magnesium atom plus 1 oxygen molecule (composed of two atoms) yields 1 molecule of magnesium oxide.

   d. To find out whether the equation is balanced, compare the number of Mg atoms on the left side of the arrow with the number on the right. There is one Mg on each side.

e. Compare the number of oxygen atoms on both sides. There are two O's on the left, but one on the right. The equation is not balanced.

f. Add another MgO by taping a blue and green dot together and placing it under the other MgO dots. You now have equal numbers of O's on each side, but the Mg numbers are unequal. Add another blue dot under the Mg on the left side of the equation to balance the Mg atoms.

g. Finish by counting the dots beneath each atom or molecule and writing the coefficients in the blanks. The equation should read:

$$2\,Mg + O_2 \rightarrow 2MgO$$

2. Follow the same process to balance this equation on the back of your card. (Use a red dot to represent an atom of aluminum.)

$$\underline{\quad} Al + \underline{\quad} O_2 \rightarrow \underline{\quad} Al_2O_3$$

❓ Follow-Up Questions

1. Write the balanced equation from step 2.

2. Do you have the same types of atoms on one side of the equation as you have on the other side of the equation? What is different about them?

➕ Extension

Use the same process and three colors of construction paper to balance this equation:

$$\underline{\quad} Al + \underline{\quad} CuCl \rightarrow \underline{\quad} AlCl_3 + \underline{\quad} Cu$$

2.7. LIMITING REACTANTS
Putting a Halt to the Reaction

When a chemist is trying to produce a certain amount of a product, she needs to be sure she has an adequate amount of each reactant. If one reactant is in short supply, it will act as the *limiting reactant* because it restricts the amount of product that can be formed. The reaction ceases when the limiting reactant is consumed. Any remaining amounts of the other reactants are called *excess reactants*.

In this activity you will see the role that limiting reactants play in a reaction by organizing basketball teams. Each player represents a reactant. The team is the product. A team must be made up of two guards, two forwards, and one center.

✔ Materials

Seven index cards

Stick-on stars: fourteen yellow, seventeen blue, and five green

1. Your task is to form seven intramural basketball teams for summer camp. After evaluating the talent of the 36 players, you find you have 14 guards, 17 forwards, and 5 centers.

2. One index card represents one team. Yellow stars are guards, blue stars are forwards, and green stars are centers. Place the five appropriate stars on each card until you have formed the seven teams. If at any point you do not have the appropriate two guards, two forwards, and one center on a team, the process should stop.

❓ Follow-Up Questions

1. How many teams were you able to form?
2. If this had been a chemical reaction, which player was the limiting reactant?
3. Name the positions and the number of players at each position that represented the excess reactants in this example.

➕ Extension

Make up your own analogy for a limiting reactant and excess reactants. Explain the analogy in detail.

2.8. WRITING IONIC FORMULAS
Equating the Ions

Ions are charged atoms or molecules. Ionic compounds are formed when positive ions (*cations*) bond to negative ions (*anions*). When the charges of the ions are added together, they equal zero. The name of the cation is always written first and the anion second. For example, calcium oxide (CaO) is an ionic compound. The cation, calcium, has a charge of +2. The anion, oxide, has a charge of −2. The sum of +2 and −2 is zero. In cases where the sum of the charges does not equal zero, a *subscript,* a small number written after the ion symbol, can be applied. In this activity you will learn to write ionic formulas.

✅ Materials

White index cards; Blue index cards; Twenty pennies

 **Activity**

1. Work through the example that follows to learn to write an ionic formula. You will write the formula for sodium sulfide.

   a. The cation, sodium (Na), has a charge of +1. Write "Na" on a blue card and place one penny on top of that card. For sodium, one penny represents a set of charges.

   b. The anion, sulfide (S), has a charge of −2. Write "S" on a white card and place it next to the Na card. Place two pennies on top of this card. For sulfide, two pennies represent a set of charges.

   c. The number of pennies on these two cards is not equal. Add one additional penny to the sodium card. Now both cards have equal sets of charges.

   d. To write the ionic formula, show that there are two pennies on the sodium card by using a subscript. The formula for sodium sulfide would be Na_2S. S does not need a subscript because it has only one set of charges.

2. Follow the same process for the following pairs of cations and anions:

   a. Calcium (Ca) with a charge of +3 and chloride (Cl) with a charge of −1.

   b. Aluminum (Al) with a +3 charge and oxide (O) with a −2 charge.

❓ Follow-Up Questions

1. What is the ionic formula for calcium chloride?
2. What is the ionic formula for aluminum oxide?

➕ Extension:
Use the index card and penny method to write all the possible formulas that could result from combinations of the following ions: magnesium (Mg) +2, aluminum (Al) +3, fluoride (F) −1, and sulfide (S) −2.

2.9. SINGLE REPLACEMENT REACTIONS
Turning Iron into Copper

One type of chemical reaction is the *single replacement reaction*, also called the displacement reaction. In this type of reaction, one element replaces a similar element in a compound. The general formula for a single replacement reaction is

$$A + BC \rightarrow AC + B$$

Reactants (what you begin with) are shown on the left side of the arrow. In this case, A is an element and BC is a compound. *Products* (what you make) are shown on the right side of the arrow. AC is the new compound, and B is the new element. In this activity you will observe a single replacement reaction.

✔ Materials

Safety goggles; Small resealable freezer bag containing 2 teaspoons of copper sulfate powder (prepared by the teacher; see Teacher's Notes); Small cup containing 2 tablespoons of water; Marble-size piece of steel wool; Paper towel

Activity

1. Put on your safety goggles.
2. Your teacher has placed 2 teaspoons of copper sulfate in a plastic bag. The chemical formula for this compound is $CuSO_4$.
3. Open the bag and pour the water from the cup into the bag. Zip the bag closed. Gently knead the bottom of the bag to mix the contents. Observe the color of the liquid produced. You now have a copper sulfate solution.
4. Open the bag and drop the piece of steel wool into the liquid. Zip the bag and observe what happens over the next couple of minutes. Steel wool is made of the element iron. The symbol for iron is Fe.
5. Note any changes to the solution and the solid in the bag.

❓ Follow-Up Questions

1. What changes occurred in the liquid? What changes occurred in the solid?
2. If this were a single replacement reaction and your reactants were copper sulfate and iron, what would your two products be?

➕ Extension: Predict the products of this single replacement reaction:

aluminum + copper (II) chloride → _____

Ask your teacher if you can observe this by adding a piece of aluminum foil to a solution of copper (II) chloride.

2.10. DOUBLE REPLACEMENT REACTIONS
Trading Partners

There are many situations in life where items are traded or exchanged. Trades also occur in chemical reactions. In *double replacement reactions*, the positive ions exchange negative ion partners. A double replacement reaction is represented by the general equation

$$AB + CD \rightarrow AD + CB$$

An example of a double replacement reaction is the reaction of iron sulfide with hydrogen chloride:

iron (II) sulfide + hydrogen chloride yields hydrogen sulfide + iron (II) chloride

$$FeS + 2HCl \rightarrow H_2S + FeCl_2$$

In this activity you will compare buying popcorn at a concession stand to a double replacement reaction.

✔ Materials

Five pink index cards; Five green index cards; One white index card

1. Prepare the index cards as follows:
   a. Write "(A) Boy" on one pink index card, "(B) money" on one pink card, "(C) concession stand" on one pink card, "(D) popcorn" on one pink card, and "+" on the last pink card. The pink cards represent the reactant side of the analogy.
   b. Write the exact same things on the five green cards. These are the product side of the analogy.
   c. Write → on the white index card.
2. Remember that the general equation for a double displacement reaction is AB + CD → AD + CB. With that in mind, here is your analogy:

   A boy at the movie theater takes his money to the concession stand to purchase popcorn. The boy leaves with his popcorn as the concession stand clerk places money in the register.
3. Using the analogy above, arrange the eleven index cards on your desk to show what happened.

❓ Follow-Up Questions

1. How did you arrange the cards?
2. What were the positive ions in the analogy? What were the negative ions?

➕ Extension:
Now that you see what happens in a double replacement reaction, predict the products of a double replacement reaction that has the following reactants:

copper (II) chloride + sodium sulfide → _____

2.11. POLARITY AND SOLUBILITY
Breaking Bonds of Packing Peanuts

Packing peanuts, which are used to cushion breakable items during shipment, may be made of either synthetic or natural materials. Cornstarch peanuts are natural polymers made of chains of glucose. They are held together by *polar* bonds, which form between particles with slight charges. Styrofoam peanuts are made from a synthetic material composed of long chains of styrene. Bonds in styrene are *nonpolar* because the particles are not charged.

Certain liquid *solvents* (chemicals that dissolve *solutes*) will break the bonds holding the peanuts together and cause them to dissolve. Following the "like-dissolves-like" rule, polar solvents dissolve polar substances, and nonpolar solvents dissolve nonpolar substances. In this activity you will determine the polarity of solvents used to dissolve Styrofoam and cornstarch packing peanuts.

 Materials

Safety goggles

Four baby food jars (or other small glass jars) with lids

Nail polish remover (acetone)

Black wax pencil

Water

Several Styrofoam packing peanuts

Several cornstarch packing peanuts

Activity

1. Put on your safety goggles.

2. Use a wax pencil to label two jars as "Cornstarch." Place two cornstarch peanuts in each of those jars.

3. Label the other two jars as "Styrofoam" and place two Styrofoam peanuts in each jar.

2.11. POLARITY AND SOLUBILITY (continued)

4. Pour two inches of water each into one of the "cornstarch" jars and one of the "Styrofoam" jars.

5. Pour two inches of nail polish remover into the remaining two jars. Replace the four lids.

6. Observe what happens in the four jars. You may need to swirl the liquid around in the jars to mix it with the peanuts.

FIGURE 2.2. Polarity and Solubility

❓ Follow-Up Questions

1. Describe what happened in the four jars.

2. Using the "like-dissolves-like" rule, indicate the polarity of water and the polarity of acetone.

➕ Extension

WD-40 is a liquid lubricant made of nonpolar bonds. Do you think balloons are made of polar or nonpolar bonds? Blow up a balloon and spray some WD-40 on it and then answer that question.

2.12. SURFACE AREA AND SOLUBILITY

Sweet Solutions

The dissolving medium in a solution is called a *solvent*, and the substance being dissolved is called the *solute*. Several factors can influence the rate at which a solute dissolves in a solvent. For example, increasing the surface area of a solute speeds dissolving. Crushing or pulverizing a large solid into smaller pieces exposes more surface area to the solvent. In this activity you will see how surface area affects the rate at which candy dissolves in your mouth.

✔ Materials

Three after-dinner mints (small size)

Clock or watch with a second hand

Paper towel

Activity

1. Place an after-dinner mint in your mouth and hold it there without chewing or moving the mint around. Use the second hand of the clock to time how long it takes the mint to completely dissolve. Record the time.

2. Place a second mint in your mouth. This time move your tongue around, but do not chew the mint. Note how long it takes for the mint to dissolve.

3. Place a third mint in your mouth and chew it. Note how long it takes the mint to dissolve.

❓ Follow-Up Questions

1. How long did it take each mint to dissolve?

2. Scientifically explain your results. Use the following words in your explanation: *surface area, agitation, chewing, solvent, solute,* and *solution.*

➕ Extension

Do some research and list all the factors that affect the rate at which a solid dissolves in a liquid. Also research some factors that affect the rate at which a gas dissolves in a liquid.

SECTION THREE

Energy of Motion

The world is full of movement, from speeding cars to birds soaring through the air. Along with movement come collisions. In this section students learn about forces, movement, and collisions. Newton recognized that movement is a basic property of the universe, and he described movement in terms of speed, direction, and mass in his equation F (force) = m (mass) × a (acceleration). Newton also recognized friction, which opposes motion. In this section students experiment with simple machines, the devices that extend the effect that humans can produce with their muscles. Simple machines are ubiquitous in modern homes, found in kitchens, workshops, and garages. This section also includes activities on potential and kinetic energy, conservation of momentum, and inertia.

3.1. POTENTIAL ENERGY AND KINETIC ENERGY
Bouncing Golf Balls

Energy is constantly being changed from one form to the other. *Potential energy,* which is stored energy, can be converted into *kinetic energy,* the energy of motion. During the conversion, some energy may be changed into sound or heat, but the energy is never completely lost. In this activity you will see how potential energy changes to kinetic energy.

 **Materials**

Golf ball

Meter stick

1. Stand the meter stick on the floor so the "0" end touches the floor.
2. Hold a golf ball at the 100-centimeter mark of the meter stick. Practice dropping the golf ball straight down and catching it at the highest point of its bounce.
3. Once you have mastered this technique, drop the golf ball from the 100-centimeter mark and catch the ball at the maximum height of its first return bounce. Note that height on the meter stick.
4. Try this drop from a couple of lower heights as well.

Follow-Up Questions

1. Did the ball dropped from the 100 cm mark bounce back up to the 100 cm mark?
2. As you reduced the drop height of the golf ball, what happened to the resulting bounce height?

Extension

Repeat this activity, but this time use a tennis ball or Ping-Pong ball. Compare the results you got from these drops with the results from the golf ball. Speculate on the reasons for the differences in data you obtained.

3.2. POTENTIAL ENERGY
The Energy of Falling Objects

Energy is constantly being transformed all around us. The *potential energy*, or stored energy, of an object is dependent on the object's mass, the height of the object above the ground, and acceleration due to gravity (10 m/sec^2 on Earth). When an object falls, the potential energy is converted into *kinetic energy*, the energy of motion. In this activity you will see how the mass of an object affects its potential energy.

 Materials

Marble

Ping-Pong ball

Steel ball (no larger than the Ping-Pong ball)

Stick or can of soft modeling clay

Meter stick

Activity

1. Make a landing zone on the floor by forming a wide rectangular blob of soft clay that is about five centimeters tall.
2. Hold the Ping-Pong ball two meters above the clay landing zone. Release the ball and allow it to strike the clay below.
3. Use your ruler to determine the indentation depth (in millimeters) that the ball made in the clay. Record this value.
4. Smooth out the clay landing zone.
5. Repeat steps 2 through 4 with the marble and then with the steel ball.

Follow-Up Questions

1. Which of the balls made the deepest indentation in the clay? Explain why you think this was so.
2. Based on the results from this activity, which of the balls had the least potential energy? Which had the greatest potential energy?

Extension

If you have access to a triple beam or electronic balance, use the mass of each ball and the potential energy formula—potential energy = mass × acceleration due to gravity × height—to calculate the potential energy of each ball at the two-meter distance above the clay.

3.3. FRICTION THROUGH A FLUID
Fluids and Falling

Friction, a force that opposes motion, is all around us. Friction affects the motion between solid or liquid surfaces. *Fluid friction* occurs when a solid moves through a liquid or gas. Several factors affect fluid friction: the *viscosity* or thickness of the fluid, the surface texture of the solid, and the shape of the solid. In this activity you will determine how shape affects the movement of a solid through a fluid.

 **Materials**

Modeling clay

Large beaker or jar of water

Stopwatch

 **Activity**

1. Roll the modeling clay into two small balls of the same size.
2. Use your hand to press one of the balls into a flat shape.
3. Put the round ball into the beaker of water. Use the stopwatch to time how long it takes the rounded ball to fall to the bottom.
4. Remove the round ball from the water. Put the flattened clay in the beaker of water and use the stopwatch to time how long it takes the flattened clay to fall to the bottom.

Follow-Up Questions

1. Which of the two clay shapes took the longer time to fall to the bottom of the container?
2. How do you think shape affects the friction of an object moving through a liquid?

Extension

Get two pieces of notebook paper. Crumple one into a ball and leave the other one flat. Stand up and drop these pieces of paper from the same height and at the same time. Does one hit the floor sooner than the other? How did friction influence this?

3.4. NEWTON'S FIRST LAW OF MOTION
Inertia—the Magician's Friend

Sir Isaac Newton is well known for his three laws of motion. The first law of motion, the *law of inertia,* states that objects at rest will remain at rest, and objects in motion will remain in motion, unless acted on by an outside force. *Inertia*, a resistance to change, depends on both mass and friction. In this activity you will observe the inertia of a penny at rest.

✎ Materials

Plastic cup; Index card; Penny

1. Place an index card on top of the mouth of the plastic cup.
2. Put the penny on top of the card, so that it sits directly above the mouth of the cup.
3. Using your finger, thump the index card horizontally so the card flies off the cup and the penny drops into the cup below.
4. Repeat this process until you have mastered this activity.

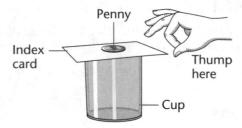

FIGURE 3.1. Law of Inertia

❓ Follow-Up Questions

1. Explain how this activity demonstrates the law of inertia.
2. How is this activity similar to the magician's trick of jerking the tablecloth from under a place setting of dishes without breaking any dishes?
3. Do you think the texture of the tablecloth is important to the magician?

➕ Extension

Try this activity with a quarter rather than a penny or with sandpaper rather than an index card.

3.5. LAW OF CONSERVATION OF MOMENTUM
Marble Collisions

If you have ever played pool or marbles, you have probably noticed that when a moving ball strikes a resting ball, the moving ball stops and the resting ball is set into motion. This phenomenon is due to the *law of conservation of momentum,* which states that the total momentum of objects that collide with each other is the same before and after the collision. Momentum affects how hard it is to stop an object that is already in motion. Momentum depends on the mass and velocity of the object and is affected by friction. If friction were completely eliminated, the total momentum would be completely conserved in collisions. In this activity you will observe the conservation of momentum in marble collisions.

 **Materials**

Ruler with a grooved top
Four marbles of equal size
Book

 **Activity**

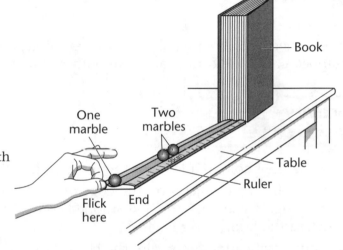

FIGURE 3.2. Law of Conservation of Momentum

1. Place the ruler flat on a table with the grooved top facing up. The ruler should be placed with the zero end near you and the other end away from you.
2. Place one marble in the grooved section about halfway down the ruler.
3. Place a book at the far end of the ruler to keep the marble from rolling off the table.
4. Put the second marble on the zero end of the ruler. Flick the marble on the zero end with your finger so it rolls down the groove and strikes the marble at the center of the ruler. Observe what happens.
5. Repeat these steps, but this time place two marbles at the center of the ruler.
6. Continue to vary the number and arrangement of marbles and observe what happens.

❓ Follow-Up Questions

1. What happened to the single center marble when it was struck by one marble? What happened to the marble that struck the one marble at rest?
2. What happened in the other collisions? How does this activity confirm the law of conservation of momentum?

➕ **Extension:** Get some large marbles and use them to strike smaller marbles. Observe what happens. Try using the small marbles to strike the large ones. Describe how the law of conservation of momentum explains the behavior of the marbles.

3.6. STATIC FRICTION
Going Against the Grain

Friction is a force that resists motion when two objects are in contact. There are two basic types of friction: static and kinetic. *Static friction* acts on objects that are not moving, and it always acts in the direction opposite to the applied force. Once an object is put into motion, the force that opposes further movement is *kinetic friction*. Static friction is much harder to overcome than kinetic friction. In this activity you will compare the static friction acting on different objects.

✅ Materials

Hardcover textbook

Three objects of about equal mass (for example, a rectangular eraser, a snack-size wrapped chocolate candy, and a smooth metal washer)

 **Activity**

1. Place the book on a table so the book binding is nearest you.
2. Place the three objects on the edge of the book that is opposite from the binding. If you have them positioned correctly, the items will slide toward you when the book cover is lifted.
3. Very slowly and gently raise the book cover. The objects on the edge will begin to slide toward you. Notice the order in which they begin to make their slide.

❓ Follow-Up Questions

1. Which object had the least static friction acting on it? Which object had the most static friction? Explain your reasoning.
2. If you wanted to increase the amount of static friction on these objects, what could you do? What could you do to decrease the static friction?

➕ Extension

In this activity you did not weigh each object to find its mass. Devise a procedure to test the effect that mass has on static friction. Perform your experiment and report your results.

3.7. NEWTON'S SECOND LAW OF MOTION
Acceleration of the Coffee Mug

Newton's second law of motion says that the acceleration of an object is directly proportional to the net force on, and inversely proportional to the mass of, the object. *Acceleration* is the change in velocity over time. Newton's law can be stated with this equation: Force (F) = mass (m) × acceleration (a). As the force acting on an object increases, the acceleration increases. As the mass of the object increases, the acceleration of the object decreases. In this activity you will observe the effect of Newton's second law of motion on a coffee mug.

✅ Materials

Large ceramic coffee mug with a handle
Spring scale
Small container of sand

1. Place the coffee mug at the end of a table farthest away from you. Hook the spring scale on the handle of the mug.
2. Pull the mug across the table at a very slow but constant speed. Look at the spring scale and read the force you are exerting. Record that force.
3. Repeat step 2, but this time increase the acceleration of the pull as you pull the coffee mug. Observe the spring scale reading.
4. Fill the coffee mug with sand and repeat steps 2 and 3. Note and record the readings on the spring scale each time.

❓ Follow-Up Questions

1. Look over your results. Did you see a correlation between force and acceleration? If so, what was it?
2. Did you see a correlation between acceleration and mass? If so, what was it?

➕ Extension

Calculate the acceleration in all three cases by using the formula F = ma. You can rearrange the formula as a = F/m. You will need to find the mass of the coffee mug without the sand and with the sand to carry out these calculations.

3.8. USING THE SPEED FORMULA
Speedy Manipulations

Speed is defined as the distance an object travels over a certain period of time. The formula to find speed is speed (s) = distance (d)/time (t). Some units used to measure speed are miles per hour, meters per second, or kilometers per hour. You will notice that miles, meters, and kilometers are all distances; hours and seconds are units of time. As long as you have two of the three values in the formula, you can calculate the third value. In this activity you will see how to use the speed formula by manipulating the values in a triangle to solve for the unknown.

✅ Materials

Large index card; Pen or pencil; Ruler; Scissors; Calculator (optional)

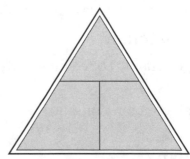

FIGURE 3.3. Using the Speed Formula

 **Activity**

1. Cut a large triangle out of the index card.
2. Draw a horizontal line about halfway down the triangle from one side of the triangle to the other.
3. At the center of the bottom half of the triangle, draw a vertical line from the horizontal line down to the base of the triangle.
4. Write the values representing the formula for speed (s = d/t) in the triangle. Write *s* in the bottom left box of the triangle. Write *d* in the uppermost box of the triangle, and write *t* in the remaining box. Look at what you wrote: s = d/t.
5. If you were asked to solve for distance and were given the speed and the time, you could calculate using the triangle. Because s and t are next to each other on the triangle, this means you multiply, so d = s × t.

❓ Follow-Up Questions

1. If you know distance and speed, how can you solve for time?
2. Use the triangle to solve this problem. A car goes an average of 60 miles per hour over a distance of 180 miles. How long has the car been traveling?

➕ Extension: Use the triangle you created and calculate the distance a runner would travel if his average speed was 8 kilometers per hour over a 2-hour time span.

3.9. NEWTON'S THIRD LAW OF MOTION
What Is a Reaction?

Newton's third law of motion, the *law of action-reaction,* says that for every action there is an equal and opposite reaction. If you use your arms to push against a concrete wall, you are exerting an action force on the wall. The wall in turn exerts a reaction force upon your hands. Since the wall does not cave in or move, the action force is equal and opposite to the reaction force. You will also notice that the action and reaction forces act on different objects. Your hands act on the wall, and the wall exerts a force on your hands. In this activity you will demonstrate Newton's third law of motion using spring scales.

 **Materials**

Two spring scales (both of which should read from 0 to 10 Newtons)

 **Activity**

1. Place the palms of your hands in front of you. Push your right hand hard against your left hand, but resist moving with your left hand. Do you feel the force of your right hand on the left? Do you feel the force of your left hand pushing back on the right? Are they equal forces? Opposite?

2. Hook the top portion of one spring scale around your right thumb. Position your right hand on the right edge of a table.

3. Hook a second spring scale to the first scale so the bottom portion of the second scale is hooked to the bottom portion of the first scale.

4. With the two scales attached, hold your right hand steady so it does not move. With your left hand pull horizontally on the top portion of the second spring scale until the reading on the scale measures 5 Newtons.

5. Look at the reading on the other spring scale. What does it read?

3.9. NEWTON'S THIRD LAW OF MOTION (continued)

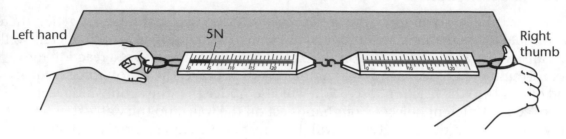

FIGURE 3.4. Third Law of Motion

❓ Follow-Up Questions

1. What did you experience when you pushed your palms together at the beginning of this activity?

2. What reading was showing on the spring scale that was being held steady? Was the reading on both scales the same? Explain the reason for this.

➕ Extension

Look at Figure 3.4, which shows the hands holding the two spring scales. Underneath the drawing, add arrows to show all of the forces at work. Remember to draw the forces interacting between the hands and the spring scales as well as the spring scales interacting with each other.

3.10. INCLINED PLANES
Making Lifting Easier

When the ancient Egyptians were building the pyramids, they created ramps to help them move gigantic blocks of stone to the upper levels. A ramp is a type of simple machine called an *inclined plane*. These flat, sloping surfaces make moving objects from one height to another easier. Inclined planes do not reduce the work done, but they do reduce the force required. In this activity you will find out how an inclined plane affects the force required to move a block.

✅ Materials

Spring scale (calibrated in Newtons); Masking tape; Wooden block; Stack of several books; Two pieces of cardboard of different lengths (for example, a twelve-inch piece and a sixteen-inch piece); Metric ruler

1. Stack several books on top of each other on a table. Measure the height of the books in meters. Make a note of the height.

2. Use masking tape to attach the wooden block to the hook on the spring scale. Once they are securely attached, pull on the scale to lift the block to the same height as the top of the stack of books. Read the force (number of Newtons) required to make that lift. Make a note of this force.

3. Select the shorter piece of cardboard and prop one end on the edge of the book stack to form a ramp. Now use the spring scale to pull the same block slowly up the ramp. Note the force required to make this pull.

4. Repeat step 3 using the longer piece of cardboard and note the force required to make the longer pull.

❓ Follow-Up Questions

1. How did the force required to lift the block straight up compare with the force required to pull the block up the first ramp?

2. Judging from your data, how does increasing the length of a ramp influence the amount of force needed to move an object from one height to another?

➕ Extension

Predict how much force would be required to lift the block if you used a piece of cardboard exactly one-half the length of the shorter piece. Cut the shorter piece in half and see if your prediction was correct.

3.11. LEVERS
First-Class Machines

A *lever* is a simple machine with a rigid arm that turns about a fixed point called a *fulcrum*. A first-class lever can be used to help lift a heavy object. This type of lever has the fulcrum located between the *effort force*, force applied to lift an object, and the *resistance force*, force created by the weight of the object that needs to be lifted. In this activity you will find out how the location of the lever's fulcrum affects the force required to lift an object.

✔ Materials

Stiff ruler; Small book; Pencil; Masking tape

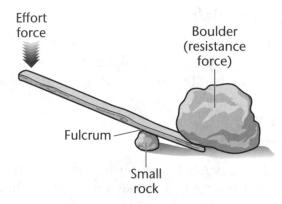

FIGURE 3.5. Lifting a Boulder with a Wooden Lever

1. Place a pencil on a table so it is horizontal to you. Tape the pencil to the table.
2. Place the ruler at a right angle across the top of the pencil so it acts like a teeter-totter or seesaw. The point where the ruler touches the pencil is the fulcrum.
3. Position one edge of a small book so it rests on one end of the ruler.
4. Arrange the ruler so that the fulcrum is six inches from the edge of the book. Push down on the effort end of the lever (the end opposite the book) to lift the book. Your push is the effort force. How difficult was it to lift the book?
5. Arrange the ruler so that the fulcrum is nine inches from the book. Push down on the effort end of the lever to lift the book. How difficult was this?
6. Arrange the ruler so that the fulcrum is three inches from the book. Push down on the effort end of the lever to lift the book. How hard was this to lift?

❓ Follow-Up Questions

1. What is the difference between effort force and resistance force?
2. How did the distance of the book from the fulcrum affect the effort needed to lift the book?

➕ Extension:
Stack six pennies on one end of a twelve-inch ruler. Place three pennies on the other end. Where must the fulcrum be located in order to make the ruler balance when placed on a pencil?

3.12. THE THREE CLASSES OF LEVERS
Lots of Levers and Lots of Class

Levers are simple machines that have a rigid arm around a fixed point or *fulcrum*. Force is transferred from one part of the arm to another. The *input* (effort) force is multiplied or redirected into an *output* (resistance) force. Levers are divided into three different classes. A first-class lever has the fulcrum between the input and output forces. A second-class lever has the output force between the fulcrum and the input force. The third-class lever has the input force between the fulcrum and the output force. In this activity you will sort different types of levers into their appropriate classes.

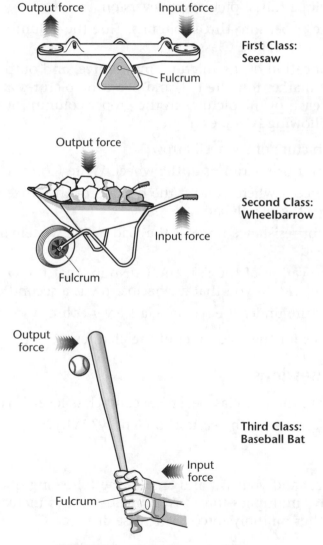

FIGURE 3.6. Three Classes of Levers

3.12. THE THREE CLASSES OF LEVERS (continued)

 **Materials**

An envelope containing pictures or illustrations of ten different types of levers (prepared by the teacher; see Teacher's Notes); White piece of paper; Magic marker; Glue or tape

Activity

1. Empty the envelope full of pictures of levers on a table.
2. Divide the white paper into three columns. Title the columns "First Class," "Second Class," and "Third Class."
3. Determine the location of the fulcrum, input force, and output force on each picture. Use the marker to write F, I, and O on the pictures at the appropriate locations. Glue each of the pictures in the proper column for the class of lever it represents. Following is one example:

   a. You have a picture of a wheelbarrow.
   b. The fixed point or fulcrum is at the wheel. Write F on the wheel.
   c. The input force is where you lift the handles of the wheelbarrow. Write I at the ends of the handlebars.
   d. The output, or resistance force, is the load in the wheelbarrow. Write O on top of the load.
   e. Look at the location of the F, I, and O. Notice that the O is between the F and the I, which tells you that a wheelbarrow is a second-class lever.
   f. Glue this picture under the second-class lever column.

4. Repeat these steps for the remainder of the pictures.

Follow-Up Questions

1. Which items were the first-class levers? Second-class levers? Third-class levers?
2. Which of the classes were the easiest to identify? Why?

Extension

Look at your pictures and your list and answer the following questions. Which class of levers always multiplies force? Which class always increases distance? Which class can either multiply force or increase distance?

SECTION FOUR

Heat, Light, and Sound Waves

Energy cannot be seen, but it is known by its effects. In this section students carry out experiments on energy and learn that energy cannot be created or destroyed, but is continuously changing forms. According to the law of conservation of energy, the total energy of a system is constant. Scientists classify the forms of energy into two major groups: energy of location (potential) and energy of motion (kinetic). Students examine both forms here, learning how lifting objects against gravity increases potential energy, as well as how kinetic energy accomplishes work. Experiments also include investigations on sound and light, comparing and contrasting the behavior of both forms of energy.

4.1. THERMAL ENERGY
What Does Temperature Really Measure?

Everything in the universe is made up of two basic components: matter and energy. Atoms and molecules make up matter. Particles of matter have *kinetic energy*, causing them to constantly vibrate or move. Because atoms and molecules are always moving, they generate heat energy. Temperature is a measurement of this heat. The temperature of a substance can be determined with a thermometer. In this activity you will see how increasing the movement of particles affects a material's temperature.

✔ Materials

Small sealable plastic container and lid

Sand

Thermometer

1. Place the bulb of a thermometer in the bottom of the plastic container. Pour enough sand into the container to completely cover the bulb.
2. After about thirty seconds, read the temperature of the sand.
3. Remove the thermometer and place the lid on the plastic container. Make sure the lid is sealed all the way around the container.
4. Shake the container vigorously for 2.5 minutes.
5. Remove the lid and submerge the thermometer bulb under the sand for about thirty seconds. Read the temperature of the sand.

❓ Follow-Up Questions

1. Did the temperature of the sand change after shaking? If so, how much?
2. Did the particles of sand experience a change in kinetic energy? Explain your answer.

➕ Extension

Design an activity that proves or disproves that the vigor with which the sand is shaken influences the temperature of the sand.

4.2. MEASURING TEMPERATURE
Human Thermometers

When you get ready to drink your hot chocolate on a cold day, you take a quick sip to see if the liquid is cool enough to drink. In other words, you make a qualitative judgment of the temperature of the liquid based on the sensation experienced by your mouth when you taste the liquid. A simple definition of *temperature* is the measure of the hotness or coldness of an object. If you had used a thermometer, you would have a more accurate, or quantitative, measure of the liquid. In this activity you will see whether human sensations are good indicators when it comes to measuring temperature.

 **Materials**

Three small Styrofoam cups labeled A, B, and C, with equal amounts of water in them, as follows:

>   A: very warm (but not scalding) water
>   B: room-temperature water
>   C: cold water

Stopwatch or clock with a second hand

Activity

1. Place the three cups of water in front of you on a table. Line them up in alphabetical order.
2. At the same time, place the index finger of your left hand into the water in cup A and the index finger of your right hand into the water in cup C. Keep these two fingers submerged for forty-five seconds.
3. After forty-five seconds, remove both fingers and alternately dip them one at a time into cup B.

Follow-Up Questions

1. How did the finger taken from the hot water feel when you dipped it in the room-temperature water?
2. How did the finger taken from the cold water feel when you dipped it in the room-temperature water?
3. Based on your findings, do you think human sensations are good indicators of temperature? Explain your answer.

Extension: Your fingers gave you a qualitative measurement of water temperature. Follow up this activity by taking a quantitative measure of the water temperature. Use a thermometer to take the temperature of each of the three cups of water. Compare the differences. The use of actual numbers to measure hotness or coldness is quantitative and a much more accurate measure.

4.3. REFRACTION
A Real Light Bender

Light normally travels in a straight line, but under certain conditions it will bend. The speed at which light is traveling changes when light moves from a medium of one density into a medium of a different density. For example, light slows when it moves from air into water, a denser medium. The slowing causes the light waves to change direction, or bend. The bending of light as it passes from one medium into another is known as *refraction*. In this activity you will observe this bending phenomenon firsthand.

✅ Materials

4″ × 6″ unruled index card; Black marker; Ruler; Drinking glass; Water

1. Lay the index card on a table.
2. Use the ruler and marker to draw a vertical line down the center of the index card parallel to the long edges of the card. The line should divide the card into two equal halves.
3. Place the bottom of the drinking glass on top of the line. Looking down into the glass, adjust its position so the line appears to divide the bottom of the glass in half.
4. While you continue to look down into the glass, pour water into the glass. Note what happens to the line in the bottom of the glass as you add water.

❓ Follow-Up Questions

1. What happened to the line in the bottom of the glass as water was added?
2. What caused the change in the appearance of the line?
3. Use what you learned today to explain why a fish you see swimming in the water is not located in exactly the place you think it is.

➕ Extension

Fill a glass half full of water. Place a drinking straw into the water. Look at the straw from both the top and the bottom of the glass. Look at it from the side of the glass. Focus on the point where the straw enters the water. Why does the straw look different depending on the angle of observation?

4.4. CONCAVE AND CONVEX MIRRORS
An Up-Close Look at the Spoon

Mirrors can be flat or curved. When you see your image in a flat mirror, it is not distorted. When you look at your image in a curved mirror, light rays leave the mirror at a different angle from the approaching rays, so distortions result. Mirrors can be curved either inward or outward. *Concave* mirrors curve inward, like the interior of a bowl. Makeup mirrors are concave mirrors because they enlarge the image. Mirrors that curve or bulge outward are called *convex* mirrors. This type of mirror gives a wide field of view and is used in security mirrors in stores as well as the side mirror on cars and trucks. In this activity you will use the opposite sides of a shiny spoon to compare the images produced by concave and convex mirrors.

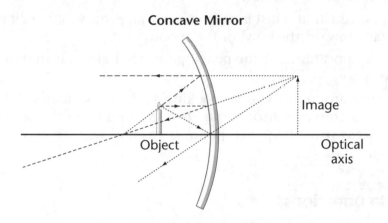

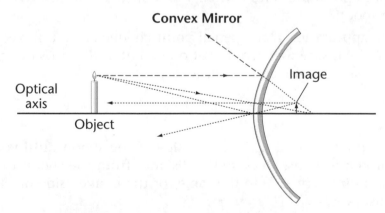

FIGURE 4.1. Concave and Convex Mirrors

4.4. CONCAVE AND CONVEX MIRRORS (continued)

✔ Materials

Shiny spoon
Sharpened pencil

Activity

1. Pick up the spoon by its handle and hold it so you are looking at the caved-in or hollowed-out side. You are looking into a concave mirror. Note whether your image appears larger or smaller.

2. With the spoon held at a distance from your face, move a pencil point slowly from your face toward the bowl of the spoon.

3. Note how the appearance of the pencil point changes as it moves closer to the bowl of the spoon.

4. Turn the spoon around so you are looking at the back side of the bowl. You are looking at a convex mirror. Note your appearance in the spoon. Repeat the same process with the pencil point as you did with the concave side of the spoon.

❓ Follow-Up Questions

1. How did your appearance differ when you looked at the concave and convex sides of the spoon?

2. How did the appearance of the pencil point change as you moved it toward the spoon? Which side was inverted at one point and right side up at another point? Which side magnified the image?

➕ Extension

Move the pencil point toward the concave side of the spoon until you get the pencil point into clear focus. Measure the distance from the spoon to the pencil. This is the focal point. Try and do the same for the convex side of the spoon. What do you discover?

4.5. MAGNIFYING LENS
Water Drop Microscopes

The invention of the microscope opened a new world to scientists. Some organisms and their structures can be seen clearly only when magnified. Early microscopes were very simple, and their quality depended primarily on the quality of their magnifying lens. The magnification of a lens is the ratio of the real object size to the image size you see through the lens. One of the simplest microscopes that you can make uses a drop of water for the lens. In this activity you will make a water drop microscope.

✔ Materials

Water; Dropper; Bottom of a clear CD case; Graph paper; Leaf; Ruler

1. Create a simple microscope by placing one drop of water in the center of the bottom of a CD case.

2. Place a leaf on a table. Position the drop of water in the CD case a few inches directly above the leaf. Position one eye directly above the water drop and see what the leaf looks like. Move the CD case and water drop up and down over the leaf until you have it in focus. Once the leaf is in focus, measure the height of the CD case and water drop. Is the leaf magnified?

3. Repeat step 2 using a piece of graph paper. Count the number of squares you can see using the water drop lens.

❓ Follow-Up Questions

1. How did the leaf look once you got it in focus? How many inches above the leaf did you position the water drop to have it in focus?

2. How many squares could you see on the graph paper using the water drop?

➕ Extension

Place a small hand magnifying lens on top of a piece of graph paper. Going from left to right, how many total boxes in one row does the widest portion of the lens cover? As you look down through the lens, raise it up from the paper. When you have the graph paper in focus, count how many boxes in one row you can see through the lens. To find the magnification of the lens, divide the number of boxes covered by the lens on the paper by the number of boxes seen when the lens was raised off the paper. How many times does this magnifying lens magnify things?

4.6. MECHANICAL WAVES
The Stadium Wave

Waves are disturbances that carry energy through a medium (whether solid, liquid, or gas). The type of waves that move through a medium are described as *mechanical* waves. Two types of mechanical waves are transverse and longitudinal. *Transverse* waves cause the particles of a medium to move perpendicularly to the direction the wave travels. *Longitudinal* waves cause the particles of a medium to move parallel to the direction the wave travels. In this activity you will mimic a stadium wave done at the ballpark.

Materials: None

1. As a class, pick a class leader to direct this activity. The leader should divide the class into team A and team B. Arrange the seats into two rows facing each other. All students will sit in the seats except for the leader.
2. The leader points to Team A. The student on the end of the row quickly stands, throws her arms overhead, and sits back down.
3. In sequence, the next students in the row, one at a time, mimic the action.
4. When the "wave" reaches the end of the row, the process repeats, moving back down the line. While Team A performs the wave, Team B observes.
5. The leader points to Team B, which repeats the process as Team A observes.

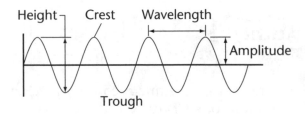

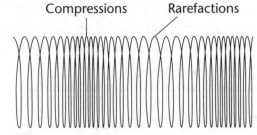

FIGURE 4.2. Transverse and Longitudinal Waves

Follow-Up Questions

1. Is the stadium wave an example of a longitudinal or transverse wave? In which direction did the wave move?
2. What was the medium in this activity? In which direction did it move?

Extension

If you were in charge of directing the class to model another type of wave, how would you do it?

4.7. TRANSVERSE WAVES
Anatomy of a String Wave

At some point you may have tossed a small stone into a pond and noticed the waves that result. A wave is a disturbance that moves from one location to another. Some waves travel through matter, called a *medium*. The medium can be a solid, liquid, or a gas. One type of wave, the transverse wave, causes the medium to move back and forth at right angles to the direction in which the wave travels. A simple transverse wave can be created by tying a rope to a door knob and snapping the free end up and down. The resulting wave will have alternating high and low points like mountains and valleys. These high points are called *crests,* and the low points are *troughs* (as shown in Figure 4.2 in the preceding activity). In this activity you will learn the parts of a transverse wave.

✅ **Materials:** Piece of string about 80 cm long; Metric ruler

1. Place the string on a table in the shape of a transverse wave. The distances between adjacent crests should be about equal.
2. Locate the crests and troughs on your transverse wave. How many crests do you have? The number of crests that pass a given point every second is called the *frequency*. We'll say that the number of crests you made represents the frequency of this wave.
3. Use the ruler to measure the distance from one crest to the next crest. This is called the *wavelength* of a transverse wave. Record that value in centimeters for the wave you just created.
4. Modify the wave you just created by halving the wavelength between each crest until you have used up all the string. You will see that your waves are closer together. What happens to the number of crests you can make?

❓ Follow-Up Questions

1. What is the difference between a crest and a trough?
2. Judging from your findings, does frequency increase or decrease when wavelength is reduced?

➕ **Extension:** Tie a rope to a doorknob or other permanent structure. Flick the rope up and down to make transverse waves with long wavelengths. Change the motion of the wave to make waves with short wavelengths. Notice what happens to the frequency.

4.8. COMPRESSIONAL WAVES
Making Waves with a Slinky

Sound requires a medium. When sound is produced, the medium vibrates in the same direction as the wave travels. This type of wave is called a *compressional* or *longitudinal* wave. You can use a Slinky to observe how energy and the medium are moving in a compressional wave. When you vibrate the coils at one end of a Slinky, the energy moves toward the opposite end and eventually rebounds back. Sound waves behave in much the same way, except that molecules of air are moving, rather than the coils of the Slinky. The sound moves by pushing molecules in the direction of the motion. In this activity you will use a Slinky to observe the characteristics of a compressional wave.

✅ Materials

Slinky; Piece of colored ribbon

1. Tie the piece of ribbon into a bow on the top of one coil on the Slinky.

2. Hold the Slinky so you have one hand on one end and your other hand on the opposite end. Place the Slinky on a table so it is horizontal to you and stretch it out as long as you can without letting go. Make sure the ribbon is still on top of one of the coils.

3. Using your left hand (and without letting go), push the Slinky toward your right hand. What do you see happening to the ribbon?

4. Allow the Slinky to come back to rest and repeat the experiment using your right hand to set the Slinky in motion toward the left hand. What is happening to the ribbon?

❓ Follow-Up Questions

1. Describe how the coils of the Slinky moved as they traveled.

2. Describe what happens to the ribbon. Does it travel along with the energy of the wave?

➕ Extension

Look back at Activity 4.7, on transverse waves. Use the Slinky to create a transverse wave on your desk. Describe how this movement is different from that produced by a compressional wave.

4.9. SOUND AND ITS MEDIUMS
Sound Matters

Sound waves travel through a medium by making its molecules vibrate. One molecule bumps into the next one and so on as the sound wave is transmitted through a series of collisions. The distances between molecules are different in solids, liquids, and gases, and these distances affect how well sound is transmitted through these different mediums. The molecules of a gas are far apart, while the molecules of a solid are packed tightly together. In this activity you will determine whether sound travels better in solids or gases.

Materials: Metal coat hanger; Two pieces of string (each about 50 cm long)

Activity

1. Turn the coat hanger so the hooked end is pointed down. Tie one string to one corner of the coat hanger and the other string to the other corner. When you finish, the strings should be almost equal in length.
2. Wrap one end of one string several times around the upper one-third of your right index finger. Wrap the end of the other string several loops around your left index finger.
3. Lift up on the two strings and make sure the coat hanger is fairly level.
4. Keeping the strings taut, swing the strings so that the hook on the coat hanger taps against the top of a table. Notice how loud a sound it makes. This represents sound traveling through a gas (the air).
5. Now place your index fingers in your ears (the string should still be wrapped around your fingers). Keeping the string taut, allow the hanger to tap on the table again. Notice the difference in the loudness or quality of the sound. This is sound traveling through a solid (the string).

Follow-Up Questions

1. Was the sound louder before or after putting your fingers in your ears?
2. In which medium—air or string—are molecules closer together?
3. Explain how the closeness of molecules in a medium could account for the difference in the sound volume.

Extension: Sound also varies depending on the composition of the solid matter through which it travels. Repeat this same activity using fishing line instead of string to hold the coat hanger. Also try a piece of metal wire to hold the coat hanger. Through which of these solids did sound travel best?

4.10. SOUND VIBRATIONS
Rubber Band Music

Sound is a form of energy that travels in waves. Sound is produced by the vibration of matter. A stringed instrument such as a guitar or violin produces sound when the strings vibrate. The pitch of the sound varies from high to low, depending on how fast the string vibrates. Pitch is dependent on factors such as the diameter, tension, and length of the string. In this activity you will find out how the diameter of a string affects its pitch.

✔ Materials

Very thick rubber band

Medium-thick rubber band

Thin rubber band

Activity

1. Put the thin rubber band over your five fingers and stretch your fingers so the rubber band is only lightly stretched.
2. Pluck the rubber band and listen for the pitch of the sound.
3. Stretch the rubber band farther by spreading your fingers. Repeat step 2.
4. Stretch the rubber band using both hands so it is very taut. Repeat step 2.
5. Repeat steps 1 through 4 with the medium-thick rubber band and then with the very thick rubber band.

❓ Follow-Up Questions

1. When you increased the stretch of each rubber band by spreading your fingers, did the pitch of the sound increase or decrease?
2. Which of the three rubber bands had the highest pitch when it was held in its tautest position?

➕ Extension

Position a wooden ruler on a desk or table so the majority of it extends off the edge. Gently push down and let go of the free end of the ruler so it vibrates up and down. Shorten the length of the ruler extended over the desk's edge and repeat this process. How is the loudness of sound affected by the length of the ruler?

4.11. SOUND AND WATER
Tuning Forks and Water

Sounds are vibrations that move through matter. When a tuning fork is struck with a rubber mallet, you cannot see the sound waves move out from the tuning fork, but you can hear them. When the mallet strikes the tuning fork, air molecules quickly bounce off the fork. The vibrations move through the air until they reach your ear, causing it to hear a sound. The vibration of air molecules is invisible to us. However, we can witness this vibration if it occurs in a denser medium such as water. In this activity you will observe the pattern of vibrations that occurs when a tuning fork is set in motion.

✔ Materials

Tuning fork; Glass of water; Rubber mallet; Paper towels

1. Place the glass of water on the paper towels.
2. Strike the tuning fork with the rubber mallet and look closely at the motion of the tuning fork. Can you see any movement of air molecules? Bring the tuning fork close to your ear and listen for the sound produced.
3. Stop the motion of the tuning fork with your hand.
4. Strike the tuning fork again and lower the upper part of the fork several inches into the water. What happens to the water?

❓ Follow-Up Questions

1. Could you see any motion of air molecules the first time you struck the tuning fork and held it in the air?
2. What happened when you struck the tuning fork the second time and lowered it into the glass of water?
3. How can you relate what you saw in the water to what happens when sound is produced in the air?

➕ Extension

Try variations of this activity by striking the tuning fork and holding it just above the surface of the water. What happens to the water? Also strike two tuning forks and place them both in the water at the same time. What happens?

4.12. ENERGY CONDUCTORS AND INSULATORS
The Cook's Choice

Because the particles in solids are very close together, they are generally better heat conductors than gases or liquids. A *conductor* is defined as a material through which energy can be transferred as heat. The denser a solid, the better it conducts heat. Cooks need some knowledge of heat conductors and insulators when working with kitchen utensils. *Insulators* are materials that transfer energy poorly. When boiling spaghetti in a pot, a cook wants plenty of heat energy to get to the food, but not to the handle. The handle needs to be a poor conductor. In this activity you will compare the heat-conducting abilities of utensils made of different materials.

✔ Materials

Large container of hot (but not scalding) water

Three spoons of about equal size: one plastic, one metal, and one wooden

1. Place the three spoons in the container of hot water so that each one is submerged to about the same depth.
2. Leave the spoons undisturbed for about one minute.
3. Carefully touch the top of each utensil to determine any temperature changes in the spoons.

❓ Follow-Up Questions

1. Which spoon was the warmest?
2. Which was the best conductor?
3. Why do you think one type of spoon conducted heat better than the others?

➕ Extension

The size and density of a material can affect its ability to conduct heat. Test this idea by forming a lightweight spoon out of some aluminum foil. Place this spoon and a regular spoon in a cup of hot water. Does the aluminum foil spoon conduct heat as quickly as the regular metal spoon? Explain your answer.

Magnetism and Electricity

The modern world relies on electricity, a form of energy that we know because of what it can do. Electric charges travel through conductors to produce heat, as in space heaters; produce magnetic fields, as in electromagnets or motors; form light-emitting chemicals, such as those in television screens; and cause chemical reactions, such as charging batteries.

Students set up electric circuits and analyze the role of the circuit components. This section also looks at magnetism, a force that is caused by moving particles. Magnetism is a property of permanent magnets and electromagnets. Other activities focus on static electricity, batteries, electrolysis, and compasses.

5.1. CHARGING BY FRICTION
Balloons and Dancing Salt Grains

Like charges repel, and unlike charges attract. You can create charges by rubbing a balloon across your hair. The balloon gains additional electrons and takes on a negative charge. Your hair loses electrons and becomes positively charged. This process is called *charging by friction*. The balloon will be attracted to other objects with positive charges or compounds containing *ions*, charged atoms. In this activity you will observe the behavior of charged objects.

✔ Materials

Balloon

Petri dish (or other small dish)

1 tablespoon table salt (approximately)

1. Sprinkle enough salt in the dish to lightly coat the bottom of the dish.
2. Blow up a balloon so it is about halfway inflated.
3. Briskly rub the inflated balloon on your hair. Notice what happens to your hair in the process.
4. Bring the balloon near the dish of salt. Observe what happens to the grains of salt.
5. Repeat steps 2 and 3, but this time look very closely and see if you can tell whether all the salt grains move with exactly the same orientation with respect to the balloon.

❓ Follow-Up Questions

1. What did you observe about your hair and the balloon? What did you observe when the charged balloon was brought near the salt grains?
2. Sodium chloride contains positive sodium ions and negative chloride ions. Which of the ions caused the change that occurred when the balloon was brought near the salt grains?

➕ Extension

Use a hole puncher and construction paper to make about twenty paper dots. Rub the balloon on your hair, then hold it near the dots. What happens? Why?

5.2. CLOSED CIRCUITS
A Battery, a Bulb, and a Paper Clip

An *electrical circuit* is a closed loop that has a power source, wires to conduct current, and a load. The *load* is anything that consumes energy flowing through the circuit, such as a light bulb. Some circuits also have switches so the power can be easily disconnected. The power source can be an electrical outlet or a battery. In this activity you will create a circuit that lights a flashlight bulb.

✅ Materials

D cell battery
Paper
Large paper clip
Flashlight bulb
Masking tape

Activity

1. Examine the materials. A battery has a positive terminal and a negative terminal. When they are connected, current flows between the terminals. A paper clip is a material that will conduct electricity. A flashlight bulb uses current. Masking tape can be used to hold parts of a circuit together.

2. Sketch a way to hook these materials together to make a complete closed circuit that will light the bulb.

3. Use the materials and assemble the circuit you sketched out. If it does not work and the bulb does not light, redraw the circuit and try again.

❓ Follow-Up Questions

1. What was the job of the paper clip in your circuit?

2. Did both the positive and negative ends of the battery have to be involved in the circuit?

3. Does an electrical circuit have to be closed? Explain your answer.

➕ Extension

Repeat this activity, but this time attempt to light two bulbs with your setup. If you find you need more batteries and/or paper clips, ask your teacher for permission.

5.3. ELECTROCHEMICAL CELL
Nine-Volt Battery Electrolysis

In *electrolysis,* electricity is used to create a chemical reaction. Electrolysis of water is the decomposition of water into oxygen and hydrogen gas. You can carry out the electrolysis of water using a battery as the power source and the points of a pencil (graphite) as the electrodes. This activity will enable you to observe bubbling of oxygen at the positive electrode, the *anode,* and bubbling of hydrogen at the negative electrode, the *cathode.*

✅ Materials

Safety goggles; Nine-volt battery; Shallow dish of water containing sodium sulfate (prepared by the teacher; see Teacher's Notes); Two pencils, sharpened at both ends; Two pieces of insulated copper wire (about six inches long) with insulation removed from the ends (prepared by the teacher); Electrical tape

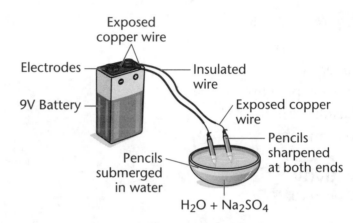

FIGURE 5.1. Electrolysis

1. Put on your safety goggles.
2. Use electrical tape to attach the two pieces of copper wire to the electrodes on the battery. Attach the free end of each wire to one of the pointed ends of each sharpened pencil.
3. Lower the free ends of each pencil into the shallow dish of water.
4. Watch for a minute until you see bubbling taking place at each end.

❓ Follow-Up Questions

1. Why did you need a power source in this experiment?
2. Complete this word equation:

   Water + Energy → _____ + _____

3. What do you think was the purpose of adding sodium sulfate to the water?

➕ Extension: In this activity we did not collect the gases. Think about a way you could have collected the gases if you had wanted to capture them. How could you have checked to see that the gases produced are oxygen and hydrogen, and not other substances?

5.4. RESISTANCE
Series and Parallel Circuits

An *electric circuit* is a complete path through which charges can flow. Circuits are classified into two basic types: series and parallel. In a *series circuit,* the charges have only one path to follow, so they must travel through each wire and *resistor*—an electrical device like a light bulb that resists the flow of electricity. In a string of lights in a series circuit, the more bulbs added to the series circuit, the greater the *resistance,* or opposition to the flow of electricity, and the dimmer each bulb shines. If one bulb burns out in a series circuit, the other bulbs go out as well because the circuit is broken. A *parallel circuit* has two or more paths through which charges can flow. If one bulb burns out in the parallel circuit, the charge can still flow along the other path. In this activity you will use drinking straws to demonstrate the difference in resistance along parallel and series circuits.

✅ Materials

Eight drinking straws (thin ones are best); Tape

1. Create a model of a series circuit by taping four drinking straws together end to end so you have created one long straw. Do not tape over the openings of any of the straws.

2. Create a model of a parallel circuit by evenly placing four drinking straws side by side on the table. Tape the four straws together in this configuration. Do not tape over the openings of any of the straws.

3. Blow through both straw models. Which of the two models was the easier to blow through?

❓ Follow-Up Questions

1. Which of the two models offered less resistance when you attempted to blow through them?

2. Judging from these models, is there more resistance in a series or parallel circuit?

➕ Extension

Carry out research on schematic diagrams. Draw a schematic of a series circuit with two light bulbs and a battery, and then draw one of a parallel circuit with two light bulbs and a battery.

5.5. MAKING ELECTRICITY
A Shocking Activity

A battery provides electrical energy by converting chemical energy into electrons' potential energy. A battery is made of metals and chemicals. You can make a simple battery out of pennies, dimes, and lemon juice. The two metals in the coins provide a source of electrons. One of the metals has a positive charge and the other a negative charge. Electrons collect at the negative metal. The lemon juice provides the chemicals to conduct electricity. When you connect the negative metal to the positive metal, electrons flow from negative to positive. In this activity you will use these materials to create a simple battery.

✅ Materials

Five dimes; Five pennies; Scissors; One paper towel; Small paper cup of lemon juice

1. Cut nine squares out of the paper towel. Each of the squares should be slightly larger than the size of a penny.
2. Place a penny flat on a table. Dip one of the paper towel squares in the lemon juice so it is saturated. Then put the square on top of the penny.
3. Place a dime on top of the lemon juice saturated square. Saturate a second paper towel square with lemon juice and place it on top of the dime.
4. Continue alternating dimes and pennies in this way. Each coin should be separated by a saturated paper towel square. Do not put a paper towel square on top of the last dime.
5. Dip the thumb and middle finger of one hand in the lemon juice. Use these two wet fingers to pick up the stack of coins. The thumb should be placed on the bottom penny in the stack and your middle finger on the dime on top of the stack.
6. Do you feel anything unusual when you pick up the stack?

❓ Follow-Up Questions

1. What did you feel when you picked up the stack of coins?
2. What did the coins and the lemon juice represent in this activity?
3. Do you think it was important to alternate the dimes and pennies in the stack? Explain your answer.

➕ Extension: Try this same activity using a lemon, a copper strip, a zinc strip, insulated wire, and a tiny light bulb. Can you figure out how to connect the materials so that the bulb lights?

5.6. SCHEMATIC CIRCUIT DIAGRAMS
Seeing the Circuit

Electrical circuits can be described with a *schematic diagram*. In this type of diagram, conventional circuit symbols are used to show the circuit and its components. The circuit symbols used in a schematic diagram are shown in Figure 5.2. In this activity you will make a model of a schematic diagram using a string and some conventional circuit symbols.

| DC Voltage | Resistor | Wires |

FIGURE 5.2. Circuit Symbols

 **Materials**

One-meter-long piece of string

Envelope containing the following items (prepared by the teacher; see Teacher's Notes):

> three resistor symbols
>
> three battery symbols (D cell)
>
> four arrows

Activity

1. You will build a model of a schematic diagram that shows a three-pack of D cell batteries used to power three light bulbs in series. You will also show the direction of conventional current flow using the arrows. Follow this procedure:

   a. Arrange the string on a table to form a rectangle. The string represents the copper wire in the circuit.

   b. On the side of the rectangle near your left hand, place the battery symbol. Position it on the string so the wide line (positive terminal) is facing north and the narrow line (negative terminal) is facing south. The current will flow out of the positive terminal and around the wire until it arrives back at the negative terminal. Place an arrow pointing upward from the positive terminal.

5.6. SCHEMATIC CIRCUIT DIAGRAMS (continued)

    c. Light bulbs are resistors. Find the three resistor symbols and place one on the top line of the rectangle, one on the right side, and one on the bottom line.

    d. Show the current flow by placing the remaining three arrows on the top, side, and bottom of the string so the current is flowing around and toward the negative terminal.

❷ Follow-Up Questions

1. What would happen to the circuit if there was a break in the string?

2. Use the model you made to draw this schematic diagram on paper.

➕ Extension

This activity connects three light bulbs in series. Get a second piece of string and show three light bulbs wired in parallel.

5.7. ELECTROMAGNETS
The Art of Magnetizing a Nail

The movement of electric charges through iron, copper, and some other metallic materials creates a magnetic field. When coils of metal wire are wrapped around an iron core, the magnetic field of the coils magnetizes the iron. Any current-carrying wire wrapped around an iron core is called an *electromagnet*. In this activity you will find out how the number of wire coils around the core of an electromagnet affects its strength.

Materials

D cell battery; Large iron nail; Insulated copper wire with about two inches of insulation removed from the ends (prepared by the teacher); Masking tape; Fifty small paper clips

Activity

1. Wrap the copper wire around the center portion of the nail ten times. Leave each end of the wire free to attach to the battery.

2. Use tape to connect one end of the wire to the positive battery terminal and the other end of the wire to the negative battery terminal. *Caution:* Over time the battery, wire, and nail can become hot, so be careful.

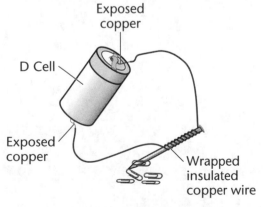

Exposed copper

D Cell

Exposed copper

Wrapped insulated copper wire

FIGURE 5.3. Electromagnet

5.7. ELECTROMAGNETS (continued)

3. Use the nail to pick up as many paper clips as possible.

4. Disconnect the wire from the battery. Wrap the copper wire around the nail twenty times. Repeat steps 2 and 3.

❓ Follow-Up Questions

1. How many paper clips could you pick up with ten loops of wire around the nail?

2. How many paper clips could you pick up with twenty loops around the nail?

3. How does the number of loops of wire affect the magnetic strength of the iron nail?

➕ Extension

Repeat this activity, but this time tape two D cell batteries end to end so the positive terminal of one touches the negative terminal of the other. Reconnect the wires to the free terminals. See how this affects the number of paper clips you can pick up.

5.8. MAGNETIC FIELD
Long-Distance Attraction

The invisible area around a magnet that attracts objects is called the *magnetic field*. The presence of the magnetic field explains why a magnet does not have to touch a magnetic object to be attracted to it. This activity will allow you to measure the size of the magnetic field of one type of magnet.

✅ Materials

Metric ruler; Paper clip; Ceramic magnet

1. Place the ruler on a tabletop so it is horizontal to you. Place the paper clip beside the ruler so the bottom end of the paper clip is just beside and touching the zero end of the ruler.

2. Place the magnet at the 10 cm mark on the same side of the ruler, so the part of the magnet nearest the paper clip is at the 10 cm mark.

FIGURE 5.4. Magnetic Field

3. Holding the ruler in place with one hand, slowly slide the magnet toward the paper clip. Continue the sliding motion until you see the paper clip begin to move toward the magnet.

4. Try this a few more times until you think you have established the exact distance where the attraction begins.

❓ Follow-Up Questions

1. How far away from the paper clip was the magnet when the attraction began?
2. Do you think all magnets have the same size magnetic field? Explain your reasoning.

➕ Extension

Repeat this activity with different types of magnets and measure the distances of their magnetic fields. Judging from the results you get, do you think some magnets are stronger than others? Which ones were the strongest, according to your measurements?

5.9. MAGNETS

What's in a Refrigerator Magnet?

All magnets are made from materials that can attract iron and other magnetic substances. However, not all magnets are constructed in the same way. The flexible rubber magnets used to post notes on refrigerator doors are made of multiple rows of tiny bar magnets embedded in flexible plastic or rubber. In each refrigerator magnet alternating rows of tiny bar magnets have opposite orientations. In other words, the magnets in one row are oriented to magnetic north; in the next row they are oriented to magnetic south. In this activity you will use iron filings to locate the rows.

✅ Materials

Two flat flexible refrigerator magnets; Piece of white paper; Iron filings

1. Pick up the refrigerator magnets and hold them so the magnetic sides are facing each other. Slowly bring the two magnets together. Does it feel like they repel or attract each other?
2. Turn one of the magnets at a 90-degree angle and repeat this process. Does this change their attraction or repulsion?
3. Place both magnets on a tabletop so the magnetic side is facing up. Place a piece of white paper on top of the magnets.
4. Scatter a light sprinkling of iron filings on the white paper that covers the magnets. Do the filings create any type of pattern?

❓ Follow-Up Questions

1. Did it matter how you turned the two magnets when you attempted to bring them together? Explain why you think this is the case.
2. What kind of pattern did you see when you sprinkled iron filings on the paper?

➕ Extension

Cut a flexible refrigerator magnet in half. Turn the two halves of the magnet so the magnetic sides face each other. Find an orientation that allows the two halves to stick together. Rub the two pieces back and forth. As you are rubbing, are there some times when the magnets move more smoothly across each other than others? Explain why you think this happens.

5.10. MAGNETIZING METALS
The Magnetic Nail

In magnets, the electrons of atoms are lined up so that they are all spinning in the same direction. This group of aligned atoms is called a *magnetic domain*. In nonmagnetic materials the electrons are oriented in different directions. Some materials, such as pieces of iron, can be temporarily magnetized with a bar magnet, which can line up the domains in the same direction. In this activity you will use a bar magnet to magnetize an iron nail so it becomes a temporary magnet.

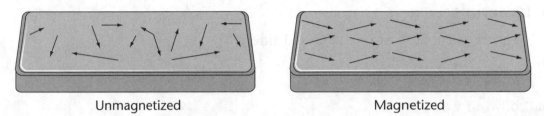

Unmagnetized   Magnetized

FIGURE 5.5. Magnetizing Metals

✅ Materials

Large iron nail; Three metal paper clips; Bar magnet; Safety glasses

Activity

1. Pick up the nail and touch its pointed end to one of the paper clips. Is the paper clip attracted to the nail?
2. Hold the head of the nail in one hand. Gently stroke the nail with the bar magnet thirty times.
3. Put down the bar magnet and attempt to pick up a paper clip with the nail again. What happens?
4. Attempt to pick up multiple paper clips with the nail. Is this possible?
5. Put on your safety glasses and drop the nail so that it strikes the floor.
6. Pick up the nail and attempt to pick up the paper clips.

❓ Follow-Up Questions

1. Were you able to pick up a paper clip in step 1? Explain why or why not.
2. Were you able to pick up any paper clips in step 3? Explain why or why not.
3. Were you able to pick up paper clips in step 6? Explain why or why not.

➕ Extension:
Determine whether the number of times you stroke the nail with a bar magnet affects the quality of the temporary magnet produced. Also try to magnetize some other substances besides a nail.

5.11. MAGNETS AND COMPASSES
Which Way Is North?

A compass is a device that indicates directions. To work properly, a compass must have a magnetic needle. Since the Earth acts like a weak magnet, the compass needle lines up with the planet's magnetic poles. A compass needle points to the magnetic North Pole of the Earth, which is very close to the geographical North Pole. In this activity you will make a compass out of cork, a metal paper clip, and a bowl of water.

 **Materials**

Piece of cork (with at least one flattened side)

Metal paper clip

Bar magnet

Small bowl of water

Compass

Note: Keep the bar magnet and compass well apart from each other when not in use so that the magnet does not damage the compass.

Activity

1. Put the bowl of water on a tabletop.
2. Place the cork in the water so the top of the cork sticking up has a flat side.
3. Bend the metal paper clip so it is no longer curved. When you finish, it should be a straight piece of metal.
4. Magnetize the straight paper clip by stroking it from top to bottom about forty times with a bar magnet.
5. Gently place the magnetized paper clip on top of the floating cork. Watch what happens.
6. Once the cork and paper clip come to rest and the paper clip is pointing in one direction, check to see if it is accurately pointing north by comparing it with a real compass. How accurate is your homemade compass?

5.11. MAGNETS AND COMPASSES (continued)

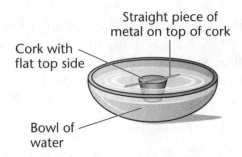

Cork with
flat top side

Straight piece of
metal on top of cork

Bowl of
water

FIGURE 5.6. Magnets and Compasses

❓ Follow-Up Questions

1. What part of a compass does the paper clip represent?
2. What happened when you put the magnetized paper clip on top of the cork?
3. Did the paper clip compass accurately point to north? How did this compare with the reading on the real compass?

➕ Extension

Check to see if the Earth's magnetic field is weaker or stronger than the magnetic field of a bar magnet. To do this, put the compass on the table in front of you. Slide a bar magnet from the side of your desk toward the compass. Does the bar magnet cause the compass reading to change? Which is stronger?

5.12. MAGNETIC FORCES
Force Blockers

A simple definition of a *force* is a push or pull. Magnetic forces, like gravity and electrical energy, can be exerted without actually touching an object. Some nonmagnetic materials may interfere with the strength of a magnetic force if they are placed between a magnet and a metal. In this activity you will determine which of several nonmagnetic materials interfere with the strength of a magnetic force.

 Materials

Two bar magnets; Ruler; Four nonmagnetic materials (for example, Styrofoam, cardboard, Plexiglas, and wood) of about equal size

Activity

1. Place the ruler on a table so it is horizontal to you. Place the north end of one bar magnet on the zero reading on the ruler. The south end of this magnet should be located away from the ruler. This is magnet A.

2. Place the second bar magnet so its south end is on the 30 cm reading on the ruler. The north end of this magnet should be located away from the ruler. This is magnet B.

FIGURE 5.7. Magnetic Forces

3. Pick up the first nonmagnetic material and place it on the 10 cm mark of the ruler. It now separates magnets A and B.

4. Holding this material in place, slowly slide magnet B along the ruler toward magnet A. Continue the slide until magnet A moves forward as a result of the magnetic force. Record the location of magnet B on the ruler.

5. Repeat these steps with the other three nonmagnetic materials.

❓ Follow-Up Questions

1. Which of the nonmagnetic materials has the least effect on the force of a magnet? Which has the greatest effect on the magnetic force?

2. Why do you think it was important to line up the two bar magnets on a ruler in this activity?

➕ Extension: Repeat this activity using different types of magnets. Do nonmagnetic materials interfere with their forces as well?

UNIT II
Life Science

SECTION SIX

The Cell

All living things show similar characteristics, such as the ability to reproduce and the need for energy. In this section students are introduced to some of the basic characteristics of living things. The use of energy is examined closely, beginning with the production of ATP within mitochondria, the transfer of this energy through the organism, and the use of energy to maintain life. Activities in this section specifically focus on the characteristics of life, conversion of ATP to ADP, the steps of the cell cycle, cell organelles and their roles, roles of enzymes, differences between plant and animal cells, photosynthesis, and respiration.

6.1. CHARACTERISTICS OF LIFE
Is It Alive?

Biology is the study of living things. Scientists have a set of criteria that an organism must possess in order to be considered alive or once living. For example, viruses are not classified as living things because they cannot reproduce without the help of a host. In this activity you will determine some of the characteristics of living things.

✔ Materials

Small animal (such as an ant) in a covered container (*handle carefully; release after the activity is done*)

Small plant (such as a potted fern or clump of grass)

Rock

Magnifying glass

1. Think of several different living things. Make a list of all the characteristics you think a living thing must possess to be considered "alive."

2. Once your list is complete, look at the ant and the fern and see whether they possess all these attributes. You may want to add to or delete characteristics from your list at this time.

3. Now examine the rock and see which attributes it lacks.

❓ Follow-Up Questions

1. What characteristics did you decide are common to living things?

2. What characteristics did the rock lack that ruled it out as a living thing? Did it have any characteristics that living things also possess?

➕ Extension

Visualize a mushroom and an amoeba. You may need to look these up in a textbook or on the Internet. Do these two organisms meet the criteria for living things that you established? Do you need to add additional characteristics or delete some you established about the animal and plant you observed earlier?

6.2. ENERGY MOLECULES

ATP and ADP

Cells require energy for chemical reactions such as respiration and photosynthesis. *Adenosine triphosphate* (ATP) is the primary energy-supplying molecule in cells. An ATP molecule is made up of three phosphate groups, each with the formula PO_4. When ATP loses a phosphate group, it becomes *adenosine diphosphate* (ADP) and releases large amounts of energy to the cell. Eventually ADP reclaims a phosphate group and becomes high-energy ATP again. In this activity you will create a model of ATP and ADP.

✅ Materials

Masking tape; Pen or marker; String (about two inches long); Small plastic container with lid

1. Place the small plastic container with lid on a table.
2. Tear off four one-inch pieces of masking tape. Write "PO_4" on three pieces of tape. Write "E" on the fourth piece.
3. Tape one PO_4 on the lid of the container. Place the second PO_4 near the bottom of the container (on the exterior) and the third near the middle of the container (on the exterior).
4. Remove the lid of the container. Tape the piece of string on the underside of the lid so it dangles downward. At the free end of the string attach the E.
5. Place the lid back on the container (with the E on the inside). The closed container represents a molecule of ATP. The E inside the container represents the energy of this molecule.
6. Remove the lid. You have removed a PO_4 and with it energy has been released. Now the molecule is called ADP. To make it ATP again, you must replace the lid.

❓ Follow-Up Questions

1. How many phosphates does ATP contain? What does an ATP molecule possess that is important to cell function?
2. How many phosphates does ADP contain? What happens to it when it gains a phosphate?

➕ Extension

Look up molecular diagrams of ATP and ADP. What elements are found in each of these energy molecules? What are some other energy molecules found in cells during cellular respiration?

6.3. ATP AND LACTIC ACID
Muscle Fatigue

The cells in your body get energy from the breakdown of carbon-rich compounds such as glucose. In the presence of oxygen, cells can completely convert glucose into large amounts of ATP, an energy molecule. During times of exercise, adequate supplies of oxygen may not be available to every cell. When oxygen levels are low, cells convert glucose to a small amount of energy and a waste product, lactic acid. When lactic acid builds up, it makes your muscles feel tired and sore. In this activity you will carry out an exercise to produce lactic acid in some of your muscles.

✔ Materials

Unopened large can of food or hand weight

Watch with a second hand

1. Pick up the can of food or a hand weight with your nonwriting hand.

2. Place your elbow on the desk and do one bicep curl by lifting and lowering the can.

3. Once you have the hang of it, do this exercise as quickly and as many times as possible for one minute. After a minute, note how your arm feels. Are you tired in any part of your arm? If not, repeat the bicep curl for another sixty seconds.

❓ Follow-Up Questions

1. The act of doing the bicep curls was a biological process, and all biological processes require energy. After the exercise, did your arm feel tired? If so, what part of your arm?

2. What do you think happened on a cellular level to account for your tiredness?

3. Do you think some people in the class felt more fatigued than others? Explain your answer.

➕ Extension

While standing, rise up and down on your toes repeatedly for one minute. How do you feel? What area of your leg is the sorest? Find out which students in your class run or exercise a lot. How did their responses to this exercise differ from those of students who do not exercise often?

6.4. THE CELL CYCLE, PART ONE

Getting Started

The life cycle of a cell includes a period of growth followed by *mitosis*, or cell division. During the growth period, called *interphase*, cells increase in size. Just before cell division, *chromosomes,* structures that hold the cell's genetic material, copy or replicate themselves so that each new cell will have a copy. This activity will summarize the first steps of the cell cycle.

✔ Materials

Paper plate; Small ball of red modeling clay; Small ball of blue modeling clay; Two thumbtacks

1. Use the red clay to make two rod-shaped chromosomes about the size of your little finger. Make two similar chromosomes from blue clay.

2. The cell cycle begins with interphase. Place one red chromosome and one blue chromosome on the paper plate. These represent the cell's genetic material during interphase.

3. When it is almost time for a cell to divide, it makes a copy of its chromosomes. To show the replication of the red chromosome, place the second red rod next to the original. The original red rod and its copy are now called sister chromatids.

4. Connect these two sister chromatids with a thumbtack to represent the *centromere,* the place where sister chromatids come in contact.

5. To show the replication of the blue chromosome, place the second blue rod next to the original. Both blue rods are now sister chromatids.

6. Connect these two sister chromatids with a thumbtack.

❓ Follow-Up Questions

1. How many chromosomes did the cell have in interphase?
2. What happened to these chromosomes?
3. What structure holds sister chromatids together?

➕ Extension

Explain how this activity would differ if your paper-plate cell had forty-six chromosomes instead of two.

6.5. THE CELL CYCLE, PART TWO

The Process

After copying its chromosomes, a cell is ready to divide into two new or daughter cells. Cell division has several steps: prophase, metaphase, anaphase, and telophase. During these steps, the original chromosomes and their copies split up. Next, the cytoplasm separates in a process called *cytokinesis*. The two new cells formed by cell division have the same number of chromosomes. They also have the same number of chromosomes as the original cell.

✔ Materials

Paper plate with sister chromatids from Activity 6.4; Two paper plates; Scissors

1. In *prophase*, the first step, the red and blue chromosomes are ready for cell division.

2. Move the red and blue chromosomes to the center of the plate to simulate *metaphase*.

3. Remove the centromere holding the two red sister chromatids together and separate them slightly. Do the same for the blue sister chromatids. This step demonstrates what happens in *anaphase*. Each sister chromatid is now called a chromosome.

4. During *telophase*, chromosomes reach opposite ends of the cell and the cell begins to divide. Further separate the chromosomes. Use scissors to partially cut the top and bottom sections of the plate.

5. Continue to drag the chromosomes off the old plate. Place each on a daughter cell plate to simulate *cytokinesis*, division of the cytoplasm.

❓ Follow-Up Questions

1. The cell in this demonstration began mitosis with two chromosomes. How many chromosomes did it have at the end of mitosis?

2. Why must a cell make a copy of its chromosomes before cell division?

➕ Extension

Look up a description of the process of meiosis. Model this process using clay and paper plates.

6.6. CELL TRANSPORT
When It Comes to Cells, Small Is Good

Why are single-celled organisms so small? Why can't an amoeba grow to the size of an elephant? Cells rely on diffusion to get nutrients. *Diffusion* is the movement of particles from areas of high concentration to areas of low concentration. Nutrients must be delivered to all parts of the cell. This activity will show why large size can be a problem.

✅ Materials

Potato cube with a 1 cm^3 volume (prepared by the teacher)

Potato cube with a 3 cm^3 volume (prepared by the teacher)

Small beaker of Lugol's solution (purchased) or iodine

Plastic knife

Forceps

Paper towel

Activity

1. Place both cubes of potato in the beaker of Lugol's solution. Potatoes contain starch, which takes on a blue-black color in Lugol's solution.

2. Leave the potato cubes in the solution for four minutes.

3. Use forceps to remove each of the cubes and place them on a paper towel on a table.

4. Both cubes should have a blue-black coloration. To see how far the solution has traveled into the potato cubes, use the knife to cut the cubes open and look inside.

❓ Follow-Up Questions

1. In which cube did the Lugol's solution (or iodine) get closer to the center?

2. The cubes represent cells. Would nutrients be more likely to diffuse to all parts of a small cell or a large cell?

3. Oxygen diffuses into cells in a similar way to how Lugol's solution diffuses into potato cubes. Would you expect a large cell to be able to supply oxygen to all of its parts?

➕ Extension

Try this activity with potato cubes of different sizes. Allow more time for soaking in Lugol's solution. Do you get similar results?

6.7. PROTEINS AS ENZYMES
Saltine Crackers and Amylase

A *protein* is a large molecule found in cells. The unique structure of a protein determines its function. *Enzymes* are proteins that speed up chemical reactions, helping transform one substance into another. The enzyme *amylase*, found in saliva, changes starch into sugar. In this activity you will experience how this transformation occurs.

✔ Materials

One-half of an unsalted saltine cracker

Small paper cup of water

1. Remove any gum or candy you may have in your mouth and drink the cup of water.
2. Place the saltine in your mouth, but do not chew it. Just hold it in your mouth.
3. Note any changes in taste you experience over the next few minutes.

❓ Follow-Up Questions

1. What did the saltine taste like when you first put it in your mouth?
2. Did you experience any change in taste over the time you held the saltine in your mouth? Explain.
3. Discuss what you think was happening in your mouth while you held the saltine.

➕ Extension

Verify what actually occurred in this activity by placing a few drops of iodine in a test tube containing a sample of cornstarch mixed with a little water. Iodine turns purple when exposed to a starch. Collect some of your saliva and mix it with cornstarch in another test tube. Allow a few minutes for the reaction. Test this with iodine. What do think will happen?

6.8. PLANT CELL OR ANIMAL CELL
Shoestring Venn Diagram

Although plant and animal cells share some basic similarities, they also have some distinctions. For instance, both plant and animal cells have a nucleus, but only plant cells have a *cell plate*, a divider that forms during cell division. In this activity you will group terms in a Venn diagram depending on whether they represent characteristics of plant cells, animal cells, or both.

✔ Materials

Two colored shoestrings; Notebook paper; Scissors

1. Write the following terms double-spaced on your notebook paper:

Animal cell	centrioles	chloroplasts	mitochondria
Plant cell	cell membrane	cell wall	cytokinesis
Both	flagella	ribosomes	large vacuoles

2. Cut out the terms so that each term is on a small rectangle of paper.

3. On a table, make a circle with each shoestring, overlapping the circles so you have three separate areas as in a Venn diagram.

4. Look over the terms you have cut out. Place "Plant cell" over the left circle, "Both" over the middle where the circles overlap, and "Animal cell" over the right circle. See Figure 6.1.

5. Place the remainder of the terms in their proper locations within the circles. Refer to Figure 6.2 if you need reminders about animal and plant cells.

❓ Follow-Up Questions

1. Which terms did you place in the animal cell region?
2. Which terms did you place in the plant cell region?
3. Which terms were characteristic of both plant and animal cells?

6.8. PLANT CELL OR ANIMAL CELL (continued)

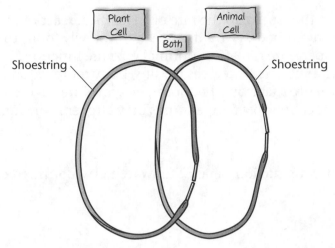

FIGURE 6.1. Shoestring Venn Diagram

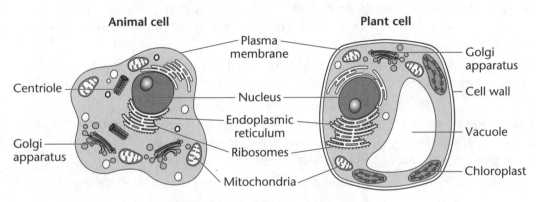

FIGURE 6.2. Animal and Plant Cells

✚ Extension

Plants and animals are made up of *eukaryotic cells*, cells with nuclei and membrane bound organelles. Bacteria are *prokaryotic cells*, cells without nuclei or membrane-bound organelles. Use your shoestring Venn diagram to classify the following terms as *prokaryotic, eukaryotic,* or *both*:

DNA   cell membrane   earliest cells on Earth

mitochondria   undergoes mitosis   chromatin

6.9. ENZYMES
Temperature and Paperase

Enzymes are proteins that speed up the rate of a chemical reaction. Without enzymes, chemical reactions in our bodies would proceed too slowly for us to survive. Factors such as pH and temperature can affect optimal enzyme function. Enzymes in the human body function best at 37 degrees Celsius, body temperature. If the temperature of the body varies too far from that point, enzymes are adversely affected. In this activity you will model how low temperatures may alter enzyme function.

✅ Materials

Two large sheets of construction paper; Stopwatch; Two or three cubes of ice in a container; Paper towel

Activity

1. Imagine that your hands represent a fictitious enzyme that we'll call *paperase*. The sole function of this enzyme is to tear paper into very small pieces about the size of peas.

2. Pick up one piece of construction paper and begin tearing it into very small pieces. Time yourself for twenty seconds. After twenty seconds, count the number of pieces of small paper. Record that number.

3. Take the cubes of ice and rub them back and forth in your hands for sixty seconds. Quickly dry your hands on a paper towel. Immediately repeat step 2 with the second piece of construction paper.

4. Compare the number of pieces you were able to tear in both cases.

❓ Follow-Up Questions

1. How many pieces of paper did paperase produce the first time? How many pieces were produced the second time?

2. What was the difference in these two trials?

3. Explain what this activity demonstrated.

➕ Extension

If you are not familiar with the words *substrate* and *active site,* look them up. What was the substrate in the above activity? Find out how the structure of an enzyme molecule is affected by high temperatures.

6.10. THE MITOCHONDRIA
Surface Area and the Folded Membrane

Mitochondria are often referred to as the "powerhouses" of cells, because they produce energy by chemically breaking the bonds in sugar molecules. Many of the energy-producing reactions occur on the mitochondria's inner membrane. The inner membrane is highly folded, giving it plenty of surface area. This activity will show how folding of the inner membrane increases its surface area.

✅ Materials

Small box of envelopes

Calculator

Metric ruler

1. Remove the envelopes from the box and set them aside.
2. Calculate the total surface area of the box in square centimeters (cm^2). To do this, multiply the length of one side of the box by the height of the box. Do this for all six sides and add the six values.
3. Calculate the total surface area of one envelope by following the procedure in step 2. When you find the surface area for one envelope, multiply that number by the number of envelopes. This will give you the total surface area of the contents of the box.

❓ Follow-Up Questions

1. What is the surface area of the box itself? What is the surface area of the contents of the box (the envelopes)?
2. How are the envelopes in the box similar to the inner membrane of the mitochondria?

➕ Extension

Try this procedure using a box of tissue. Is the surface area greater or less in this case? Explain.

6.11. PHOTOSYNTHESIS AND RESPIRATION
Formula Scramble

Autotrophs, such as plants, produce organic compounds (like glucose) through the process of photosynthesis, in which light and carbon dioxide combine to make glucose and release oxygen. Respiration is the opposite process in which living organisms use oxygen to break down organic molecules (like glucose) to produce energy needed for survival and release carbon dioxide and water. This activity will allow you to construct the chemical formula for these two processes.

✔ Materials

An envelope containing the following words and symbols on individual pieces of paper (prepared by the teacher; see Teacher's Notes):

oxygen	carbon dioxide	glucose	water	+ +	⟶
sunlight	chlorophyll	energy			
oxygen	carbon dioxide	glucose	water	+ + +	⟶

Activity

1. Empty the envelope of words and symbols on the desk.
2. Begin by combining pieces to form the word equation for photosynthesis.
3. Underneath this equation use the remaining words to form the equation for respiration.
4. If you did it correctly, you will not have any leftover pieces of paper. If you do, reexamine your equations to find your error.

❓ Follow-Up Questions

1. Write the word equation for photosynthesis. Write the word equation for respiration.
2. How do plants and animals depend on each other for survival?

➕ Extension

Respiration produces carbon dioxide gas. One way you can verify the production of carbon dioxide in your own respiration is by blowing into a container of bromthymol blue solution (prepared by the teacher; see Teacher's Notes). Use a straw to bubble air into a large test tube partially filled with bromthymol blue. What happens to the color? If it changes to yellow, this is evidence of the addition of carbon dioxide. If you want to see it change back to blue, put a radish seedling in the yellow chemical, stopper it, put it in the sun, and leave it twenty-four hours. What do you think will happen?

SECTION SEVEN

Genetics

Since Gregor Mendel's groundbreaking work that revealed basic genetic principles, the field of genetics has grown into a science that encompasses research into genetic diseases and technology used to make recombinant DNA. To truly understand genetics, students must see how cellular structures access the genetic code within the nucleus and use it to make the proteins that drive a cell's processes. The activities in this section explore the structure of nucleotides and DNA molecules, chromosomes, mitosis, meiosis, the process of crossing over that provides genetic diversity, the use of Punnett squares to predict offspring, Mendelian inheritance and the law of segregation, pedigrees, sex-linked traits, recombinant DNA, and protein synthesis.

7.1. DNA
Candy Nucleotides

DNA is a large molecule that is twisted into the shape of a double helix (see Figure 7.1). When the molecule is unwound, it resembles a ladder. The ladder rungs represent pairs of bases in DNA. The four bases that can be found in DNA are thymine, adenine, guanine, and cytosine. The sides of the ladder correspond to alternating sugars and phosphate groups. Close inspection of the DNA molecule shows that it is made of many smaller units called nucleotides. Each *nucleotide* consists of one base, one sugar, and one phosphate group. In this activity you are going to build the four types of nucleotides that compose DNA. In a later activity you will form the molecule itself.

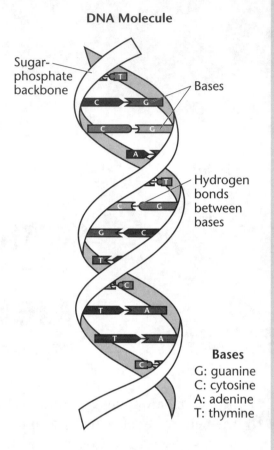

DNA Molecule

Sugar-phosphate backbone

Bases

Hydrogen bonds between bases

Bases
G: guanine
C: cytosine
A: adenine
T: thymine

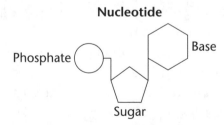

Nucleotide

Phosphate

Base

Sugar

FIGURE 7.1. Double Helix Structure of a DNA Molecule (*top*) and a Nucleotide (*bottom*)

7.1. DNA (continued)

✅ Materials

Toothpicks broken in half

Four small white marshmallows

Four orange jelly beans

Yellow, green, black, and red gumdrops

Paper towel

Activity

1. To form the first nucleotide, stick a toothpick vertically into the bottom of the marshmallow. At the free end of the toothpick, place an orange jelly bean. The marshmallow represents a phosphate group; the jelly bean, a sugar. These two parts compose the sides of a DNA molecule.

2. The third piece of a nucleotide is a nitrogenous base. Insert a toothpick horizontally from one side of the orange jelly bean. Attach a yellow gumdrop to the free end of the toothpick. This yellow gumdrop represents a thymine base. The sugar, phosphate group, and thymine form one nucleotide.

3. Repeat steps 1 and 2, but change the base each time. Green gumdrops are adenine, black are cytosine, and red are guanine.

❓ Follow-Up Questions

1. How are the nucleotides alike? How are they different?

2. What are the three parts of any nucleotide?

➕ Extension

Now that you have created four nucleotides, do some research and see how they go together to form a DNA molecule. What is meant by the base pairing rule?

7.2. CHROMOSOMES
Learning to Speak "Chromosome"

The genetic material DNA is found in structures called *chromosomes*. During cell division, chromosomes undergo some changes. This activity will help you become familiar with those changes. The paper plate in this activity represents the nucleus of the cell. Red modeling clay represents a chromosome from the father and blue modeling clay is a chromosome from the mother.

 **Materials**

Paper plate

Small ball of red modeling clay

Small ball of blue modeling clay

Four thumbtacks

Activity

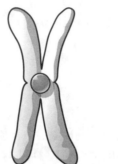

FIGURE 7.2. Homologous Chromosomes (Duplicated)

1. Form two rod-shaped chromosomes about the size of your little finger from red clay. Form two more chromosomes from blue clay.

2. Place one red and one blue rod of clay on the paper plate in any locations. These represent two chromosomes.

3. During interphase, a period of the cell cycle in preparation for cell division, these chromosomes will replicate. Match up your second red chromosome to the one on the plate to show replication. Once a chromosome has replicated, the two pieces are called sister chromatids. Position the two pieces of clay so that they form the shape of an X. Place a thumbtack in the center of the X. The thumbtack represents a centromere, a structure that holds sister chromatids together.

4. Repeat step 3 with the blue chromosome.

5. Place the two replicated chromosomes side by side. Notice they are the same size and shape. One chromosome came from the mother and one came from the father, meaning they carry genes at the same locations. These two chromosomes are now called *homologous chromosomes*. (See Figure 7.2.)

Follow-Up Questions

1. How many chromosomes do you have in the cell you made?
2. Why do you think the chromosome replicates prior to cell division?

Extension: Look up the term *tetrad*. During meiosis, chromosomes form tetrads. Use your modeling clay chromosomes to form a tetrad and explain its function.

7.3. GENETIC DIVERSITY
Crossing Over During Meiosis

A population of organisms such as gray squirrels shows *genetic diversity:* no two animals are exactly alike. One mechanism that contributes to genetic diversity is crossing over during *meiosis*, cell division that produces eggs and sperm. During meiosis, matching chromosomes from each parent, *homologous chromosomes*, form pairs or tetrads. The two homologous chromosomes then swap *alleles* of genes in a process called crossing over. An *allele* is one of the forms of a gene. Because of this swapping, the cells produced by meiosis contain chromosomes with traits of both parents. In this activity crossing over will be demonstrated in a model.

 **Materials**

Small ball of red modeling clay
Small ball of blue modeling clay
Masking tape
Ruler
Pen

 **Activity**

1. Use the red modeling clay to make a 12 cm tube. This represents a chromosome.
2. To show that this chromosome has replicated, make another red clay tube the same length. Connect the two tubes at the center by pinching the clay together. The two parts of a replicated chromosome are called sister chromatids.
3. Show three genes on each of the sister chromatids. Begin as follows:

   a. Place a small piece of masking tape on each of the sister chromatids at the following locations: 2 cm from the top, 4 cm from the top, and 10 cm from the top.

   b. Label the tape from top to bottom as A, B, and C to represent three genes on the chromosome.

7.3. GENETIC DIVERSITY (continued)

Chromosome

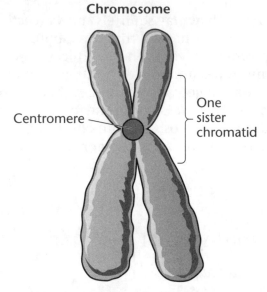

Centromere

One sister chromatid

FIGURE 7.3. Pair of Sister Chromatids

4. Use the blue modeling clay and masking tape to make another replicated chromosome to match the red one. The red and blue chromosomes represent a homologous pair.

5. Place the two homologous chromosomes side by side to represent a tetrad.

6. Simulate crossing over by pinching off the blue modeling clay labeled C on one chromatid and swapping it with the red modeling clay labeled C on one chromatid.

❓ Follow-Up Questions

1. What are homologous chromosomes?

2. How many genes were located on each chromosome in this activity?

3. In this simulation, how many genes were exchanged during crossing over?

➕ Extension

Use your clay models of chromosomes to represent the entire process of meiosis.

7.4. GENETIC COMBINATIONS
Tall and Short Pea Plants

Genetics is the study of how characteristics are passed from parents to offspring. Geneticists use Punnett squares to predict the likelihood that offspring will inherit *alleles*, forms of genes, from their parents. A Punnett square is a box divided into four parts. The alleles of one parent are written across the top of the box. The alleles of the second parent are written along the side. The combination of alleles formed within the four parts predicts the traits of offspring.

 Materials

Pencil; Paper

1. To predict the traits of the offspring of two tall pea plants, you will use the Punnett square shown in Figure 7.4. One plant's alleles for height, Tt, are written across the top. The other plant's alleles, Tt, are written on the side of the square. One of the predicted combinations of alleles is shown inside the box. Complete the rest of the square.

2. Draw another Punnett square. Write TT across the top and tt along the side. Fill in the four parts of the square.

❓ Follow-Up Questions

1. In step 1, what percentage of the offspring would you expect to inherit tt?

2. In step 2, what percentage of the offspring would you expect to inherit tt?

3. Why are Punnett squares useful?

➕ **Extension:** Use a Punnett square to predict the offspring of one parent with the alleles Tt and the other parent tt.

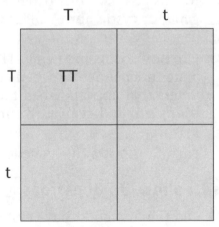

FIGURE 7.4. Punnett Square

7.5. MENDEL'S LAW OF SEGREGATION
Cystic Fibrosis

Gregor Mendel (1822–1884) studied the inheritance of traits. In his Law of Segregation, Mendel stated that "factors" segregate independently of each other when an individual produces sex cells. We now call these factors *alleles*, or alternate forms of a gene. Understanding the independent segregation of alleles helps explain why certain diseases such as the lung disease *cystic fibrosis* show up in offspring even when both parents are healthy. Cystic fibrosis is carried on a *recessive* gene, a gene that is not expressed if a *dominant* gene is present. A child can inherit cystic fibrosis if she receives one recessive gene from each parent.

✔ Materials

Two coins; Masking tape; Black marker

1. The two coins represent the mother and father in a genetic cross. The sides of each coin represent the alleles for lung function. "C" stands for the allele for normal lung function. The allele for cystic fibrosis is represented by "c."

2. In this activity both parents have normal lung function, but carry the recessive gene for cystic fibrosis. Place a piece of tape on both sides of each coin. Write a capital "C" on one side of each coin and a small "c" on the other side.

3. Flip both coins in the air. Flipping the coins shows that pairs of alleles separate independently when eggs and sperm are formed. The combination of letters that appears when the coins land represents the alleles contributed by the sperm and egg for the first child.

4. Flip the coins seven more times and record your combination each time. Each flip shows the alleles contributed to the next seven children.

❓ Follow-Up Questions

1. Did the first child have cystic fibrosis?
2. Out of the eight children produced, how many of them had cystic fibrosis?

➕ Extension

Repeat this activity, but this time label one coin as "C" on both sides and the other coin as "c" on both sides. Answer the same follow-up questions.

7.6. DOMINANT AND RECESSIVE GENES IN CAT BREEDING
Curly-Eared Cats

In *artificial selection*, animal breeders choose the traits they want to appear in the off-spring of plants or animals. For example, cat breeders are interested in a trait that controls whether ears are curved or straight. A gene that causes a cat's ear to curve inward is dominant over the recessive gene for straight ears. A dominant gene completely masks the presence of a recessive gene. Cat breeders can use their knowledge of genetics to produce kittens that display the curly-eared trait. In this activity you will simulate the breeding of two cats, one with curly ears and one with straight ears.

✅ Materials

Small paper bag; Two red pipe cleaners (5 cm long); Two white pipe cleaners (5 cm long)

1. Place a red and a white pipe cleaner in the paper bag to represent the genes of a female cat. The red pipe cleaner is the dominant gene for curly ears. The white pipe cleaner is the recessive gene for straight ears.
2. Place another red and another white pipe cleaner in the same bag. These represent the genes of a male cat.
3. Close the top of the bag and shake it to simulate breeding. Without looking, reach into the bag and draw out two pipe cleaners. The pipe cleaners you have in your hand represent the genes of the cats' first kitten. Record the colors of the pipe cleaners. A red-red or red-white combination indicates that the kitten has curly ears. A white-white combination tells you that the kitten has straight ears.
4. Replace the two pipe cleaners in the bag and repeat this process seven more times. Record your results each time.

❓ Follow-Up Questions

1. Describe the ears of the two parents.
2. How many curly-eared kittens did you produce? How many straight-eared kittens?
3. Which of the kittens could become parents of curly-eared offspring only if they mated with another curly-eared cat?

➕ Extension

Repeat this activity, but begin with a white-white combination of pipe cleaners to represent the female and use red-red pipe cleaners for the male. Simulate breeding to produce eight kittens, then answer the follow-up questions.

7.7. PEDIGREES
The Higgenbothum Hairline

A *pedigree* is a type of graphic organizer or diagram that shows how a particular trait is passed from one generation to the next. Scientists can use a pedigree to help determine the genetic makeup of specific individuals in a family.

 **Materials**

Pedigree (see Figure 7.5)

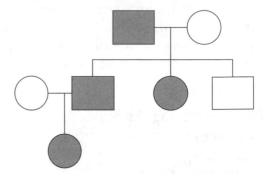

FIGURE 7.5. Pedigree

Activity

Look closely at the pedigree. Use the following information to learn how to read the pedigree of Jethro and Geraldine Higgenbothum and their descendants. The pedigree follows the inheritance of a *widow's peak*, a type of hairline in which hair comes to a point at the top of the forehead.

a. Boxes represent males, and circles represent females. When boxes or circles are filled in, the widow's peak trait is expressed in that person.

b. Horizontal lines connecting males and females indicate mating. Vertical lines from the horizontal lines indicate the offspring of that couple.

Follow-Up Questions

1. How many children did Jethro and Geraldine have?
2. How many of their children had a widow's peak hairline?
3. Judging from this pedigree, would you expect the widow's peak hairline to be a dominant or recessive trait? Explain your reasoning.

Extension

Freckles are a dominant trait. Write a short story about a fictitious couple, their children, grandchildren, and great-grandchildren and the inheritance of freckles in this family. Draw a pedigree to accompany your story.

7.8. SEX-LINKED TRAITS
Flipping Over Color Blindness

The sex chromosomes of a female are XX, and those of a male are XY. Traits controlled by genes located on the sex chromosomes are called *sex-linked traits*. *Red-green color blindness*, an inability to distinguish the color red from the color green, is a recessive sex-linked trait. A male needs only one recessive sex-linked gene to express color blindness. A female must have two recessive genes to show the trait. In this activity you will use coins to demonstrate color blindness in a family.

✅ Materials

Two pennies; Masking tape; Pen

1. Select one of the pennies to represent the male parent in this activity. Place a piece of masking tape on both sides of that penny. On one side of this penny write X^c. On the other side write Y. This is Paul, and he is color blind.

2. Place masking tape on each side of the second penny. On one side of the penny write X^c and on the other side write X^C. This is Jane, and she has normal vision but carries the gene for color blindness.

3. Paul and Jane marry and begin to raise a family. Toss the two pennies and allow them to land on the table. The combination of traits shown on the coins represents the traits of their first child. Was the first child a boy or girl? Was the child color-blind? Record your result.

4. Flip the coins seven more times and record your results.

❓ Follow-Up Questions

1. How many boys and girls did Paul and Jane have?

2. How many of the children were color-blind, and how many had normal vision?

3. Do you think color blindness is more common in boys or girls?

➕ Extension

Draw a Punnett square—a diagram showing the expected results of a genetic cross—based on Paul's and Jane's genes for color vision. To do so, draw a square and divide it into four equal sections. Write Paul's genes—X^c and Y—across the top. Write Jane's genes—X^C and X^c—along the side. Write the combinations of genes inside the four boxes. How many of the girls and how many of the boys would you expect to be color-blind?

7.9. GENE SPLICING
Human Growth Hormone and Recombinant DNA

Today's scientists can insert genes of one organism into the DNA of another organism. This technique, *gene splicing,* is used in research on human DNA to produce large quantities of human growth hormone, a protein. In gene splicing, a *plasmid*, a small piece of circular DNA in a bacterial cell, is opened with a restriction enzyme. *Restriction enzymes* cut strands of DNA at particular base sequences. Once the plasmid is open, the human gene that codes for the production of human growth hormone is inserted. The plasmid with its new gene is described as *recombinant DNA*. The recombinant plasmid is inserted into a bacterium. As the bacterium grows and divides, it and its descendants produce human growth hormone. This activity will simulate that process.

✅ Materials

Piece of white legal-sized paper; Scissors; Clear tape; Piece of red construction paper; Ruler

Activity

1. Use scissors to cut a one-inch-wide strip of paper from the longer side of the legal-sized paper. Shape the strip into a circular loop and secure it with tape. This represents a bacterial plasmid.

2. Use scissors to cut a one-inch-wide strip from the short end of the red construction paper. This represents the gene coding for human growth hormone.

3. To simulate gene splicing, use the scissors to cut open the plasmid. The scissors represent the restriction enzyme opening the plasmid.

4. Tape the red paper into the place where the plasmid was opened, reforming the loop. The tape represents the enzyme *ligase* that affixes the new gene into the plasmid. This new plasmid with recombinant DNA is ready to be reinserted into a bacterium so it can make growth hormone.

❓ Follow-Up Questions

1. Describe the process of gene splicing.
2. What are the functions of a restriction enzyme and ligase?

➕ Extension

Expand this activity by researching how the restriction enzyme knows where to cut the plasmid. Also, find out the gene code for growth hormone and write it on the red construction paper.

7.10. PROTEIN SYNTHESIS
Modeling Transcription

The genetic information within each cell is carried in the nucleus on that cell's DNA. When decoded, DNA tells the cell how to make specific proteins. Ribosomes are small organelles outside the nucleus where proteins are made. Although a cell's DNA carries the blueprint that directs the production of proteins, DNA cannot leave the nucleus. For a cell to get DNA's blueprint for proteins to the ribosomes, a strand of messenger RNA (mRNA) is created. The process in which DNA makes mRNA is called *transcription*. DNA and mRNA are both large molecules. Each is made of strands of nucleotides, subunits that consist of a sugar, a phosphate group, and a base. Both DNA and mRNA nucleotides contain the same type of phosphate group. However, the sugars and some bases vary. The sugar in DNA is deoxyribose; RNA contains ribose. The four bases that are found in DNA are adenine, thymine, cytosine, and guanine. In mRNA, thymine does not appear; it is replaced with uracil.

✓ Materials

Envelope of DNA nucleotide bases (prepared in red by the teacher; see Teacher's Notes); Envelope of RNA nucleotide bases (prepared in blue by the teacher; see Teacher's Notes)

Activity

1. Empty the red DNA nucleotides on your desk. The nucleotides are labeled with the bases they contain: **A** for adenine, **T** for thymine, **C** for cytosine, and **G** for guanine. Arrange them horizontally in the exact letter sequence seen here:

ACGCTTCCA

   This represents part of the base sequence of a DNA molecule. The DNA is ready to form a strand of mRNA.
2. Remove the blue RNA nucleotides from the other envelope. The labels on these also represent the bases within the nucleotides. Unlike DNA, mRNA contains uracil, which is represented by **U**. Create a strand of mRNA bases that is complementary to the DNA strand using the base pair rule for RNA: **A** binds to **U**, and **G** pairs with **C**.

❓ Follow-Up Questions

1. What were the nine letters in the mRNA strand that you created from the DNA strand?
2. According to the base pair rule, what nucleotide base is found in DNA, but not in RNA?

➕ Extension: Find an mRNA amino acid chart in a textbook. Name the three amino acids that would be coded for by the mRNA chain you assembled.

SECTION EIGHT

Evolution

After traveling the world and observing organisms in their natural habitats, Charles Darwin challenged the generally accepted theory that all living things were put on Earth in their present form. Darwin's theory of natural selection offered an explanation of how living things might have developed into their present forms. Students of evolution must understand the concept of fitness and the essential roles of adaptation. The activities in this section focus on the topics of natural selection, fitness, adaptations, adaptive radiation, evidence of evolution from fossil dating, and an example of present-day evolution—the development of antibiotic resistance.

8.1. NATURAL SELECTION

Life as a Peppered Moth

There are two types of peppered moths in England: one has light-colored wings and the other, dark-colored wings. Prior to the Industrial Revolution in the 1850s, the light-colored moth was more prevalent. By 1900, sooty pollutants had changed the bark of trees from light gray to dark gray. The dark tree bark provided camouflage for dark moths and enabled them to hide from predators. The number of dark moths rose dramatically as the number of light-colored moths declined. This increase in dark moths is an example of *natural selection*, a concept introduced by Charles Darwin that explains how organisms best suited to the environment survive and reproduce. In this activity you will see how a change in the color of tree bark affected the populations of moths.

FIGURE 8.1. Light and Dark Peppered Moths

✅ Materials

Sheet of tan or gray construction paper

Sheet of black construction paper

Thirty tan or gray beans

Thirty black beans

Watch with a second hand

Activity

1. Place the sheet of gray or tan construction paper on a table. Spread all sixty beans around the paper.

2. Close your eyes and count to ten. Open your eyes and pick up as many beans as you can in twenty seconds. You can only pick up one bean at a time. Record the number of each color of bean that you picked up.

3. Repeat this process, but this time use the black paper as your background.

❓ Follow-Up Questions

1. How many of each color bean did you pick up on light-colored paper? How many of each color bean did you pick up on dark-colored paper?

2. If you imagine the beans were moths and the paper was tree bark, explain how these results help illustrate natural selection.

➕ Extension

Eventually antipollution laws were enacted in England. Do you think this changed the number of each type of moth there? Do some research and see what actually happened and which species is more prevalent today.

8.2. ADVANTAGEOUS TRAITS
Which Creature Is the Fittest?

In his theory of natural selection, Charles Darwin (1809–1882) said that individuals who are best adapted to their environment are the ones that are most likely to survive and pass on traits to their offspring. Darwin pointed out that individual organisms of a species show *variations*, slight differences in traits. Some of these variations improve the ability of individuals to survive. One type of variation is size. This activity will help you understand how large size might be an advantageous trait in some environments.

✅ Materials

Styrofoam cup with a lid and a hole the size of pencil eraser in the bottom; Ten grains of uncooked rice, ten dry pinto beans, and ten dry black-eyed peas; Piece of masking tape; Small bowl or other container

Activity

1. Place a piece of masking tape over the hole in the bottom of the cup (on the outside of the cup).
2. Place the rice, beans, and peas in the Styrofoam cup. These items represent three variations in a species that lives in an earthquake-prone environment. To survive in this environment, individuals must avoid being swept in the holes created by the earthquakes.
3. Hold the cup right side up over the top of the bowl and remove the masking tape from the bottom of the cup. Gently shake the cup back and forth for twenty seconds. At the end of that time, retape the hole. Count the number of individuals of each type that remain in the cup.

❓ Follow-Up Questions

1. How many of each variation—rice, pinto beans, and black-eyed peas—remained in the cup?
2. Explain how this activity illustrates natural selection.
3. Which individuals were most likely to survive in the earthquake-prone environment? Why?

➕ **Extension:** Continue this activity as before, but after each period of twenty seconds, assume the organisms that survived reproduced. Double the number of each species that survived, then shake the cup for another twenty seconds. Repeat this for several generations and see what the future holds for these organisms.

8.3. PRIMATE ADAPTATIONS
The Importance of the Opposable Thumb

Adaptations are inheritable characteristics that help organisms survive in the environments in which they live. One important adaptation in primates is the opposable thumb. Opposable thumbs enable primates such as monkeys to grasp tree branches effectively. Humans use their opposable thumbs to manipulate tools. This activity will help you see how important the opposable thumb is for humans.

✔ Materials

Duct tape

Shoelace

Stopwatch

1. Place the shoelace on a table in front of you. Use the stopwatch to see how quickly you can pick up the shoelace, tie it in a bow, and place it back on the desk.
2. Now use the duct tape to tape the thumbs of both hands to the sides of your hands. (Taping your thumbs simulates hands with no opposable thumb.)
3. Repeat step 1 without the use of your thumbs.

❓ Follow-Up Questions

1. How much time difference was there between tying the bow with your thumbs and tying the bow without thumbs?
2. List as many activities as you can think of that would be affected if humans did not have opposable thumbs.

➕ Extension

Another primate adaptation is binocular vision, which means there is slight separation between the two eyes to better view objects. Scientists believe this adaptation has enhanced primates' eye-hand coordination and the ability to judge distance. Test this claim by having one of your classmates hold two pencils in front of you at different distances. Quickly grab one of the pencils from him. Now repeat this with one eye closed. What does this tell you about the advantages of binocular vision?

8.4. STEPS OF NATURAL SELECTION
Natural Selection Sequencing

In the mid-1800s Charles Darwin (1809–1882) developed his theory of evolution based on natural selection. *Natural selection* means those organisms with traits (*variations*) that are best suited to the environment are more likely to survive and reproduce. In most populations, there are more organisms than can survive, and each organism is unique. For this reason, the environment selects the organisms that will be the survivors. In this activity you will arrange the principles of natural selection in the proper order.

✅ Materials

Sheet of notebook paper; Scissors; Pencil

Activity

1. Copy and cut out the five steps of natural selection that follow. (They are not listed in any particular order.)

   ⟳ Organisms produce more offspring than can survive.

   ⟳ Over time offspring with helpful variations expand the population and can eventually become a separate species.

   ⟳ Differences or variations occur among individuals of a species.

   ⟳ Some variations are helpful, and individuals with helpful variations survive and reproduce.

   ⟳ Variations among parents are passed to offspring.

2. Arrange these steps in a logical sequence as Darwin might have done.

❓ Follow-Up Questions

1. What was the sequence of your steps?
2. Could any of the steps be omitted? Why or why not?

➕ Extension

Do some research and find a real-life event that illustrates the principles of natural selection. Match the steps of the event you researched to the principles you sequenced in this activity.

8.5. PLANT ADAPTATIONS
Features for Survival in the Rain Forest

Because of natural selection, individuals that are the best fitted to their environment survive and reproduce offspring. In the tropical rain forest, more plants are produced than can survive. The plants that possess useful characteristics or adaptations are the ones that are successful. For example, the leaves of many plants in the upper levels of the rain forest have specially shaped tips called "drip tips." Rainfall is high in this region. The tips permit water to run off the leaves quickly, preventing the growth of mold and mildew. In this activity you will compare the leaf of a plant in a temperate forest with one from the tropical rain forest.

✅ Materials

Piece of green card stock

Scissors

Pencil

Paper towel

Small spray bottle of water

 Activity

1. Divide the card stock into two equal halves.
2. On one half draw an oval leaf with a gently rounded tip. On the other half draw an equal size leaf, but give it a very pointed tip.
3. Cut out both leaves.
4. Hold one leaf in your hand so the tip is pointed away from you. Lower your hand at an angle so the leaf is inclined downward toward a paper towel on the desk top. Mist the top side of the leaf with a couple of quick sprays of water. Note how quickly the water runs off the end of the leaf.
5. Repeat this process with the other leaf.

❓ Follow-Up Questions

1. Which one of the two leaves allowed water to run off quicker?
2. Which one of the leaves represented the "drip tip" leaf? Explain your answer.

➕ Extension

Do some research and find three other plant adaptations that enable plants to survive in the tropical rain forest.

8.6. ADAPTIVE RADIATION
The Beaks of Darwin's Finches

On the Galapagos Islands there are thirteen species of finches. When Charles Darwin visited the Galapagos, he noticed that each island was home to a specific species of finch. The diverse species differed in the shapes of their beaks. The beak of each species was adapted to the food sources on their particular island. All the finches are believed to have evolved from a single species that inhabited the mainland of South America. The evolution of one species to fill many different niches is called *adaptive radiation*. Darwin's finches are a perfect example of this concept. In this activity you will use four different tools to represent the beaks of four species of finches living on one Galapagos island. On this island worms are the main source of food. You will decide which finch has the best beak adaptation for gathering worms.

✅ Materials

Large cup of yarn "worms" (prepared by the teacher; see Teacher's Notes); Plastic fork; Plastic spoon; Tweezers; Plastic knife; Clock or watch with second hand

Activity

1. Spread the yarn worms on a table, which represents one of the Galapagos Islands.
2. You will play the roles of four different species of finches feeding on the worms. Each finch species has a differently shaped beak. The different beak shapes are: fork-shaped, spoon-shaped, tweezer-shaped, and knife-shaped.
3. You will have twenty seconds to pick up worms with the fork, which represents a fork-shaped beak. When your teacher says "Go," begin picking up yarn worms with the fork and placing them in a cup. Cease collecting worms when your teacher says "Stop."
4. Count and record the number of worms you picked up. Return the yarn worms to the cup.
5. Repeat this process for each of the other three tools: spoon, tweezers, and plastic knife.

❓ Follow-Up Questions

1. Which of the tools picked up the most worms? What was it about that particular "beak" that allowed the finch to gather the most worms?
2. What do you think might happen to the other three types of finches over time if worms were the only possible food source?

➕ Extension: Gather some actual birdseed and determine which beak adaptation would be the most effective in gathering this type of food.

8.7. VARIATIONS AND SURVIVAL
Pine Needle Variation

If you look at the individual organisms within a species, you will see some differences among them. Some of these differences, called *variations*, may be advantageous to the survival of an individual. A variation that provides an advantage is called an *adaptation*. Adaptations are passed down from one generation to the next. In this activity you will look for variations among pine needles from the same tree.

 **Materials**

Metric ruler

Pine needles on a twig

Pencil

 **Activity**

1. Remove twenty pine needles from a pine twig.
2. Measure and record the length of each needle in millimeters.

? **Follow-Up Questions**

1. What was the most common length of the twenty pine needles?
2. How might leaf length affect the ability of the plant to store food? To photosynthesize?

+ **Extension**

Gather twenty bean pods filled with beans. Open each pod and count the number of beans inside. What was the most common number of beans in the pods? What advantage do you think this might have to survival of the beans?

8.8. HORSE EVOLUTION
Horse Height Over Time

Horses have not always looked the way they do today. The modern horse is the result of more than fifty-five million years of evolution. Modern horses are quite different from their prehistoric relatives in height, foot shape, back configuration, and dental characteristics. In this activity you will see how horse height has changed over evolutionary time.

 **Materials**

Metric ruler

 **Activity**

Study the following information about the evolution of horses. Each time a new genus of horse is described, use the ruler to see what its approximate height would have been.

a. About 55 million years ago, the first horse was *Hyracotherium*. It stood about 38 cm tall and lived in swampy areas with dense forests.

b. Approximately 30 million years ago, *Miohippus* appeared on Earth. It stood about 65 cm tall and lived in dry areas among trees and shrubs.

c. *Merychippus* walked the Earth about 13 million years ago. It stood about 100 cm high and lived in the grassland.

d. Today's horse, *Equus*, stands about 140 cm tall and also resides in the grassland.

❓ Follow-Up Questions

1. What modern-day animal would be about the same size as *Hyracotherium*?

2. What characteristics of the environment of *Hyracotherium* favored the smaller size?

➕ Extension

Expand your research on horse evolution and find out exactly how foot shape and tooth shape have changed from fifty-five million years ago up until today. Draw some sketches of the differences you see.

8.9. FOSSIL DATING
Stacking Up Rock Layers

Paleontologists, scientists who study fossils, have found many fossil remains in rocks. Scientists rely on the *law of superposition* to help them determine the ages of these fossils. This law states that younger layers of rocks are deposited on top of older layers. This relative dating technique enables paleontologists to infer the ages of rocks and thus the fossils in those rocks. This activity shows how the law of superposition works.

 **Materials**

Scissors

Pictures of organisms (see Figure 8.2)

 **Activity**

1. Cut out the pictures of different organisms. The pictures represent fossils of these organisms.

2. Without referring to the table below, stack these pictures in the order in which you think they appeared on Earth. Put the oldest organisms on the bottom of the stack and the youngest on the top of the stack.

3. Compare your stack to the dates in the table. If necessary, rearrange your stack to make it accurate.

4. Add the dates these organisms appeared on Earth to the pictures.

Appearance of Organism	Time in Millions of Years Ago (mya)
Bacteria	3,000 mya
Jellyfish	600 mya
Shark	400 mya
Earthworm	300 mya
Small mammal	210 mya
Archaeopteryx (birdlike reptile)	140 mya
Ants	100 mya
Camel	35 mya
"Lucy" (early manlike primate)	4 mya

8.9. FOSSIL DATING (continued)

❓ Follow-Up Questions

1. What were the first living things?
2. How much time passed between the appearance of the first living things and the appearance of insects?
3. If you found one fossil embedded in the top of a rock layer and another one embedded in the bottom of the layer, which fossil would be the oldest? Explain your answer.

➕ Extension

Carry out research to learn how fossils are formed. Use clay to demonstrate what you learn.

FIGURE 8.2. Various Organisms

Shark

Archaeopteryx
(birdlike reptile)

Small mammal

Lucy
(early manlike primate)

Bacteria

Earthworm

Ants

Jellyfish

Camel

8.10. ANTIBIOTIC RESISTANCE
Present-Day Evolution

You know that all humans are not the same; their differences are pretty obvious. It is harder to see that not all bacteria are the same. Some contain characteristics that others do not have. In a population of bacteria, it is likely that a few organisms carry the gene for antibiotic resistance. *Antibiotics* are chemicals used to kill bacteria, and they are important in treating infections. In this activity you will see why some disease-causing bacteria survive and thrive, even when antibiotics are used for treatment.

✅ Materials

Paper cup filled with dried beans
Red marker

1. Spread eleven dried beans on a table. Each bean represents a bacterium.
2. Mark one of the beans with the red marker. This bean represents a bacterium that carries the gene for antibiotic resistance.
3. Show that the bacteria are reproducing by adding eleven more dried beans to the tabletop. Mark one of the beans red.
4. Assume that an antibiotic is used to get rid of the bacteria. Remove all the beans except those marked in red.
5. Show that the bacteria are reproducing by adding two more beans. Mark both these beans in red.

❓ Follow-Up Questions

1. Why didn't all the bacteria die after the first treatment with antibiotics?
2. What would happen to the remaining bacteria if they were exposed to antibiotics?

➕ Extension

Conduct research on pesticide-resistant insects. Find out how the use of pesticides is changing some insect populations.

SECTION NINE

Diversity of Life

All living things share basic characteristics, including the need for energy. However, the manner in which organisms meet their survival needs varies. Some are adapted for life deep in the soil where there is no oxygen, while others live on the oxygen-rich surface. Most of the living things on Earth are unicellular, yet millions of species are multicelled. Large organisms face challenges unknown to the one-celled creatures. If an organism is made of one cell, food and other requirements simply diffuse through its plasma membrane. In large multicelled organisms, however, not all the cells are in contact with the environment, so their needs must be met through special structures. In this section students learn about the many ways organisms have of meeting their needs. These activities focus on the diversity of life and the structural modifications that support this diversity.

9.1. THE SIX KINGDOMS
Kingdom Match Game

The broadest group in the classification system of living things is the *kingdom*. Scientists have placed all living things into one of these six kingdoms: *Eubacteria, Archaebacteria, Protista, Fungi, Animalia*, or *Plantae*. In this activity you will use what you have learned through your study of living things to sort organisms or characteristics of organisms into the proper kingdoms.

✅ Materials

Sheet of legal-sized paper
Sticky notes
Ruler
Pencil

1. Turn the legal-sized paper so the long side is horizontal to you. Use the ruler and pencil to divide the paper into six columns. Write the name of a different kingdom at the top of each column.

2. Write the following words or phrases on separate sticky notes:

   humans
   has no nucleus *[write this on two notes]*
   E. coli
   all have cell walls and chloroplasts
   mushroom
   most, but not all, are unicellular
   all are multicellular heterotrophs
   likes extreme environments
   fern
   Euglena

9.1. THE SIX KINGDOMS (continued)

  cell wall of chitin

  first organisms on Earth

  algae

  mildew

  tick

3. Place each of these notes in the correct Kingdom column. Look up any unfamiliar terms or phrases.

4. Write your own terms on six more blank notes and then place these notes in the correct columns.

❓ Follow-Up Questions

1. Briefly describe the characteristics of all plants.

2. In what kingdoms can you find unicellular organisms?

➕ Extension

Use the titles in the columns and information on the notes to make a concept map. You can add more terms if you need to.

9.2. VASCULAR PLANTS
Checking Out a Fern Frond

Ferns were probably the first vascular plants on Earth. *Vascular plants* have special vessels to carry water and nutrients throughout the plant. Ferns reproduce by spores, rather than seeds. The production of spores is an asexual method of reproduction. In this activity you will examine a fern *frond*, the leaf of a fern.

 **Materials**

Fern frond
Ruler
Magnifying glass

1. Use the magnifying glass to look for the main vessels or veins in the fern frond. How many main vessels do you see?
2. Ferns reproduce by way of spores. Look on the underside of the frond for small, round, brown structures. These structures, called *sori*, are packets containing spores.
3. Describe the appearance of the sori.
4. Note any other structures you observe on the fern.

❓ Follow-Up Questions

1. How are the vascular tissues of ferns like the blood vessels of animals?
2. How many vessels did you see on one frond?
3. Describe the sori.

➕ Extension

Obtain a sample of moss. Use the magnifying glass to look at the moss. These plants are nonvascular. Compare their appearance and structures to those of a fern's. If they have no vascular tissue, how is water transported throughout the moss?

9.3. FLOWER PARTS
Dissecting the Flower

Angiosperms are flowering plants. The seeds of these plants are produced within the *flower*, the reproductive structure of the plant. Many flowers contain colorful structures called *petals*. Within the petals is a central female structure, the *pistil*, which is made up of an *ovary* at the base, a stalk-like *style*, and a swollen top called the *stigma*. Surrounding the pistil are multiple male structures called *stamens*. Each stamen is made up of a long stalk called a *filament* that is topped with a buttonlike structure called an *anther*. The stamen produces pollen that fertilizes the ovule in the ovary of the pistil. In this activity you will examine a flower and identify its parts, as shown in Figure 9.1.

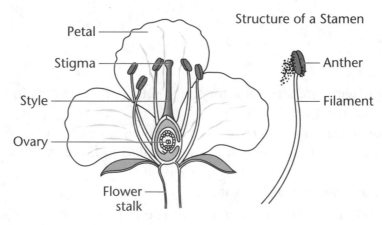

FIGURE 9.1. Parts of a Flower

 **Materials**

Flower
Tweezers
Paper towel

9.3. FLOWER PARTS (continued)

Activity

1. Find the petals of your flower. Note the number of petals. You may remove the petals if you cannot see inside the flower.
2. Locate the pistil in the center of the flower and note its appearance and shape. Examine the pistil to see if you can distinguish between the ovary, style, and stigma.
3. Locate a stamen of the flower and note its appearance. How many stamens do you see? Can you see any pollen on top of the stamens?
4. Examine the stamen more closely to see if you can locate the anther and filament.

❓ Follow-Up Questions

1. Describe the appearance of the stamen and the pistil.
2. Compare the number of stamens and pistil(s) in the flower. Can you think of a reason for the difference in numbers of each?
3. Suggest some ways that pollen might be transferred from the stamen to the pistil.

➕ Extension

Obtain other flowers and compare the number of pistils and stamens in different species. Does the number of stamens vary from one type of flower to the next? Does the number of pistils vary from one type of flower to the next? Do all flowers have both stamens and pistils?

9.4. FOOD STORAGE IN SEEDS
Dissecting a Dicot

Bean plants are called *dicotyledons* because they have two food storage structures, *cotyledons*. The developing bean plant, the *embryo*, is found between the two cotyledons. The embryo has tiny leaves at one end. It also has a shoot called the *epicotyl*. The two halves are held together by an external seed coat. In this activity you will examine the structure of a lima bean.

✅ Materials

Safety glasses; Lima bean (soaked in warm water overnight); Iodine; Medicine dropper; Paper towel; Magnifying glass; Black crayon

1. Dry the bean with a paper towel. Peel off the outer skin.
2. Using your thumbs, open the bean so it falls into two halves.
3. With the help of the magnifying lens, locate the parts of the bean discussed above. You will be asked to sketch these parts in the first follow-up question.
4. Put on your safety glasses. To determine the part of the cotyledon that contains food, place a drop of iodine at several locations on the inside of the bean. Iodine turns black in the presence of starch (stored food).

❓ Follow-Up Questions

1. Draw a sketch of the inside of the dicot you examined. Label the cotyledon, embryo, and epicotyl.
2. Using the crayon, color your sketch in areas where starch was located.

➕ Extension

Conduct an experiment in which you compare the growth of bean plants to the amount of cotyledon. You will need a control group of seeds that have normal cotyledons, a group with only one-half cotyledons, and a group with only one-quarter cotyledons.

9.5. SEED DISPERSAL
Where Plants Come From

You may have seen plants growing in unusual places and wondered how they got there. Plants have many ways of dispersing, or spreading, their seeds. Many seeds simply drop to the ground from the parent plant, but some seeds travel great distances before germinating. Wind and water can disperse seeds miles from their source. Animals also help spread seeds. Some seeds "hitchhike" to a new location on the fur of animals, feathers of birds, or clothing of people. In this activity you will design a method of seed dispersal.

✔ Materials

Empty chewing gum sleeve

Index card

Pencil

Activity

1. Pretend the chewing gum sleeve is a seed.
2. Study the seed. On the index card, describe or draw one method of dispersing this seed. For example, you might describe how the seed is carried by wind or water, or your seed might be transported by animals.
3. Be prepared to demonstrate this later for your teacher using the chewing gum sleeve.

❓ Follow-Up Questions

1. How was your seed dispersed?
2. Describe how this process would occur and what characteristics your seed possesses that makes that dispersal possible.

➕ Extension

Set up a demonstration that shows exactly how your chewing gum sleeve seed will move from one part of the room to another.

9.6. ANIMAL SYMMETRY
What Symmetry Is This?

All animals, whether simple or complex, show some type of *symmetry*. The simplest animals, the sponges, have an irregular shape, and scientists describe them as *asymmetrical*. All other animals have a more definite body design. A sea anemone is considered to have *radial symmetry* because all its body parts are arranged around a central axis, much like the spokes of a bicycle wheel. Humans and many other advanced animals show *bilateral symmetry*. If a plane were passed through the midline of the body, the left and right sides would be almost exact mirror images of each other. In this activity you will show your understanding of the three types of symmetry by imagining that each letter of the alphabet is an animal and deciding which type of symmetry each represents.

 **Materials**

Large index card

Pen or pencil

Ruler

 **Activity**

1. Turn the index card so the longest portion of the card is horizontal to you.

2. Use the ruler and pencil to divide the card into three equal columns. Label column 1 as "Asymmetry," column 2 as "Radial symmetry," and column 3 as "Bilateral symmetry." Draw a horizontal line beneath all three of these words.

3. Starting with the letter A and going through letter Z, identify the type of symmetry shown by each letter. Place all twenty-six letters in one of the three columns.

Follow-Up Questions

1. Which letters of the alphabet represented the same symmetry as a sponge?

2. Name three animals that have the same type of symmetry as the letter A.

Extension

Look at the letter O. What type of symmetry does it have? Name three animals that have the same symmetry as the letter O. Do you think this letter could have more than one type of symmetry?

9.7. VIRUSES
Nuts and Bolts of a Bacteriophage

A *virus* is a nonliving particle that depends on a host to reproduce. There are different types of viruses, but all consist of a *capsid,* an outer protein coat, and some genetic material. Some viruses contain DNA and others RNA. In this activity you will build a simple model of a *bacteriophage*, a virus that infects bacteria.

 **Materials**

Small bolt

Two nuts

One washer

Six small pieces of pipe cleaners

Activity

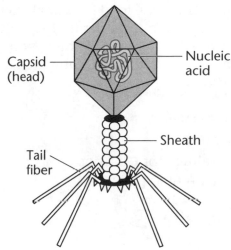

FIGURE 9.2. Parts of a Virus

1. Use the materials provided to build a bacterio-phage model, referring to the illustration in Figure 9.2 as needed for guidance. Your model should have a capsid, a tail, and tail fibers.

2. Judging by their appearance, what do you think the function of each of the parts in the model might be?

❓ Follow-Up Questions

1. What did you use for the capsid of the virus? What materials make up the capsid of a virus?

2. If you could have cut away part of the capsid, what do you think would be found inside the capsid?

3. What two parts do all viruses have in common?

➕ Extension

Viruses are generally classified according to their DNA or RNA content. Do some research, then illustrate and name two common viruses that contain DNA and two others that contain RNA.

9.8. BIRD DIGESTION
Why Birds Don't Need Teeth

If you have ever watched a bird eat, you might have noticed that it does not chew. Birds do not have teeth. The food a bird eats is ground up in a section of its stomach called the *gizzard*. Birds occasionally swallow grit and small rocks by instinct, and these are stored in the gizzard. This muscular digestive organ then grinds and pulverizes the food into small pieces. The toughness of a bird's gizzard varies with the species. In species that eat soft food, the gizzard is small. Once food has passed through the gizzard, it moves on into the intestines. In this activity you will make a model gizzard and see how well it works to grind up a bird's food.

✅ Materials

Two small towels

Gravel

Small cup of Cheerios

Two rubber bands

1. Make a model gizzard by placing one towel flat on a table. Sprinkle some gravel in the center of the towel. Place the second towel on top of the gravel.

2. Sprinkle a small cup of Cheerios in the center of the second towel and roll up the towels so they form a long cylinder. Wrap a rubber band tightly around each end of the towels.

3. Simulate the gizzard grinding food by using your hands to roll the towels back and forth on your desk. Also pick up the towels and squeeze them.

4. Unwrap the towel roll and note the appearance of the Cheerios.

❓ Follow-Up Questions

1. How did the Cheerios look after you rolled them?

2. Judging by your experience in this activity, do you think the bird's gizzard is a rough or a smooth organ? Explain your answer.

➕ Extension

Repeat the gizzard activity, but this time attempt to grind up tougher foods, such as walnuts or sunflower seeds. Do you think the size and amount of gravel in the gizzard has an influence on the grinding process?

9.9. EXAMINING A FUNGUS
Close-Up Look at a Mushroom

Mushrooms belong to the Fungi kingdom. Most members of this kingdom are *multicellular*, meaning they have more than one cell. Fungi are not able to produce their own food, so they are called *heterotrophs*. A mushroom has an umbrella-shaped top called a *cap*. The underside of the cap has *gills* that produce *spores*, reproductive structures. The stem or stalk, also called the *stipe,* is made up of many hairlike filaments called *hyphae*. In this activity you will examine a mushroom to become acquainted with its parts.

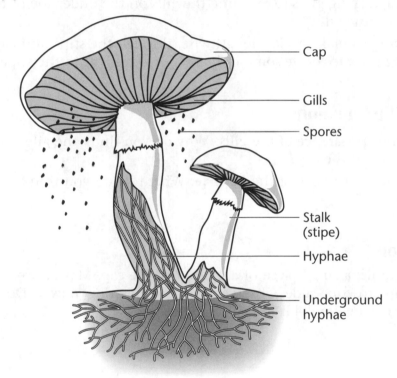

FIGURE 9.3. Parts of a Fungus

 **Materials**

Mushroom (common grocery-store variety)

Paper towels

Plastic knife

Magnifying glass

Index card

9.9. EXAMINING A FUNGUS (continued)

Activity

1. Examine the mushroom carefully and locate the cap, gills, spores, stipe, and hyphae. Make a sketch of the mushroom on an index card and label the cap, stipe, and gills.

2. Use the magnifying glass to examine the gills on the underside of the cap. Look for spores on the gills.

3. Use the knife to make a slice, lengthwise, through the stipe and cap. Use the magnifying glass to locate some individual hyphae within the stipe.

❓ Follow-Up Questions

1. Describe the appearance of the gills. Why do you think the gills are located on the underside of the cap?

2. Describe the appearance of the hyphae. What role do you think they serve in the mushroom?

➕ Extension

Use tweezers to lift a small piece of a gill out of the cap. Make a wet mount of the gill on a microscope slide. Observe the slide under low power. Do you see any spores? What do they look like?

9.10. TAXONOMIC CATEGORIES
Addressing Classification

Taxonomists, scientists who classify organisms, use an ordered hierarchical system that ranges from broad to specific. This system first puts organisms into large groups called *kingdoms*. Each kingdom is subdivided into several *phyla*. A phylum is further divided into *classes*, which are broken down into *orders*. Each order is split into *families*, which are divided into *genera*. A genus contains several *species*, the smallest subdivision. In this activity you will learn more about this hierarchical system by comparing the U.S. Postal Service address system to the biological classification system.

✔ Materials

Envelope; Pen; Box of markers

1. Address the front of an envelope as though you are sending a piece of mail to yourself at school.
2. On the first line write your name. On the second line write the street address of your school and on the third line write your city and state. On the fourth line, write the country—USA.
3. Highlight the following by using markers in the colors specified:
   a. Use yellow to underline the country. This represents the kingdom.
   b. Use green to underline the state. This is the phylum.
   c. Use blue to underline the city. This is the class.
   d. Use red to underline the street name, but not the street number. This is the order.
   e. Use gray to underline the street number. This is the family.
   f. Use pink to underline your last name. This is the genus.
   g. Use orange to underline your first name. This is the species.

❓ Follow-Up Questions

1. How does the postal address represent a hierarchal system?
2. If you had used the ZIP Code in your address, what color would you have used to underline it? Why?

➕ Extension

What is your favorite animal? Do some research and find the taxonomic hierarchy for that animal, starting with kingdom and ending with species.

SECTION TEN

Ecology

*E*cology is the study of how living things interact with each other and with their environments. To understand ecology, students must appreciate the "big picture" of life, the flow of energy and the cycling of nutrients in the biosphere. In addition, they must also see how individual ecosystems function. Therefore, ecology examines the lives of organisms on many levels and in all environments. In this section students will analyze the flow of energy through ecosystems, as well as the relationships found in food chains and food webs. Activities demonstrate the roles of individuals, populations, and communities, highlighting symbiotic relationships. This section also takes a look at the roles of humans in ecosystems.

10.1. ENERGY FLOW THROUGH THE FOOD CHAIN
The 10 Percent Rule of Energy Flow

Food chains show how energy moves through an *ecosystem*, the combined physical and biological elements in an environment. In a food chain, *producers,* organisms that make their own food, provide food for animals called *first-level consumers*. These animals are then eaten by *second-level consumers*, which may be consumed by *third-level consumers*. Scientists estimate that only 10 percent of the producers' energy is passed to the first-level consumer. This activity will help put that amount into perspective.

✅ Materials

10 ml graduated cylinder; Cup filled with 100 ml of water; Medicine dropper; Three small paper cups

1. Label cup 1 "first-level consumer," cup 2 "second-level consumer," and cup 3 "third-level consumer." The large cup filled with 100 ml of water represents the producer. For this activity we will assume that the producer possesses 100 units of energy.
2. A first-level consumer eats the producer and absorbs only 10 percent of its energy. Use the graduated cylinder to pour 10 ml of the producer's water into cup 1.
3. The second-level consumer eats the first-level consumer and gets only 10 percent of its energy. Use the graduated cylinder to pour 1 ml of water from cup 1 into cup 2.
4. The third-level consumer eats the second-level consumer and gets only 10 percent of its energy. Use the medicine dropper to transfer 0.1 ml of water from cup 2 into cup 3.

❓ Follow-Up Questions

1. If the food chain had continued to the next level, what percentage of energy would the fourth-level consumer have received from the third-level consumer? How much water would you have transferred into the fourth-level consumer's cup?
2. Judging from this activity, why do you think most food chains never go higher than second- or third-level consumers?

➕ Extension

Do some research and draw a pyramid of energy showing the following organisms in the correct order: caterpillar, grass, snake, lizard, and hawk. Label the percentage of energy each organism gets through the food chain.

10.2. POPULATION GROWTH RATE
Growing Exponentially

A population's growth rate describes how fast a population is expanding. Populations show two types of growth. *Exponential* growth begins slowly but eventually increases rapidly. During the rapid phase of exponential growth, the population quickly uses up valuable resources. The second type of growth, *logistic*, increases rapidly until a population reaches the carrying capacity of its environment. *Carrying capacity* refers to the population size that an environment can sustain over a long period of time. This activity will help you understand exponential growth.

 **Materials**

Calculator

1. Imagine that you are searching for a job where you can work about fifteen hours a week after school. You get two job offers. You have to decide in the next five minutes which one you will accept—Offer A or Offer B.

   a. *Offer A:* The job pays a flat rate of $10 per hour with a minimum of fifteen hours a week.

   b. *Offer B:* The job pays in increasing increments. The first hour you are paid only 1 cent. The second hour you are paid 2 cents, the third hour 4 cents, and so on. In other words, the rate doubles for each hour you work. The rate starts over with each new week.

2. Do the math and quickly decide which job offer to accept.

❓ Follow-Up Questions

1. How much would you earn weekly from Offer A? How much would you earn weekly from Offer B?

2. Which job pay scale is descriptive of the pattern seen in exponential growth in populations? Explain your answer.

3. Why do you think the Offer B employer would be more likely to limit your number of hours each week than the Offer A employer?

➕ Extension

Graph your earnings per hour for one week of work.

10.3. FOOD WEB
Piecing Together a Food Web Puzzle

Feeding relationships cannot be depicted adequately with simple food chains, because many organisms have multiple food preferences. (See Activity 10.1 for more on food chains.) A better representation of feeding relationships in an ecosystem is a *food web,* because it shows all the interconnected food chains and the pathways of energy flow. This activity will enable you to see the complexity of a food web.

✅ Materials

Envelope containing jigsaw pieces of a food web (prepared by the teacher; see Teacher's Notes)

Activity

1. Your teacher has selected an illustration of a food web and cut it into jigsaw puzzle pieces.
2. Open the envelope and empty the pieces on your desk.
3. You have only a few minutes to put the puzzle together and answer the questions that follow.

❓ Follow-Up Questions

1. What ecosystem do you think you are looking at in the picture?
2. While you look at the picture, answer the following questions:
   a. What producers do you see?
   b. What are some herbivores in the picture?
   c. Which animal(s) are both carnivore and herbivore in the picture?
   d. Which animal(s) have at least three different direct food sources?
3. Which animal in the food web receives the least energy?

➕ Extension

Think of an ecosystem close to where you live. Draw a food web of the organisms that live in that area. If it is accurate, your teacher may have you make a jigsaw puzzle from it and share it with your classmates.

10.4. POPULATION ESTIMATIONS
Mark and Recapture of Wildlife

Wildlife biologists use the mark-and-recapture method to estimate the number of organisms of a certain species living in an area. In this method a random sample of the species under study is trapped. These animals are then marked or ear-tagged and released back in the population. At a later date, animals are captured again. The number of recaptured animals can be used to determine population size. In this activity you will simulate the mark-and-recapture technique and use a simple formula to estimate the population size. In the formula $N/M = n/m$, N stands for the estimated population size, M represents the number of animals marked on the first sample, n is the number of animals captured in the second sample, and m is the number of marked animals captured in the second sample.

✔ Materials

250 ml beaker or medium-size jar; Coffee scoop; White beads; Red beads

1. Fill the beaker or jar about half full of white beads. Estimate how many beads you think you have in the beaker.
2. Collect one scooper of white beads. This represents the number of animals marked in the first capture (M).
3. Count the beads in the scoop and record the number. Set these beads to the side. Replace them in the beaker with the same number of red beads. Gently agitate the beaker to mix up the beads.
4. Without looking, scoop out another sample of beads from the beaker. Count the total number of beads in the scooper and record the count. This is the number of animals captured in the second sample (n).
5. Count and record the number of red beads in the scoop. This is the number of marked animals that were recaptured (m).
6. Use the formula and solve for "N" in the equation.

❓ Follow-Up Questions

1. How many white beads did you estimate were in the beaker before the activity started?
2. How many beads did you calculate with the formula?

➕ Extension

Go back and count the actual number of beads in the beaker. How close did your calculations come to the actual amount?

10.5. THE IMPORTANCE OF NICHES
Extinction and the Paper Clip Niche

All organisms in an ecosystem are interconnected and depend on one another. The role that an organism has in an ecosystem is called its *niche*. If one species in the ecosystem becomes *extinct,* all other organisms are affected. In this activity you will see why it is so important that all organisms fill their respective niches.

✅ Materials

Envelope A, containing ten regular paper clips (prepared by the teacher; see Teacher's Notes)

Envelope B, containing ten paper clips that have been elongated from their bent form (prepared by the teacher; see Teacher's Notes)

Stopwatch

Activity

1. Your role in the ecosystem is to construct a chain made up of ten paper clips. Other organisms in your ecosystem have the job of shaping the paper clips into their typical, rounded style.

2. In envelope A, you will find paper clips that have been prepared for you by other organisms in the ecosystem. Make a chain from these paper clips and time how long it takes.

3. In envelope B, you will find paper clips that are not shaped—the organisms that usually mold paper clips into curves have become extinct. Despite this problem, you must make a chain. Time how long it takes you to make your chain of ten paper clips.

❓ Follow-Up Questions

1. What is your niche in this activity?

2. How did the extinction of one species in your ecosystem affect your ability to fill your niche?

➕ Extension

Do some research and cite a real example of an extinction of one organism that negatively affected the niches of the other organisms.

10.6. SYMBIOSIS
Want Ads for Mutualism

Some organisms live in symbiotic relationships—close associations of two different species. The type of symbiotic relationship in which both organisms benefit is *mutualism*. One example of mutualism exists between the clown fish and the sea anemone. The anemone provides a habitat and protection for the clown fish, while the clown fish attracts prey for the anemone. In this activity you will write a want ad for a mutualistic relationship. Following is one way a want ad from the clown fish to the sea anemone might read.

> Brightly colored marine organism looking for place to live. Will provide all meals by luring prey to our home in exchange for protection and shelter from predators. Call 1-800-CORAL REEF or wave me down next time I'm in the area.

✔ Materials: Index card; Pencil or pen

1. Read the following information about the relationship between the Egyptian plover and the Nile crocodile:

   Birds known as Egyptian plovers live around the Nile River. They feed on parasites that live in the mouths of Nile crocodiles. The consumption of the parasites gives the plovers much-needed food and also relieves the crocodiles of harmful parasites that suck their blood.

2. On the index card write a brief want ad from the plover to the crocodile or from the crocodile to the plover.

❓ Follow-Up Questions

1. How does living with a crocodile benefit an Egyptian plover?
2. How does living with an Egyptian plover benefit a crocodile?
3. What kind of relationship does the crocodile have with the organisms in its mouth? Explain.

➕ Extension

Do some research and find more examples of mutualism. Pick an interesting one and write a want ad from one of the animals. See if your classmates can guess the relationship from the want ad.

10.7. HUMAN POLLUTION
Plastic Killers

Some of the trash we throw away eventually finds its way to the ocean. The plastic loops that hold together six-packs of drinks can be deadly to ocean animals. These plastic rings decay very slowly, taking about three hundred years to break down. These rings can slip over the heads of birds, seals, and fish, binding their jaws or forming nooses around their necks. To protect these animals, six-pack plastic rings should always be cut into pieces before they are placed in the trash. This activity will simulate the struggle ocean animals experience when they become entangled in this debris.

✅ Materials

Plastic rings to hold a six-pack of drinks (cut into six separate rings; see Teacher's Notes)

1. Tightly close the fingers of your dominant hand. Hold your thumb out to the side.
2. Slide the ring over your tightly closed fingers (but not over the thumb). The ring should be positioned so it is just below the first knuckles on your hand and around the bottom of your fingers. This simulates what happens when the ring is caught around the neck of a bird or a seal in the ocean.
3. Try to get the plastic ring off your hand without using your thumb or the other hand. This illustrates the ordeal an ocean animal goes through in this situation.

❓ Follow-Up Questions

1. Explain why you should always take a few minutes to cut the plastic loops from six-packs into pieces before disposing of them.
2. If your hand had been the mouth of a seal, what would happen to the seal if it was unable to remove the plastic loop?

➕ Extension

Imagine that someone polluted a waterway near your school. Find some local maps of the water systems near you and trace the path that the pollutants might take on their way to the nearest ocean.

10.8. PLANT GROWTH REQUIREMENTS

When Seeds Get Too Crowded

Plants, like all living things, require food, water, space, and warmth. When seeds are planted too close together, not all will germinate. A fast-growing population of plants can result in overcrowding that can quickly deplete basic resources. In this activity each member of the class will represent plants attempting to exist with a limited number of resources.

✔ Materials

Hula hoop; Small plate holding twenty jelly beans

Activity

1. One student acts as the class leader who prepares and begins the activity. The leader should place the hula hoop in the center of the room. This will represent the growing zone for the plants.

2. Each person in the room is a plant that needs nutrients to survive. The leader holds the plate of jelly beans and gets inside the hula hoop circle. The jelly beans are nutrients that are available in the growing zone.

3. The leader eats one jelly bean.

4. The leader invites two students to join her in the circle to demonstrate plant reproduction. The leader and the two new plants each take an additional jelly bean.

5. The leader invites four new plants to join the circle, and jelly beans are consumed again.

6. Continue this process until the jelly beans are gone or no more space is available.

❓ Follow-Up Questions

1. Did you run out of room or nutrients first?

2. What would happen if these plants continued to reproduce?

3. Explain in your own words the significance of this activity.

➕ Extension

Try this activity using real plants. Place soil in three small paper cups. In one cup plant one radish seed. In a second cup plant five radish seeds, and in the third cup plant fifty radish seeds. Water each equally and see how germination and the growth of the seeds are affected by overcrowding.

10.9. PACKAGING AND THE ENVIRONMENT
Convenience or Conservation?

Marketing experts know that consumers want convenience. What impact does convenience packaging of food and drink items have on the environment? Think about the way milk is packaged. A half-pint milk carton, like the ones served with many school meals, requires energy and resources to manufacture. Eventually the container ends up in a landfill. In just one school day millions of these cartons are discarded. If milk could be served in reusable containers, natural resources and landfill space could be conserved. In this activity you will compare the materials in a single-serve container and a bulk-serve container.

✔ Materials

One empty, clean half-pint carton of milk; One empty, clean quart carton of milk; Ruler

Activity

1. Unfold the empty half-pint milk container and place it flat on a table.
2. Measure the length and width of the container in centimeters. Record your measurements.
3. Multiply the length by the width and record this value. This is the area of the packaging in a half-pint container of milk.
4. Repeat steps 1 through 3 for the quart container of milk. This is the area of the packaging in a quart of milk.
5. Since four half-pints of milk equal one quart of milk, multiply the area of the half-pint carton by 4. This is the packaging required for four half-pints of milk.
6. How does the amount of packaging in four half-pint cartons of milk compare with the packaging in one quart carton of milk?

❓ Follow-Up Questions

1. What is the area of packaging in the quart container? What is the area of packaging in the pint container?
2. Which packaging uses more natural resources—four half-pints or one quart?

➕ Extension

Repeat this activity, but select some other items that can be purchased in single-use size and in bulk size. List some items that you believe are overpackaged for the sake of convenience.

10.10. ARTHROPOD BEHAVIOR
Response of the Pill Bugs

Pill bugs are members of the Arthropod phylum. All *arthropods* are invertebrates with jointed appendages and hard external skeletons made of *chitin*. A pill bug is a small animal that can roll up into a ball when threatened. Pill bugs live in dark environments, and they breathe with gills. Because they eat dead organic matter, pill bugs play important roles in ecosystems. In this activity you will see whether pill bugs show a preference for dry or moist environments.

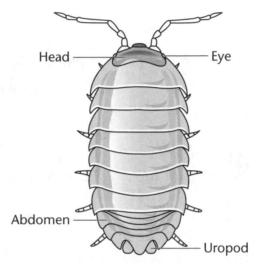

FIGURE 10.1. Pill Bug

✅ Materials

Petri dish

Crayon

Scissors

Filter paper (such as from a coffee filter)

Spray bottle of water

Five pill bugs *(handle carefully; release after the activity is done)*

10.10. ARTHROPOD BEHAVIOR (continued)

Activity

1. Fold the piece of filter paper in half and cut it into two equal parts. You may have to trim the pieces a little to get the right fit in the petri dish.
2. Use a crayon and draw a bold line on the filter paper down the center so that the petri dish is divided into two equal halves.
3. Thoroughly wet one half of the filter paper. Place this half on one side of the line in the dish.
4. Place the dry piece of filter paper in the other half of the dish. You should be able to see the line you drew down the center of the dish. If not, trim the pieces of filter paper.
5. Place the five pill bugs on the center line.
6. Over the next few minutes, see which side the pill bugs move toward.

❓ Follow-Up Questions

1. Did the pill bugs seem to prefer a wet or dry environment? Why do you think this was the case?
2. Pill bugs are members of the subphylum Crustacea. Do you think most crustaceans prefer this type of environment? If you were to go outside and hunt for pill bugs, where might you look?

➕ Extension

See if pill bugs prefer light or dark conditions. Use aluminum foil to cover up one side of the petri dish and see if the pill bugs move toward the light or the dark. Remember to use either all wet or all dry filter paper in the bottom of the dish so that you are testing only one variable.

SECTION ELEVEN

Body Systems

The human body is a testament to the close relationship between structure and function. From the digestive system to the reproductive system, structures in the human body have evolved to carry out their jobs efficiently. To maintain its balance with the external and internal environments, the body constantly tweaks the systems that maintain temperature, chemical reactions, immunity, nutrition, digestion, and all other functions. This section includes activities that show how bile aids in digestion, how the brain and visual systems work to produce images, the jobs of the heart and blood vessels, and the functions of muscles and tendons.

11.1. THE ROLE OF BILE IN DIGESTION
Emulsifying Fat

Food does not physically pass through every organ involved in the digestive process. Some body parts are described as accessory organs because they produce materials that aid digestion. One of these accessory organs is the liver, which secretes and sends *bile* to the small intestine to help with the breakdown of fats. Bile's main role is to *emulsify* fats, separating them into small droplets so the body can use them as nutrients. In this activity you will see how bile breaks up fats.

✅ Materials

Two small clear cups, each filled with 50 ml of water
Two medicine droppers or pipettes
Small container of cooking oil
Small container of dishwashing detergent
Plastic spoon

1. Add two medicine droppers full of cooking oil to each cup of water.
2. Observe the appearance of the oil in the water.
3. Add a dropper full of dishwashing detergent to one of the cups, stirring with the spoon as you release the detergent. Do not add anything to the other cup.
4. Compare the appearance of the oil in both cups.

❓ Follow-Up Questions

1. What did the oil look like when you first added it to the water?
2. What happened to the oil after you added dishwashing detergent to one cup?
3. In the process of digestion, what nutrient do you think the cooking oil represents? What chemical do you think the dishwashing detergent represents?

➕ Extension

Bile is stored in a small sac, the gall bladder, until needed. How do you think the surgical removal of the gall bladder and the subsequent loss of bile might affect a person's digestion? The liver is a multifunctional organ. Research some of the other roles of the liver aside from fat emulsification.

11.2. TENDONS
Visualizing How the Fingers Work

Skeletal muscles are responsible for the movement of bones. As a muscle contracts, it pulls on the bone to produce movement. Cordlike bands of tissue called *tendons* connect muscles to bone. The tendon transmits the force of the muscle contraction to the bone, allowing the muscle action to work from a distance. Your hands contain many little bones in a small space. The tendons in the hand are long and skinny, but extremely strong. The muscles that work these tendons are located higher up the arm. This activity will enable you to see some tendons in action.

 Materials

None

 **Activity**

1. Look at the top of your hand. Extend your fingers out as far as you can. Tense your hand and really stretch to elongate the fingers and hand. Do you see some structures that look like cords or bands on top of your hand? Take the index finger of your opposite hand and rub over the top of these structures.

2. Curl your hand into a clawlike shape. Do you see the tendons on top of the hand?

3. Wiggle your index finger up and down. Try to trace the path of the tendon.

4. Wiggle all your fingers up and down. Try and trace the path of the tendons to each finger.

Follow-Up Questions

1. What do the tendons on the top of your hand look like?

2. When you wiggled your fingers, where did the muscle action seem to originate when you traced the tendon back up the hand?

Extension

One very important structure in the heel is the Achilles tendon. A tear in the Achilles can end the career of a professional athlete. Wiggle your foot up and down and use your hand to try to locate that tendon. What do you think this tendon allows your foot to do?

11.3. THE HEART
The Strongest Muscle of the Body

The circulatory system consists of the blood, a series of vessels to transport the blood, and the heart. The heart, about the size of a fist, works twenty-four hours a day to pump blood throughout the body. The heart of an average person pumps about seventy times a minute. In this activity you will see why it is vital that the heart be an extremely strong muscle.

✔ Materials

Tennis ball

Watch with a second hand

1. Pick up the tennis ball and squeeze it. The force required for you to squeeze the ball is very similar to the force needed to squeeze blood out of the heart.

2. Using the clock to time yourself, count how many times you can squeeze the tennis ball in a period of sixty seconds.

3. How close did you get to seventy times? If you didn't get at least seventy squeezes in, try it again.

❓ Follow-Up Questions

1. How many times were you able to squeeze the tennis ball in the first minute?

2. How did your hand feel after sixty seconds of squeezing?

3. Imagine that you had to squeeze the tennis ball twenty-four hours a day without a break. Compare the heart's strength as a muscle with the strength of the muscles in your hand.

➕ Extension

Calculate how many times your heart has beat over the course of your lifetime. Use seventy beats per minute in your calculations. Multiply 70 by 60 minutes in an hour to get beats per hour. Multiply the result by 24 to get the number of beats per day. Multiply this answer by 365 to get beats per year. Multiply the beats in a year by your age.

11.4. PARTNERING OF THE BRAIN AND EYES
Putting the Fish in the Bowl

The eyes and the brain can work together to create an optical illusion. When you see a picture, your brain and your eyes retain the image for just a fraction of a second after the picture is removed from your line of sight. This phenomenon is called *persistence of vision*. If two pictures are introduced quickly and withdrawn, these images actually overlap in your brain, creating a blended appearance or optical illusion. In this activity you will demonstrate persistence of vision by making a simple *thaumatrope* that will allow you to blend images of a fish and a fishbowl.

 **Materials**

Sharpened pencil

Clear tape

Two index cards

Colored pencils (optional)

 **Activity**

1. Follow these directions to make your thaumatrope:

   a. Turn the two index cards over so the unlined sides are facing up. On one index card draw a picture of a fishbowl that takes up the majority of the card. On the other index card draw a picture of a fish. The fish should be smaller than the fishbowl you drew.

   b. Attach these drawings to the top half of a pencil by firmly taping the lined sides of both cards together with the pencil sandwiched between the cards. The two drawings should be showing on opposite sides of the pencil.

2. Hold the bottom end of the pencil between the palms of your hands. Roll the pencil briskly back and forth between your hands while you look at the index cards. What do you see?

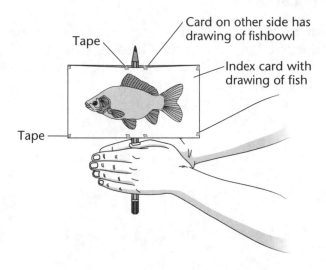

FIGURE 11.1. Fishbowl Thaumatrope

❓ Follow-Up Questions

1. What happened to the two pictures as you twirled the pencil around in your hands?

2. Producers of movies can make still images appear to move by using persistence of vision. How do you think this process works?

➕ Extension

Design your own thaumatrope. Try using circular cardboard rather than rectangular index cards. Do you get the same results?

11.5. LUNG CAPACITY DURING EXERCISE
Balloons and Vital Capacity

The volume of air you breathe out after taking a deep breath is much greater than the quantity you exhale after taking in a normal breath. This maximum volume of expelled air is called the lungs' *vital capacity*. In this activity you will use a balloon and some math skills to determine your vital capacity.

✔ Materials

Large round balloon

Metric tape measure

Calculator (optional)

1. Blow up the balloon a few times to stretch it. Take several deep breaths. When you are ready, take the deepest breath possible, then exhale forcefully into the balloon. Pinch the neck of the balloon so no air escapes, then tie it off with string.

2. Wrap the tape measure around the balloon and measure the circumference in centimeters. Calculate the radius by dividing the circumference by 6.28 (which is pi × 2).

3. Calculate your vital capacity using the formula $V = (4/3)3.14 (radius)^3$.

4. The answer you calculate will be in cubic centimeters (and one cm^3 is equal to 1 milliliter.)

❓ Follow-Up Questions

1. What is your vital capacity?

2. If you had to explain vital capacity to a classmate, what would you say?

➕ Extension

Compare your vital capacity to that of your classmates. Compare your value to other students of different heights, weights, and fitness levels.

11.6. BLOOD VESSELS
Arteries or Veins?

The cardiovascular system includes two kinds of blood vessels. *Arteries* are vessels that carry blood away from the heart. Blood is returned to the heart by way of the *veins*. In this activity you will examine the vessels in your arm.

 **Materials**

None

 **Activity**

1. Place your arm on a table with the palm facing up.

2. Find a blood vessel near the inner surface of your elbow that is clearly visible. If you have trouble seeing one, use your free hand to lightly pat the underside of your arm.

3. Once you find a vessel, use the index finger of your free hand to press firmly on it. Notice what happens to the appearance of the vessel over the next ten seconds.

4. While still pressing on this vessel, slide your index finger down your arm toward your wrist. What happens to the appearance of the vessel above the point you were originally pressing down?

Follow-Up Questions

1. What happened to the vessel as you pressed down on it near the elbow?

2. Judging by what happened as you moved your finger down the vessel, in what direction do you think the blood was flowing (away from or toward the heart)?

3. Were you pressing on an artery or a vein?

Extension

Do some more research about arteries and veins. Are veins and arteries also found deeper in the skin, buried below muscle and connective tissue? Why or why not?

11.7. MUSCLE INTERACTIONS
Pairing of the Biceps and Triceps

Skeletal muscles are voluntary muscles that are directly attached to the skeleton. These muscles work in pairs. In the upper arm, the biceps and triceps muscles work together to bend and straighten the elbow. When the biceps (on the front of upper arm) is contracted, or shortened, the triceps (on the back of upper arm) is elongated, or made longer, and the elbow bends. When the triceps is contracted, the biceps is elongated, and the elbow is straightened. Since neither muscle can stretch itself, it must be stretched by its partner, and for this reason these muscles are called *antagonist (partner) muscles*. In this activity you will see how the biceps and triceps muscles work together when pushing and pulling.

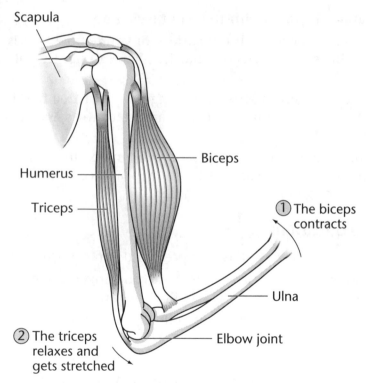

FIGURE 11.2. Muscle Interactions

11.7. MUSCLE INTERACTIONS (continued)

✅ Materials

A table

1. Place one hand under the table so your palm is flat against the underside of the table. Keep your elbow bent. Use that hand to push upward on the table as if you were attempting to lift it. As you do this, use your other hand to feel the muscles being used in the upper arm. Feel both of the biceps and triceps muscles as you pull upward. Attempt to determine which one is being contracted and which one is being elongated.
2. Next take that same hand and put it palm down on top of the table. Push downward on the table. Again, feel the muscles of that upper arm. Determine what the biceps and triceps are doing during this process.

❓ Follow-Up Questions

1. During which of the two activities did the biceps muscle feel harder? During which activity did the triceps muscle feel harder?
2. Using the words *contract* and *elongate,* describe what the biceps and triceps muscles were doing during both of the activities performed today.

➕ Extension

Think of an activity you can do to see how the muscles of the upper leg (quadriceps and hamstrings) work in pairs. Perform the activity and describe what is happening.

11.8. MECHANICAL DIGESTION
The Initial Breakdown of Digestion

As soon as you eat, the digestive process of breaking down food particles begins. The first digestive process, *mechanical digestion*, involves the actions of the teeth and tongue to break food particles into smaller pieces. Later the smaller pieces of food will be further broken down by enzymes during chemical digestion. In this activity you will see how mechanical digestion aids chemical digestion.

✅ Materials

Two paper cups, each filled with 100 ml water

Two sugar cubes of equal size

Spoon

Paper towel

Watch with a second hand

Small plastic bag

 **Activity**

1. Place one sugar cube in a plastic bag and use your textbook and hand to crush it until only sugar particles remain.

2. Simultaneously, drop a whole sugar cube into one cup of water while pouring sugar particles from the baggie into the other cup of water.

3. Wait thirty seconds. Examine the contents of the cups by swirling gently. In which cup was the sugar more effectively dissolved?

❓ Follow-Up Questions

1. Which part of the digestive process do you think crushing the sugar cube represented in this activity?

2. In which cup was more of the sugar dissolved?

3. How does this demonstration represent what happens to food particles in the body after you ingest them?

➕ Extension

Some medications are taken as powders, while others are taken as pills. Why do you think this is so?

11.9. PERISTALSIS DURING DIGESTION

Moving Food Through the Esophagus

Both mechanical and chemical digestion begin in the mouth immediately after we ingest food. The partially digested food travels from the mouth through the esophagus on the way to the stomach. The *esophagus*, a muscular tube-shaped organ, facilitates this process through involuntary, wavelike contractions called *peristalsis*. This activity will simulate how peristalsis occurs through the esophagus.

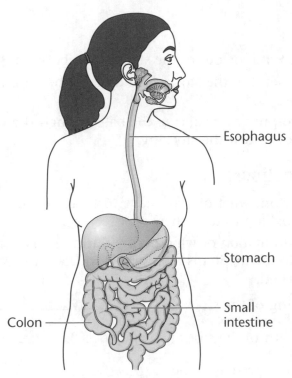

FIGURE 11.3. Digestive System

11.9. PERISTALSIS DURING DIGESTION (continued)

✅ Materials

Tennis ball
Nylon knee-high stocking
Scissors

Activity

1. Use scissors to clip the toe out of the stocking so both ends are open.
2. Hold up one open end of the stocking and place the tennis ball in the opening of the stocking.
3. Use your hands to push and squeeze the ball through the stocking to the other end. Be careful not to tear the stocking.

❓ Follow-Up Questions

1. In the demonstration, what did you have to do to move the tennis ball from one end of the stocking to the other?
2. Since this was a simulation of what occurs during peristalsis, indicate which part each of the following items represented in the digestive tract, referring to Figure 11.3 as needed.

   a. The top opening of the stocking was the _____.

   b. The entire length of the stocking was the _____.

   c. The tennis ball represented the _____.

   d. Your fingers represented the _____.

   e. The bottom end of the stocking represented the _____.

➕ Extension

The muscles of the esophagus are involuntary muscles. Do some research and come up with a list of other involuntary muscles in the human body.

11.10. WHY WE SWEAT
Staying Cool with the Sweat Glands

On hot days or during times of heavy exercise or exertion, glands in the skin help keep us cool by producing sweat. The evaporation of sweat from the skin removes heat and helps us avoid overheating. *Evaporation* is a change in the physical state of a substance from liquid to gas. The rate of evaporation varies depending on the *humidity* (amount of water) in the atmosphere. In this activity you will see how sweat helps keep you cool.

✔ Materials

Thermometer
Cotton ball soaked with rubbing alcohol
Paper towel

Activity

1. Place the thermometer on a paper towel in front of you.
2. Read the air temperature as shown on the thermometer.
3. Thoroughly rub the bulb of the thermometer with rubbing alcohol.
4. Blow on the surface of the bulb for about ten seconds.
5. Read the temperature on the thermometer again.

❓ Follow-Up Questions

1. How did the temperature change in this activity?
2. Rubbing alcohol has a fast rate of evaporation. How do you think this activity demonstrates what happens when we sweat?
3. Why do you think we used rubbing alcohol instead of water in this demonstration?

➕ Extension

Repeat this activity, but do not blow on the bulb of the thermometer. How long does it take to see a temperature decline? Explain why you think it is harder to get cool in humid climates than in dry climates after you sweat.

UNIT III
Earth Science

SECTION TWELVE

Structure of Earth Systems

In the study of earth systems, students learn about planet Earth and its components. This nonliving system is run by the mechanical and thermodynamic laws of the universe. The system is highly energetic and constantly changing. Some of the energy responsible for these changes comes from the Earth's hot core and strong magnetic field. The constantly rotating magma deep in the Earth move the crust, building mountains and creating seas. The sun provides energy that creates air currents and moves water through cycles of precipitation and evaporation. In this section students study soil and processes that form soil, along with the differences between rocks and minerals, the structure of the Earth, and the properties of oceans.

12.1. CORE SAMPLING
Seeing Inside the Cupcake

Rather than digging up a region of land to see what is beneath the surface, geologists can "see" into the Earth by *core sampling*. During this process a special drill is lowered into the Earth to remove a cylindrical piece of subsurface material. The sample taken by the drill is then analyzed to map the contents of the area in question. In this activity you will take a core sample of a cupcake.

✅ Materials

Three clear stiff drinking straws; A cupcake with cream filling; Drawing paper; Colored pencils

1. Sketch what you think the inside of the cupcake looks like. Include details and indicate exactly how much of the cupcake is filled with cream and how far below the top of the cake the filling is located.

2. Use a straw to take a core sample by gently twisting the straw to penetrate the entire depth of the cupcake. Gently pull the straw out and observe the contents through the sides of the straw.

3. Repeat step 2 with the other 2 straws in a different part of the cupcake.

4. Look at your original drawing of the inside of the cupcake. Do you need to change it? If so, what changes do you need to make?

5. Break the cupcake in half and check the accuracy of your drawings.

❓ Follow-Up Questions

1. How are the components of the cupcake similar to the components of Earth?

2. If you had been getting ready to drill for oil, would the core sample technique help you prepare for the drilling process? Explain the ways it might help.

➕ Extension

Have a classmate select a solid object such as a ball, a toy car, or a small pencil. Ask the classmate to wrap modeling clay around the object so you cannot see it. Use toothpicks to penetrate the clay to touch the object. See if you can guess what the object is by making a mental picture of it through probing.

12.2. METAMORPHIC ROCKS
Pressure and the Candy Bar

Rocks undergo transformations, depending on the physical conditions surrounding them. If *sedimentary* rocks, which are made of layers of material, or *igneous* rocks, which are made of cooled lava or magma, are exposed to high pressures and temperatures, they can be changed into *metamorphic* rocks. The process of changing is a very slow one that occurs deep within the Earth. This activity will help you visualize what happens when a rock morphs into its metamorphic form.

✔ Materials

Snack-size candy bar that has been cut in half (a candy bar with several ingredients, like peanuts, caramel, and so on, works best); Two blocks of wood (larger than the candy bar); Two pieces of wax paper (about the same size as the blocks of wood); Crayons

Activity

1. Look at the cut side of the candy bar. Sketch the appearance of the cut side, including any layers, and color the layers to differentiate what you see.
2. Place one piece of wax paper on the block of wood, then put the candy bar on the wax paper. Place another piece of wax paper on top of the candy bar, then the second block of wood.
3. Use your hands to press down on the top block of wood to flatten the candy bar. You may need to stand on the block if you cannot exert sufficient pressure with your hands.
4. Reexamine the cut side of the candy bar. Sketch its appearance once again.

❓ Follow-Up Questions

1. Did your original sketch have layers? If so, describe them.
2. After you exerted pressure on the candy bar, how many layers could you see in the cut side?
3. Explain how this activity describes what happens during the formation of metamorphic rocks.

➕ Extension:
Sedimentary rocks are made from tiny particles of soil washed down streams into deposits that become thicker each year. Over time these deposits form sedimentary rocks. Think of a demonstration you could do to show a classmate how sedimentary rocks are formed.

12.3. SEDIMENTATION
Making Sedimentary Rocks

Most sedimentary rocks are made up of a combination of several types of sediments. Sediments may be composed of mud, sand, and pebbles, as well as the remains of dead plants and animals. These sediments are usually deposited in the sea by rivers and waves. As millions of years pass, the sediments accumulate layer by layer. The processes of compaction, the compression of material, and cementation, the "glueing" together of sediment grains by dissolved minerals, eventually convert the layers into sedimentary rock. In this activity you will observe the process of sedimentation.

✔ Materials

Jar with a lid
Water
Tablespoon
Fine silt (about 5 tbsp)

 **Activity**

1. Fill the jar about three-quarters full of water.
2. Add the silt and put the lid on the jar securely.
3. Shake the jar briskly back and forth for about twenty seconds.
4. Place the jar on the table and watch what happens for the next two to three minutes.

❓ Follow-Up Questions

1. What did the shaking of the silt in the jar represent?
2. What does the silt represent in this activity?
3. What happened when you left the jar undisturbed after the shaking?
4. The sedimentary accumulation rate for an area is about 0.15 centimeter a year. How long would it take for 10 centimeters of sediment to deposit?

➕ Extension

Repeat this activity a few times, each time varying the temperature of the water in the jar. Does the temperature of the water make a difference in the sedimentation rate?

12.4. SOIL CONSERVATION
How Much of the Earth Is Usable Soil?

Humans depend on the soil for food, because it supports both plant and animal life. It may seem that soil is in abundant supply because we see it everywhere. What we do not often realize is that soil is not really that plentiful. The process of soil formation takes hundreds of thousands of years. Water and wind erosion are constantly depleting the amount of soil that is available for use. This activity will help you put into perspective how little of the Earth's crust contains usable soil.

 **Materials**

Paper plate; Ruler; Scissors

 **Activity**

1. Look at the paper plate and imagine that this paper plate represents a one-dimensional view of the surface of the Earth. As you read the statements below, use the scissors to cut away the parts of the Earth's surface that have unusable soil.

   a. Cut away three-fourths of the paper plate. This represents the fact that 75 percent of the Earth is water.

   b. Of the one-fourth remaining, half is composed of deserts, mountains, bogs, cities, and other areas that do not have usable soil. Cut away one-half of the slice that remains.

   c. Of the small slice you have left, 75 percent has temperatures and weather conditions that prevent it from being used for cultivation. Cut away three-quarters of the remaining plate.

2. Look at the slice of paper plate you have left in your hand. It represents only about one thirty-second of the Earth's surface.

❓ Follow-Up Questions

1. What are some ways that humans use the soil?
2. What are some ways that humans abuse the usable soil supply?

➕ Extension

Do some research and look up the areas of the Earth that have the greatest amount of fertile soil. How are we trying to conserve the soil in these areas?

12.5. PHYSICAL WEATHERING OF ROCKS
Sugar Cube Breakdown

The rocks that compose the Earth's crust are subjected to a variety of forces. Depending on the environmental factors at work, the rocks can be altered in size or in composition. Factors such as wind, water, plants, and animals cause *weathering*, physical changes in rocks that affect their size. However, physical changes do not affect the composition of rock. In this activity you will see the effect of physical weathering on rocks.

✅ Materials

Piece of sandpaper; Tape; Small jar with a lid; Three sugar cubes; Paper plate

 **Activity**

1. Open the jar and line the inside of it with the piece of sandpaper so that the rough surface is facing the interior and the smooth surface is against the glass. Tape the sandpaper onto the inside walls of the jar.
2. Look at the sugar cubes and note their sizes.
3. Drop the three sugar cubes in the jar and close the lid.
4. Shake the jar vigorously for two minutes.
5. At the end of two minutes, open the lid and carefully pour the contents of the jar onto the paper plate.

❓ Follow-Up Questions

1. How did the size and consistency of the sugar cubes change after being agitated in the jar?
2. What type of environmental force do you think you were simulating when you shook the jar? What did the sugar cubes represent in this activity?
3. *Chemical weathering* changes the composition of rocks. How do you know that the type of weathering in this activity was physical and not chemical?

➕ Extension

Plan another activity to show the physical weathering of sugar cubes in which you can collect quantitative data by finding the mass of the chunks of sugar cubes before and after the activity. Show your plan to your teacher.

12.6. MINERAL HARDNESS
Mineral Ranks

Minerals can be identified by a variety of characteristics, but one of the most useful ways is to test their hardness. *Hardness* is the measure of the resistance of a mineral to being scratched. Geologists use a standard hardness called the *Mohs scale* to rank minerals from 1 (softest) to 10 (hardest). The scale indicates which common objects can scratch certain minerals. If you are just comparing the hardness of minerals with each other, you can do so without using the Mohs scale. Just remember a harder mineral is capable of scratching a softer mineral, and a softer mineral may leave a streak on the harder mineral. In this activity you will arrange five unidentified minerals in order of hardness, from softest to hardest.

Mineral	Hardness
Talc	1
Gypsum	2
Calcite	3
Fluorite	4
Apatite	5
Feldspar	6
Quartz	7
Topaz	8
Corundum	9
Diamond	10

FIGURE 12.1. Mohs Scale of Hardness

12.6. MINERAL HARDNESS (continued)

✔ Materials

Cup containing five unidentified minerals of different hardness (prepared by the teacher and labeled A, B, C, D, and E; see Teacher's Notes)

Pencil

Paper plate

Activity

1. Empty the minerals from the cup onto the paper plate.

2. Your task is to arrange the minerals in order, starting with the softest mineral and ending with the hardest mineral.

   a. Rub any two minerals together and see which of the two is capable of scratching the other mineral. (Note: After rubbing two minerals together, rub your finger over the mark left on one to determine whether the mark is a scratch or a streak. A streak can be rubbed off, but a scratch cannot.)

   b. Continue this process until you are able to rank the minerals from softest to hardest.

❓ Follow-Up Questions

1. What was the softest mineral? What was the hardest?

2. Based on the scratch and streak test, list the minerals you examined in this activity from softest to hardest.

3. Look at the Mohs scale in Figure 12.1. Which mineral can be scratched with your fingernail?

➕ Extension

Using the Mohs scale and some common objects you have on hand, attempt to determine the actual hardness of the five minerals you ranked today.

12.7. CROSS SECTION OF THE EARTH
Egg Modeling

The interior of the Earth is composed of three primary layers: the crust, the mantle, and the core. The outermost layer is the *crust*. This thin layer, composing only 1 percent of Earth's mass, is made of hard, solid rock. Beneath the crust is the *mantle*, a layer of solid and molten rock. The mantle is about two-thirds of the mass of Earth. The center of the Earth beneath the mantle is called the *core*. The core, almost one-third of the mass of the Earth, is divided into a liquid outer region and a solid inner region. Scientists speculate that the core is made primarily of iron and nickel. In this activity you will use a boiled egg to model a cross section of Earth.

✔ Materials

Boiled egg (in its shell); Plastic knife; Small cup of water; Pushpin; Paper plate

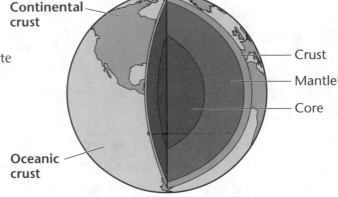

FIGURE 12.2. Cross Section of the Earth

Activity

1. Look at the boiled egg and imagine that it represents the Earth. Look at the shell surrounding the egg. What part of the Earth do you think this represents?
2. Dip the blade of the plastic knife in water and carefully cut the egg in half lengthwise. Do not peel the egg; cut through the shell as well.
3. Examine the inside of one half of the egg. Set the other half aside for the extension activity.
4. Use the pushpin to make a small indention in the center of the yolk in the interior of the egg.

❓ Follow-Up Questions

1. What does the shell of the egg represent? What does the egg white represent? What is represented by the majority of the egg yolk? What does the pinprick inside the yolk represent?
2. How is the egg model similar to the real Earth? Which elements in this model are wrong?

➕ Extension

Gently crack the external shell of the unused egg half so that it has several broken segments. What do you think this now represents? Note that these segments can push against one another. What does that represent?

12.8. POROSITY OF SOIL SAMPLES
Soil's Holding Power

Soil is made up of particles of different sizes, shapes, and composition. These particles do not fit together snugly. The vacant areas between particles are called *pore spaces.* When water seeps into the soil, it gets stuck in these pore spaces. Pore spaces support life in the soil such as plants, fungi, small animals, and microscopic organisms. In this activity you will determine soil's *porosity*, the percentage of pore spaces.

 Materials

Two 500 ml beakers

Dry or sandy soil (400 ml)

Water

Activity

1. Place 400 ml of dry soil in one of the beakers.
2. Pour exactly 400 ml of water in the other beaker.
3. Set the beaker of soil on a flat surface in front of you.
4. Slowly pour water from the second beaker into the soil sample. Continue to pour water into the beaker of soil until the water level reaches the top of the soil sample.
5. Determine the amount of water left in the beaker.

Follow-Up Questions

1. How much water remained in the beaker of water after the activity? How many milliliters of water fit in the pore spaces of the soil sample?
2. Calculate the porosity of the soil sample by dividing the volume of the pore space by the total volume of soil. In other words, divide the amount of water taken up by the soil by 400 ml (the total volume of the soil).

Extension

Compare the porosity of several different types of soils by collecting soil samples from different areas and repeating the process you used today. Which samples would be the best for supporting living things?

12.9. GROUNDWATER AND PERMEABILITY
Just Passing Through

Water permeates soil and accumulates beneath the surface of Earth as *groundwater*. *Permeability* refers to the rate at which water flows through the soil. Different surfaces and rock types hold different amounts of water. Surface permeability is very important for geologists to monitor because water is more likely to pool on top of ground surfaces that are impermeable, a factor that increases the risk of flooding. Water that does penetrate the surface of the earth will flow downhill until it comes in contact with impermeable rock. At this point the water will flow in a lateral direction in locations called *aquifers*. It is in these aquifers that our groundwater is stored. In this activity you will observe the difference between impermeable and permeable substances.

✅ Materials

Two paper cups; Modeling clay; Ruler; Potting soil; Water

1. Put modeling clay in one cup to a depth of two inches.
2. Put potting soil in the other cup to a depth of two inches. Do not pack down the soil.
3. Pour 50 ml of water into both cups.
4. Over the next thirty seconds, observe what happens to the water in the two cups.

❓ Follow-Up Questions

1. What happened to the water in each cup?
2. Which of the cups represented the permeable substance? Which represented the impermeable substance?
3. Explain what you learned from this activity.

➕ Extension

Place some gravel, sand, and clay in three different paper cups to a depth of two inches each. Use your pencil tip to punch three holes in the bottom of each cup. Position one cup in a tall, narrow drinking glass so that it is suspended above the bottom of the glass. Pour 60 ml of water into the cup. Do the same with the other two cups. After twenty-four hours see which glass has collected the most water. The soil in this glass is the most permeable.

12.10. WATER IN THE OCEAN
Sink or Float?

Ocean water is described as "salty" because it contains many dissolved minerals, including sodium chloride. But the ocean's salinity is not constant. Areas near rivers receive large volumes of fresh water. When these two types of water intermingle, they do not immediately mix. In this activity you will see how freshwater and salt water interact.

✔ Materials

Two transparent plastic cups (one half-filled with salt water, the other half-filled with freshwater—both of them labeled)

Medicine dropper filled with freshwater mixed with blue food coloring

Medicine dropper filled with salt water mixed with red food coloring

Activity

1. Place a few drops of blue freshwater into the cup of salt water. Do not stir or mix.
2. Observe the behavior of the blue freshwater for a few minutes.
3. Place a few drops of red salt water into the cup of freshwater. Do not stir or mix.
4. Observe the behavior of the red salt water for a few minutes.

❓ Follow-Up Questions

1. Did the blue freshwater sink or float in the salt water?
2. Did the red salt water sink or float in the freshwater?
3. Density refers to the mass of a material per unit volume. Which type of water is denser—fresh or salt? How do you know?

➕ Extension

Design an experiment to find out how the amount of salt in water affects its density.

12.11. OCEAN CURRENTS
Temperatures Start the Motion

Ocean currents are regular streams of water that move throughout the ocean. One factor that causes ocean water to move is the difference in the *density* of cold and warm water. The sun does not heat the Earth evenly: water near the equator receives more direct sunlight than water at the poles. Cold water is denser than warm water, so the heavier polar water sinks and moves along the sea floor toward the equator. This sets up density-driven ocean currents. In this activity you will see how cold water behaves.

✔ Materials

Ice cube tinted with food coloring

250 ml beaker or medium-size jar of room-temperature water

1. Place the colored ice cube in the beaker of water.
2. Observe the ice cube for a few minutes. Note what happens to the tinted water as the ice cube melts.

❓ Follow-Up Questions

1. What happens to the tinted meltwater?
2. Eventually the beaker of water and the meltwater will be the same temperature. What would you expect to happen then?

➕ Extension

Do some research on the molecular structure of water and find out why cold water is denser than ice.

12.12. BOTTLE ERUPTION
Volcanic Activity

A volcano is a point on Earth's surface where *magma*, or molten rock, erupts through the surface. On the surface, the magma is called *lava*. Some volcanoes erupt slowly, sending out a steady stream of lava. Others spew lava into the sky, where some of it cools and becomes ash. In this activity you will create a model of a volcanic eruption.

✔ Materials

Three or four sheets of newspaper

Small soft drink bottle, washed and label removed

1/4 cup water

1/4 cup vinegar

Few drops of red food coloring

Few drops of dishwashing detergent

Toilet tissue (one square)

1 tbsp baking soda

Goggles

 Activity

1. Sit on the floor and spread three or four layers of newspaper in front of you.
2. Put on your goggles.
3. Pour the water, vinegar, food coloring, and detergent in the bottle.
4. Wrap the baking soda in the tissue. When you are ready for the eruption, drop the tissue into the bottle.

❓ Follow-Up Questions

1. In this activity, what does the bottle represent?
2. What does the red foam coming out of the bottle represent?
3. What part of the experiment represents the magma?

➕ Extension

Find out how varying the amounts of vinegar and baking soda affect the rate of your model volcanic eruption.

SECTION THIRTEEN

Earth's History

Unlike the Moon and the other planets, Earth has undergone dynamic changes since its formation 4.6 billion years ago. The constant evolution of Earth means that its present state is very different from past conditions. To understand how the Earth has changed, scientists remotely study its interior and directly examine its exterior. Rock layers and fossils provide a lot of information. Shifting tectonic plates help explain many geological features. In this section students examine the processes that form fossils, and the relationships of fossils to rock layers. They also find out how Earth's magnetic field has, and is still, changing. Glaciers, volcanoes, and rockslides also provide insights into Earth's development and present character.

13.1. INFERENCES FROM FOSSILS
Who Was Here?

One way scientists learn about the past is from the evidence they find. *Fossils*, the remains or traces of organisms that lived in the past, provide *evidence* that you can gather directly. If you are examining a fossilized dinosaur and find the remains of insects in its stomach, you have evidence that the dinosaur ate insects. However, direct evidence from fossils can only tell a scientist so much. Scientists must also draw some inferences from the fossils. *Inferences* are conclusions that are drawn from the evidence. If the insects in the dinosaur's stomach are a type typically found around swamps, the scientists might infer that the dinosaur lived in a swampy region. In this activity your teacher will show you a bag filled with items. You will examine the evidence and then make some inferences.

✔ Materials

Bag of items prepared by the teacher (see Teacher's Notes)

1. Examine the direct evidence, the items in the bag. List the items.
2. Draw some inferences about the bag of items by answering these questions:

    a. Does anything in the bag suggest whether the owner was male or female?

    b. Does anything in the bag suggest the age of the owner?

    c. Does anything in the bag suggest the size of the owner?

    d. Does anything in the bag suggest where the owner lived?

❓ Follow-Up Questions

1. What is the difference between *evidence* and *inference*?
2. If you examined a fossilized animal that had sharp teeth, claws, feathers, two long rear legs, two short front legs, and a tail, what might you infer from this evidence about the animal?

➕ Extension

Using the evidence and your inferences about the animal described in follow-up question 2, draw the organism.

13.2. MAGNETIC ROCKS

Lodestones

Lodestones are naturally occurring magnetic rocks. These iron-bearing rocks became magnetized by their positions in Earth's crust in relation to its magnetic field. Lodestones have both north and south poles. For this reason, these rocks were used in the first compasses. In this activity you will see how to magnetize a rock that contains iron so it becomes a lodestone.

✅ Materials

Iron-bearing rock (such as magnetite or hematite); Iron filings (about 1 tbsp); Sheet of paper; Strong bar magnet

 Activity

1. Hold the rock to be magnetized in your left hand. Sprinkle the iron filings on top of the rock. Quickly turn the rock over to allow the filings to fall onto a piece of white paper. Note whether any of the iron filings stick to the rock.
2. Remove the filings from your desktop.
3. Hold the bar magnet in your right hand and stroke the stone gently with one pole of the bar magnet. Do this 75 to 100 times. Then put away the bar magnet.
4. Hold the rock in your left hand and place the teaspoon of iron filings on the side of the rock you were stroking with the magnet.
5. Turn the rock upside down above the white paper. Examine the rock to see whether any iron filings stayed attached.

❓ Follow-Up Questions

1. Did any iron filings stay attached to the rock when you flipped it over before you stroked it with the magnet?
2. Did any iron filings stay attached to the rock when you flipped it over after you stroked it with the magnet?
3. Could you now use this rock to make a magnet? Explain.

➕ Extension

Repeat the above activity, but test different types of rock. Test other iron-bearing rocks such as limonite, siderite, and taconite. Also test rocks that do not contain iron. Determine whether all types of rocks can be magnetized.

13.3. RADIOACTIVE ROCKS
The Age of Rocks

Old rocks and new rocks look alike. One way scientists determine the ages of rocks is through radioactive decay analysis. Every radioactive element decays at a unique rate, a period of time known as the sample's *half-life*—the time required for one-half of the nuclei of a radioactive sample to decay. Scientists can calculate how many years a rock has existed by the amount of radioactive element that still remains in the rock. By comparing these values with the known values, scientists can determine the age of the rock. In this activity you will determine the half-life of a fictitious radioactive element that we will call Paperium.

✅ Materials

Piece of graph paper; Scissors

1. Cut a square area out of the graph paper that is 16 blocks wide and 16 blocks tall. This square contains 256 blocks. Set aside the rest of the graph paper.

2. You are now looking at a whole sample of the element Paperium. This element has a half-life of one thousand years, so every thousand years one-half of the element decays. You will represent the decay by cutting out some of the squares with scissors. Following is the procedure:

    a. Cut the paper in half and throw away one-half. This represents the sample that remains after one thousand years. What fraction of the element remains?

    b. Cut the sample in half again to indicate that another one thousand years have passed. Two half-lives of the element have now gone by. Throw the decayed portion away. What fraction of the original element now remains?

    c. Repeat this for a third half-life. What fraction of the original remains?

    d. Repeat this for a fourth half-life. What fraction of the original remains?

❓ Follow-Up Questions

1. What fraction of the original element remained after the second half-life? The third half-life? The fourth half-life?

2. If scientists discovered a rock that contained Paperium, but only one-eighth of the original sample remained, what would be the age of that rock?

➕ Extension

Solve this problem: radium-226 has a half-life of 1,599 years. If a rock was discovered that contained one-sixteenth of the original amount of radium-226, how old would the rock be?

13.4. CONTINENTAL DRIFT
Puzzling Over the Continents

In 1912 German scientist Alfred Wegener proposed the theory of *continental drift*, saying the continents of the Earth must once have been joined together in a single landmass, which he called Pangaea. Wegener believed that millions of years ago Pangaea started breaking apart. Over time the continents moved to their present-day locations. If you observe the shape of the boundaries of the continents, you can see that they look like jigsaw pieces that appear to fit together. In this activity you will piece together the continents of the Earth back into one land mass.

✅ Materials

Envelope filled with cutouts of the continents of the Earth (prepared by the teacher; see Teacher's Notes)

Map of the world

1. Empty the contents of the envelope onto a table.
2. Fit the pieces into one large landmass by piecing them together in the best configuration you can find. (Note: The fits will not be exactly perfect. Over time sedimentation and deformation have changed the outlines of the continents.)
3. After you have pieced the landmass together, take out the map of the world.
4. Look at your puzzle pieces and compare them with the map. Do you think you put the pieces together correctly?

❓ Follow-Up Questions

1. Which two continents seemed to fit together best when you pieced them together?
2. When you compared your assembled pieces with the map, did you have your puzzle pieces arranged properly?

➕ Extension

Do some research and read about the theory of plate tectonics. Find a picture of the boundaries of the plates on a world map. If you put the plates together (rather than the edges of the continents), would the fit be better? What do scientists say happens as these plates move against each other?

13.5. STRENGTH OF EARTHQUAKES

It's the Cracker's Fault

Earthquakes are vibrations of the Earth that result when large areas of the Earth's crust, called *plates*, move against each other. The fractures along which movement occurs are called *faults*. Vibrations produced by earthquakes vary in intensity depending on the amount of movement along the fractures. In weaker earthquakes, the fracture lines are fairly even and the plates slide past each other with minimal grinding and displacement. In the case of larger earthquakes, the fracture lines may be uneven, blocking movement of the plates. Once movement begins, there can be a rapid release of energy that sends out the strong vibrations characteristic of intense earthquakes. In this activity you will observe the forces that create earthquakes of different intensities.

✔ Materials

Large paper plate; Graham cracker (or other cracker with a perforated line down the center)

Activity

1. Place the paper plate on a table.
2. Break the cracker in half along the perforated line.
3. Place the two pieces of the cracker on the paper plate so they look as they did before you broke them apart. Be sure the pieces are touching.
4. While keeping the two pieces on the plate and in contact with one another, push them together so that one piece moves upward and the other piece downward. Observe what happens during this process.
5. Dispose of one-half of the cracker and keep the other half for the extension activity. Break the cracker you saved into two pieces. Look at the edges along the break. Are they smooth or uneven?
6. Repeat steps 3 and 4 with this cracker.

❓ Follow-Up Questions

1. What did the breaks in the cracker represent?
2. Which cracker movement created the most debris? Which cracker movement represented the stronger earthquake?
3. What does this activity demonstrate?

➕ Extension

Get two small wood blocks and glue a piece of sandpaper to each. Press the blocks together so the rough sandpaper sides are in contact. While pushing the blocks together, try and slide the blocks in opposite directions. What does this activity tell you about the pressure and energy created along a fault line prior to movement of the plates?

13.6. FOSSIL MOLDS AND CASTS
Making Fossils

Fossils are the remains or impressions of once-living plants and animals. The best impressions are made from the hard parts of an organism, but the soft areas, such as skin and scales, can also be preserved under the right conditions. An impression of a fossil is called a *mold*, the space or hole left by an organism's body. Over time that space can be filled with minerals and sediment that harden into a *cast*. In this activity you will make molds of both soft and hard objects.

✔ Materials

Coin or some other hard object

Leaf

Modeling clay

1. Divide the modeling clay into two piles.
2. Mold both clay piles into pancake shapes.
3. Put the coin on the desk and press one clay pancake over the coin.
4. Carefully peel the clay away from the coin, trying not to deform the mold you made.
5. Repeat this process with the leaf.
6. Compare your two molds.

❓ Follow-Up Questions

1. Which made the better impression, the coin or the leaf? Why?
2. Explain how this activity is similar to what occurs when a fossil is being made.
3. If you filled in your mold with plaster of paris, what would the hardened material inside the mold be called?

➕ Extension

Make a cast from the molds you made. Mix 10 teaspoons of plaster of paris with 5 teaspoons of water. Pour the liquid material into the molds and allow them to harden. Separate the clay from the plaster of paris cast. How does the cast compare to the original items?

13.7. GLACIERS
Ice in Motion

Glaciers are large masses of moving ice. In areas with deep layers of snow and grainy ice, the pressure of the overlying areas flattens the ice grains and squeezes out air bubbles. As snow and grains of ice continue to stack, the glacier may either move outward under its own weight or move down a slope. Like rivers, glaciers can be agents of erosion as they begin to move, picking up sediment and rock along the way. As a result of the abrasive action of a moving glacier, new landforms may be created. In this activity you will observe the effect that the movement of a glacier can have on landforms.

✅ Materials

Lid from a shoe box; Index card; Double-sided tape; One-quart resealable plastic bag filled with a mixture of table salt, sand, small pebbles, and rock salt (in about equal proportions)

Activity

1. Place the shoe box lid on a table to serve as a small rectangular container. Empty the mixture of salts, sand, and pebbles into the shoe box lid. Spread them out with your hand until you have a level surface.

2. Completely cover one side of the index card with double-sided tape. Do not put tape on the other side of the card.

3. With the sticky side of the card touching the salt-sand mixture in the box, move the card along the length of the box, exerting even pressure as you move it across.

4. Notice how the sand-salt mixture changed after the card was moved across it. Inspect the underside of the card.

❓ Follow-Up Questions

1. What did the salt-sand mixture represent in this activity? How did it change after the card was moved across it?

2. What did the sticky card represent in this activity?

3. Explain how glaciers cause erosion to the surface of the Earth.

➕ Extension

Make a model glacier by freezing a water-sand-pebble mixture in an ice cube tray. When it is frozen, try rubbing it over different surfaces to see what effect it has. Vary the amounts of sand and pebbles you put in individual cubes and note how this changes the effect of your "glacier."

13.8. DEFORMATION OF ROCKS
Rocks Under Stress

The Earth's crust and its rigid upper mantle, the *lithosphere*, are broken into sections or blocks called *tectonic plates*. As the lithosphere moves, rocks in the crust are squeezed, stretched, and twisted. The force put on the rocks by these actions is called stress. There are three different types of stress in the rocks of the lithosphere: tension, compression, and shear. During *tension stress*, rocks are pulled in opposite directions. *Compression stress* squeezes and shortens rock as they are pushed together. *Shear stress* distorts the shape of rocks by pushing certain sections in opposite directions. In this activity you will model the three types of rock stresses using large marshmallows.

 Materials

Three large marshmallows
Paper towel

 **Activity**

1. Model tension stress by holding a marshmallow between the fingers of both hands. Slowly pull the edges of the marshmallow in opposite directions as if you were attempting to pull it apart. Observe what happens.

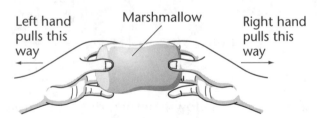

Left hand pulls this way

Marshmallow

Right hand pulls this way

FIGURE 13.1. Tension Stress

2. Model compression stress by holding a second marshmallow between your thumbs and forefingers. Push the edges of the marshmallow toward each other as if you were trying to make them meet. Observe what happens.

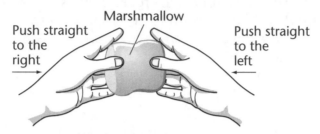

FIGURE 13.2. Compression Stress

3. Model shear force by holding the last marshmallow between your thumbs and forefingers. Push one edge of the marshmallow downward while you push the other edge upward. Observe what happens.

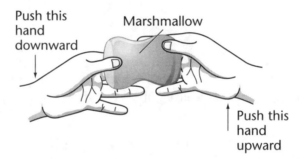

FIGURE 13.3. Shear Force

❓ Follow-Up Questions

1. Does the shape of the marshmallow lengthen during compression or tension stress?

2. What happens to the shape of the marshmallow during shear stress?

3. Describe the differences between the three types of stresses that can occur to rocks as the lithosphere moves.

➕ Extension

Do some research and find out what happens to different types of rocks when put under these three types of stresses.

13.9. GEOLOGIC TIME SCALE MODEL
Earth's History on a Football Field

Earth is about 4.6 billion years old. In its infancy, the planet was made of hot molten rock that slowly cooled. When Earth was about 3.5 billion years old, life began to appear in the form of simple cells. Billions of years are difficult to visualize. To put that time frame of Earth's history into periods that we can comprehend, we can make a scaled-down model. In this activity you will fit the entire history of the Earth on a football field.

✔ Materials

Pencil; Ruler; Paper

1. Draw an imaginary football field on your paper. The length of a football field from one goal line to the other is 100 yards. Turn the paper horizontally and draw two goal lines at opposite ends of the paper. Now make equal spaces in between the goal lines so you have lines indicating 10, 20, 30, 40, 50, 60, 70, 80, and 90 yards. The first goal line is 0 and the last goal line represents 100 yards.
2. On the 0 yard line, write "today." On the opposite goal line, write "origin of the Earth."
3. To position some of the important events in the history of the Earth on the football field, use the following formula and solve for X. In each calculation, X represents the location of the event on the football field.

$$\frac{\text{Event in real time age of Earth}}{4{,}600{,}000{,}000 \text{ years (Earth age)}} = \frac{\text{Event location of football field (X)}}{100 \text{ yards (length of field)}}$$

4. Use the formula above to calculate three important Earth events on the football field. Once you solve for X, write each event in the correct place on the football field. Following are the three events:

   ⮕ Oldest evidence of life: 3,800,000,000 years ago

   ⮕ Oldest fish fossils: 510,000,000 years ago

   ⮕ *Homo sapiens* (humans) appear in fossil record: 100,000 years ago

❓ Follow-Up Questions

1. What values did you get for the three events you calculated?
2. How far away in yards is the appearance of humans from the first life form?

➕ Extension: Do some research to find other important events in Earth's history. Position the events on the appropriate yard lines on your imaginary football field.

13.10. GRADED BEDDING
Breaking the Law

Layers of rock can hold clues about the sequence of events in Earth's past. The *law of superposition* says that when you look at layers of sedimentary rock, the upper layers are younger than the bottom layers. This law applies most of the time, because sedimentary rocks are generally formed in horizontal layers. However, sedimentary rocks that have been tilted or deformed by crustal movements defy that law because older layers may have been pushed up above younger ones. In these cases scientists can look at graded bedding to find clues about the original position of the rock layers before deformation. In many environments the heavy and coarse particles will be deposited on the bottom layers. The arrangement of heavy and coarse layers at the bottom is called *graded bedding*. If scientists find the heavy particles on the top layers, they can assume that the layers were overturned by tectonic forces. In this activity you will observe the formation of graded bedding.

✅ Materials

Tall plastic container with a tight-fitting cap or lid

Mixture of equal amount of small pebbles, sand, and silt to cover several inches of the bottom of the container

Water

1. Put the pebble, sand, and silt mixture in the container to a depth of several inches.
2. Put enough water in the container to rise one inch above the solid material.
3. Secure the lid tightly. Vigorously shake the container for about thirty seconds.
4. Place the container flat on a table and watch what happens. Note the sequence in which the sand, pebbles, and silt settle to the bottom of the container.

❓ Follow-Up Questions

1. What did this activity represent about the age of rock layers?
2. What is graded bedding? In what order did the particles settle to the bottom of the container?

➕ Extension

Cross-bedding and *ripple marks* are also clues to determining the original arrangement of rock layers. Do some research to find out what these terms mean and what they tell scientists about rock layers and their ages.

13.11. SEISMIC WAVES
Human Wave Form

Earth's crust is made up of several large, slow-moving plates. When two plates collide, earthquakes result. Earthquakes produce two basic types of seismic waves: surface waves and body waves. As the name suggests, *surface waves* travel along the exterior of the crust. *Body waves*, which can be P-waves or S-waves, travel through the interior of the Earth. *P-waves* are compressional, so the ground is alternately squeezed and dilated, similar to the motion of a wave traveling along a Slinky. *S-waves* are transverse, so the ground moves perpendicular to the direction of the wave, like an ocean wave. In this activity you and your classmates will model P-waves and S-waves.

✔ Materials: None

FIGURE 13.4. Simulating Seismic Waves

1. Stand side-by-side in line with ten to fifteen other students.
2. Put your arms on the shoulders of the students on both sides of you. Be sure to keep your arms this way through the entire activity.
3. To demonstrate a P-wave, the teacher will gently push the student on one end of the line toward the line, beginning a compression. Notice what happens to each person in the line.
4. To demonstrate an S-wave, the person at one end of the line bends at the waist at a 90-degree angle, then straightens back up. Notice what happens to each person in the line.

❓ Follow-Up Questions

1. How did you and your classmates demonstrate the action of a P-wave?
2. How did you and your classmates demonstrate the action of an S-wave?

➕ Extension

The time it takes for a wave to travel is called its *period* and the distance the wave travels is the *wavelength*. *Wave velocity,* the distance traveled per unit time, is another important measurement. Get a stopwatch and meter stick to find the velocity of each of the waves you made.

13.12. MOUNTAIN BUILDING
Paper Peaks

The Earth's crust is not one solid layer. The crust is broken into several tectonic plates that float on top of the *mantle*, the layer of half-molten rock beneath the Earth's surface. The floating plates continuously change the shapes of continents, islands, and oceans, though they do so at the rate of only about one inch each year. The slow movement of two plates towards each other crumples the edges, pushing up the crust and creating mountains. All the great mountain ranges on Earth were formed by colliding plates. Some of the oldest rocks on the planet, located at the bases of these mountains, have been pushed upward in the folding processes. In this activity you will see how mountains are formed.

❓ Materials

Several sheets of newspaper

1. Place the unfolded newspaper sheets on the floor.
2. Place the palms of your hands about one foot apart on the newspaper.
3. Slowly push your hands, and the paper, together.

❓ Follow-Up Questions

1. In this activity, what do you hands represent? What does the newspaper represent?
2. As you push your hands together, what happens to the paper between your hands?
3. How does this motion model mountain building?

➕ Extension

When plates collide, they may produce folded mountains or faulted mountains. Do a little research to find out what will cause a rock to fold or fault.

SECTION FOURTEEN

Meteorology

The science of *meteorology* is the study of changes in the atmosphere, especially as these changes relate to weather and climate—the average weather of an area. To understand weather, students must understand how the Sun's energy affects the air around Earth. Uneven heating of the atmosphere causes air to move, creating winds. The Sun's energy also causes water to evaporate, putting it into motion in the water cycle. The activities in this section help students understand how the Sun moves water and how rain and dew are formed. This section also examines the formation of temperature inversions, the behavior of air, and the causes of winds.

14.1. TEMPERATURE INVERSIONS
Weather Patterns and Pollution

Combustion of fossil fuels is one of the main contributors to air pollution. *Temperature inversion*, the layering of warm air on top of cold air, is a weather event that can worsen atmospheric pollutants. Cool air is denser than warm air, so cool air and its pollutants can get trapped beneath warm air currents. Since the cool, polluted air cannot circulate upward and away from the Earth, the ground-level atmosphere becomes thick with unhealthy pollutants. In this activity you will use hot and cold water to model an atmospheric temperature inversion.

✓ Materials

Beaker or medium-size jar half-filled with cold water

Beaker or jar half-filled with hot (but not scalding) water

Red food coloring

Spoon

Pencil

 Activity

1. Stir two drops of red food coloring into the beaker of hot water.

2. Scoop up a spoonful of the colored hot water. Carefully and gently pour the spoonful of hot water down the inside of the beaker of cold water. Observe what happens.

3. Repeat the process of spooning hot water down the inside of the beaker several more times. Continue to observe what happens.

❓ Follow-Up Questions

1. What did the cold water and the hot water represent in this activity?

2. What happened when you spooned the hot water on top of the cold water?

3. Using what you observed in this activity, describe how this is similar to an atmospheric temperature inversion.

➕ Extension

Some areas of the Earth are more prone to temperature inversions than others. Do some research and see which areas of the Earth have the most temperature inversions. What does the research say about the health consequences for citizens living in areas where inversions are frequent?

14.2. CLOUD FORMATION
The Cloudy Bottle

Clouds form when warm, moist air rises and cools. Near the surface of the Earth, heat is exchanged rapidly between the ground and the atmosphere. In the evening the Earth's surface radiates heat and air begins to cool. This cooling allows the water vapor molecules in the air to stick together more easily and form tiny suspended water droplets, the beginning of clouds. In addition, as air rises in the atmosphere, the pressure drops. In this activity you will see how cool temperature and low air pressure make a cloud in a bottle.

✔ Materials

Safety glasses; Empty 16-ounce clear plastic bottle with a tight-fitting cap; Graduated cylinder; Match; Rubbing alcohol; Black paper

1. Put on your safety glasses.
2. Place about 25 ml of rubbing alcohol in the bottle. Tightly replace the cap.
3. Shake the bottle to saturate the bottle's air with alcohol.
4. *Under adult supervision:* Light a match and blow it out. (Be sure that the match is extinguished.) Quickly remove the cap from the bottle and drop the smoking match in the bottle. Replace the cap.
5. Squeeze and release the bottle several times until you see the cloud form.
6. After the cloud forms, squeeze the bottle and hold it. What happens? Now release the bottle. What happens?

❓ Follow-Up Questions

1. What did you do in the activity to create high humidity in the bottle?
2. Which event influenced the pressure in the bottle?
3. Did the cloud form when the pressure was increased or decreased?

➕ Extension

Condensation of water vapor in air also causes the formation of dew. Carry out some research to learn how dew forms on grass in the mornings. Use a glass, some ice, and some water and see how long it takes for condensation to occur. How does the humidity of the atmosphere influence that time?

14.3. WARM AIR RISES
Refrigerated Balloons

Most weather patterns are set into motion by the movement of air masses, which may be cold or warm. Warm air is not so dense as cold air, so it rises. The *density* of air and other materials is a measure of the mass of the material per unit volume. Warm air is not dense because its molecules are moving quickly, bouncing off of each other. When air is cool, the molecules move much more slowly and can exist in a smaller space. In this activity you will see how the temperature of air affects its density.

✔ Materials

Two inflated balloons of the same size, one at room temperature and one that has been refrigerated for thirty minutes

Tape measure

 Activity

1. Use the tape measure to find the circumference of the room-temperature balloon. Record the circumference.

2. Use the tape measure to find the circumference of the refrigerated balloon. Record the circumference.

3. Hold one balloon in each hand. Try to determine whether one is heavier than the other.

❓ Follow-Up Questions

1. Volume refers to the amount of space a material occupies. In which balloon does air have more volume: the room-temperature balloon or the refrigerated balloon?

2. Assume that the mass of the two balloons is the same. Which balloon is denser?

3. Explain what happens to the air molecules in a balloon when it is put in the refrigerator.

➕ Extension

Write a procedure for finding the actual density of each balloon. Base your procedure on the equation for density, as follows:

$$\text{density (d)} = \text{mass (m)} / \text{volume (v)}$$

14.4. WATER VAPOR
Dew on the Beaker

The humidity of air is included in almost every weather report. The most common way of reporting humidity is as *relative humidity*, the amount of water vapor in the air compared with the amount of water vapor that the air could hold. If the relative humidity is 100 percent, air is completely saturated with water. The humidity is less than 100 percent unless it is raining. When relative humidity is high, some of the water vapor may condense during the night to form dew. Dew forms at night because the air cools in the evenings and cooler air cannot hold so much water as warm air. In the daytime water vapor from the air can form on cool objects. In this activity you will cause daytime condensation to form on a beaker.

✔ Materials

Beaker or medium-size jar of water; Five or six ice cubes; Thermometer; Stopwatch or watch with a second hand; Paper towel

1. Dry the outside of the beaker with the paper towel.
2. Add the ice cubes to the beaker.
3. Gently add the thermometer to the beaker.
4. Start the stopwatch.
5. Observe and record the temperature of the water.
6. Observe the outside of the beaker for several minutes. If there is enough humidity in the air, condensation will form on the beaker. To check for condensation, run one finger over the beaker's exterior.
7. Once you see condensation, record the temperature and the time.

❓ Follow-Up Questions

1. At what temperature did condensation form?
2. How long did it take for condensation to form?
3. Dew forms on outdoor plants during the night, but not during the day. Why do you think this is so?

➕ Extension

Dew will often form on the top of a car before it forms on grass or plants. What reason can you think of for this event?

14.5. RAIN GAUGE
Let It Pour

The amount of water on Earth is constant; no new water is ever added. This water continuously moves through the *water cycle*. Water in the oceans and on the land evaporates and changes into water vapor. As water vapor moves up in the atmosphere, it cools, condenses, and changes back into tiny droplets of liquid water. In the atmosphere suspended droplets of water form clouds. When clouds become very heavy, the water falls back to Earth as *precipitation*. All living things on Earth rely on water to support life. A change in the amount of rainfall an area receives has a drastic effect on the organisms that live there. In this activity you will see how rainfall is measured.

✔ Materials

Tall jar (such as an olive jar)

Six-inch ruler

Rubber bands

Funnel that will completely cover the top of the jar

Activity

1. Use the rubber bands to attach the ruler to the outside of the tall jar so that the bottom of the ruler and the bottom of the jar are even.

2. Insert the funnel in the mouth of the jar. The top of the funnel should cover the entire opening of the jar.

3. The next time rain is in the forecast, set the jar outside. Be sure to put it in an open area away from buildings or trees. If you want to reuse the rain gauge, empty it after each rain.

❓ Follow-Up Questions

1. What are three reasons you might need to know how much rain falls in your area?

2. Can your rain gauge be used to measure the amount of snow that falls? Why or why not?

➕ Extension

Do some research to find out how much rain your area gets each year. In one year, how many times would this amount of rain fill your rain gauge?

14.6. THE LOSS OF OZONE
Oxygen Is Not Just for Breathing

The oxygen we breathe, whose chemical formula is O_2, is abundant near Earth's surface. *Ozone*, another form of oxygen with the chemical formula O_3, exists in the upper atmosphere. Upper-level ozone plays the critically important role of protecting the Earth from ultraviolet (UV) radiation. Even though ozone has existed for millions of years, it is being destroyed faster than nature can repair it. Human-made compounds that contain chlorine, such as *chlorofluorocarbons* (CFCs), break down ozone. In this activity you will see how CFCs damage ozone molecules.

✅ Materials

Scissors; Tape; Envelope containing six molecules: two ozone molecules, two free oxygen atoms, and two CFC molecules (prepared by the teacher; see Teacher's Notes)

Activity

1. Remove the molecules from the envelope.
2. Follow these steps to model the destruction of ozone molecules:
   a. UV radiation breaks off a chlorine (Cl) atom from the CFC. To show this, cut the chlorine atom off the CFC molecule.
   b. The chlorine atom breaks off one oxygen atom from ozone. Cut one oxygen atom off an ozone molecule. What you have left is an ordinary oxygen molecule (O_2).
   c. The chlorine atom bonds to a free oxygen atom, forming chlorine monoxide. Tape the chlorine to a free oxygen.
   d. Another free oxygen atom breaks the bond in chlorine monoxide, releasing the chlorine atom. Cut the tape holding chlorine and oxygen together.
   e. The free oxygen binds to the oxygen released from the breakup of chlorine monoxide. Tape these oxygen atoms together.
   f. The free chlorine breaks apart another ozone molecule. Repeat step b.
   g. UV radiation breaks apart another CFC molecule. Repeat step a.

❓ Follow-Up Questions

1. How does a free chlorine atom damage ozone?
2. What is the source of free chlorine atoms?
3. What can people do to slow the destruction of upper-level ozone?

➕ Extension

Each chlorine atom can lead to the destruction of thousands of ozone molecules, increasing the levels of UV radiation on Earth. Carry out some research to find out what kind of damage UV radiation can cause.

14.7. TEMPERATURE
Do You Want That in Celsius or Fahrenheit?

How can you tell the temperature? Without a thermometer, you have to rely on how you feel and how your body responds to the conditions. Sweating suggests that the temperature is high; shivering indicates cool temperatures. A thermometer makes it possible for you to accurately read the temperature. Two temperature scales are commonly used: Fahrenheit and Celsius. In this activity you will take readings from both types of thermometers.

✔ Materials

Celsius thermometer

Fahrenheit thermometer

Beaker of ice water

Beaker of very warm (but not scalding) water

1. Place both thermometers on a table. After thirty seconds, read the thermometers. When you read a thermometer, your eyes should be level with the top of the fluid in the thermometer. Record the temperature on each thermometer.

2. Place both thermometers in the cup of ice water. After one minute, read the thermometers. Record the temperatures.

3. Place both thermometers in the cup of hot water. After one minute, read the thermometers. Record the temperatures.

❓ Follow-Up Questions

1. What is the purpose of a thermometer?

2. On which thermometer is the boiling point 100° and the freezing point 0°?

3. Why would the following individuals need to be able to read a thermometer: farmers, auto mechanics, cooks, and nurses?

14.7. TEMPERATURE (continued)

➕ Extension

If you know the temperature in degrees Fahrenheit, you can convert it to Celsius with this formula:

$$Celsius = 5/9 \, (F - 32)$$

The reverse is also true. To change from Celsius to Fahrenheit, use this formula:

$$Fahrenheit = 9/5C + 32$$

Use the first formula to convert 70°F to Celsius. Use the second formula to change 30°C to Fahrenheit.

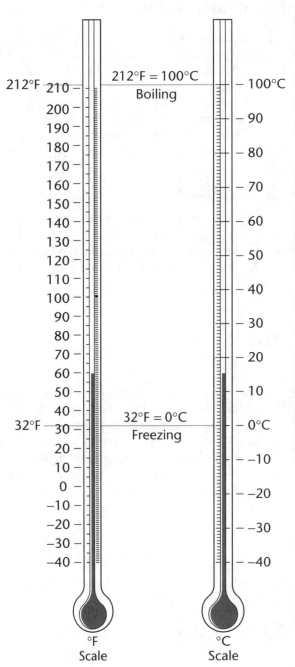

FIGURE 14.1. Thermometers

14.8. HEAT TRANSFER
Spiraling Upward

The Sun warms Earth's surface, but it does so unevenly. Heat is transferred from hot areas to cooler regions. This transfer of heat around the globe causes our changes in weather. Heat transfer can occur in three ways: radiation, conduction, and convection. *Radiation* is the transmission of energy as waves or particles. The Sun's energy travels to us through radiant energy waves. You feel these energy waves every time you walk into the sunlight. In *conduction*, heat travels from one molecule to another. Rocks absorb heat and release it by conduction. *Convection* is heat transfer that results from differences in densities: warm air rises and cool air sinks. In this activity you will observe heat transfer by convection.

 **Materials**

Paper; Pencil; Scissors; String; Tape; Candle or lamp (take care when working with candles; do not let paper or other flammable objects touch candle flames); Heat-proof base for the candle

 **Activity**

FIGURE 14.2. Heat Transfer Spiral

1. Draw a spiral on your paper similar to the one in the Figure 14.2. Your spiral should cover the entire sheet of paper. Cut out the spiral along the solid lines.
2. Tape the string to the innermost point of the spiral.
3. Holding it by the string, suspend the spiral a few inches above the candle or lamp. *(Be careful to keep the paper away from the flame.)* Steady your hand so that you can hold the spiral still.
4. Observe the spiral and notice any motion.

Follow-Up Questions

1. How did the spiral move when you held it over the candle?
2. Why did the spiral move?

Extension

Get a beaker of warm water and add a few drops of red food coloring, stirring to mix. In a separate beaker, mix some ice-cold water with a few drops of blue food coloring. Slowly pour the cold blue water into the warm red water. Describe what happens. How is this an example of convection?

14.9. READ A CLIMATOGRAM
Quick Take on Climate

A *climatogram* is a graph that summarizes the lows, highs, and average temperatures of a region. It also shows precipitation by month. The values on a climatogram are gleaned from data collected over a period of thirty years or more, so they reflect the *climate*—the average weather over a long time—not just the current weather. On a climatogram, precipitation by month is shown as a bar graph. The precipitation scale is shown on the left *y*-axis of the graph. Temperatures are depicted as line graphs, and the temperature scale is located on the right *y*-axis. Months are listed on the *x*-axis. In this activity you will examine and interpret a climatogram.

✔ Materials

Climatogram of Rio de Janeiro, Brazil (see Figure 14.3)

1. Examine the climatogram of Rio de Janeiro, Brazil.
2. On the left side of the graph, find the precipitation scale.
3. On the right side of the graph, find the temperature scale.
4. Locate the months along the *x*-axis.

❓ Follow-Up Questions

1. What is Rio de Janeiro's rainiest month? What is its driest month?
2. Judging by the mean temperature, what is Rio de Janeiro's coolest month? What is its warmest month?
3. In your opinion, what would be the best month to vacation in this locale? Explain your reasoning.

➕ Extension

Collect average rainfall and temperature data for your city or county and create a climatogram.

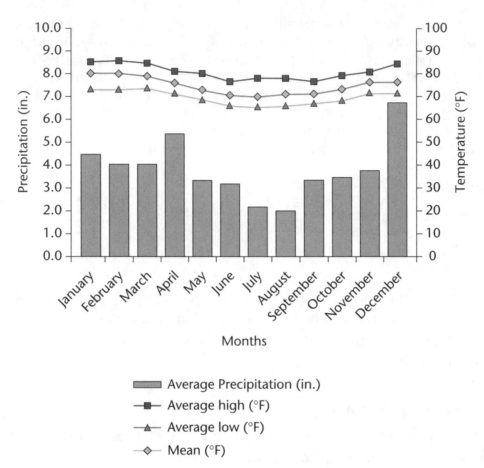

FIGURE 14.3. Climatogram: Rio de Janeiro, Brazil

14.10. AIR HAS WEIGHT
Living Under Pressure

Air is pressing down on you all the time. *Standard air pressure*, the weight of air at sea level, is one atmosphere. This value is equal to 14.7 pounds per square inch. We are so accustomed to the weight of air that we never notice it. However, you can see the effects of air pressure. In this activity you will demonstrate the strength of air pressure.

Materials

Meter stick
Several sheets of newspaper
Roll of newspaper

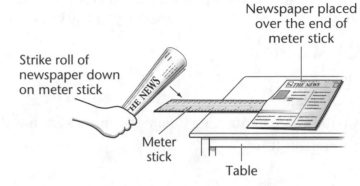

FIGURE 14.4. Air Has Weight

Activity

1. Place a meter stick on a table so that about five centimeters extend over the edge.
2. Hit the extended edge of the meter stick with the roll of newspaper. (Be sure your meter stick does not fly up and hit you or another student.)
3. Put the meter stick back in its original position. Lay several sheets of newspaper over the part of the meter stick on the table.
4. Repeat step 2.

Follow-Up Questions

1. What happened to the meter stick in step 2?
2. What happened to the meter stick in step 4?
3. Newspaper is not heavy enough to hold a meter stick to the desktop. How can you explain the difference in the meter stick's behavior in steps 2 and 4?

Extension

Calculate the weight of the air in your classroom. Measure the room's length, width, and height. Multiply the three values to find the volume of the air in the classroom. If you measured the room in meters, multiply the volume by 1.2 (because a cubic meter of air weighs 1.2 kilograms). If you measured the room in feet, multiply the volume by 0.07 (because a cubic foot of air weighs 0.07 pounds).

14.11. MAKE IT RAIN
Bottle Rainstorm

Warm air can hold a lot of water vapor. When warm moist air rises, it eventually reaches cold air high in the sky. As a result, the warm air begins to cool. Since cool air does not hold so much moisture as warm air, water vapor condenses into the tiny droplets of water that form clouds. Over time millions of miniscule cloud droplets fuse and become so heavy that they can no longer remain suspended in the air. These large droplets fall as rain. In this activity you will create rain in a bottle.

✔ Materials

Quart jar

Small plate

Small beaker containing about 150 ml of very hot (but not scalding) water

Several ice cubes

1. Carefully pour the hot water into the quart jar.
2. Cover the jar with the small plate so the plate is facing upward.
3. Wait a minute or two, then place the ice cubes on the plate.
4. Observe the jar.

❓ Follow-Up Questions

1. What happened on the underside of the plate?
2. Which parts of the experiment represent the following elements?

   ⮑ Warm, moist air rising through the atmosphere

   ⮑ Cold air high in the atmosphere

   ⮑ Rain

✚ Extension

Repeat this experiment, using cold water instead of hot water. Describe and explain your results.

14.12. WINDS
Air Masses in Motion

Gravity holds the atmosphere to the Earth. As the planet rotates on its axis, the atmosphere travels with it. Air masses within the atmosphere move because the Sun's energy warms the atmosphere unevenly. Direct rays strike the equator, heating that zone a great deal. Oblique rays hit the polar zones, resulting in much less heating. When the warm equatorial air rises, it flows toward the poles. Cold polar air sinks below the warm air and moves toward the equatorial zones. This movement of air masses creates wind. However, these winds do not move directly to their destinations. Because of Earth's rotation, winds are deflected to the right in the Northern Hemisphere and to the left in the Southern Hemisphere. In this activity you will see how air deflection occurs.

 **Materials**

Cardboard disc with a diameter of about 20 centimeters and a hole in the center; Pencil with eraser; Few drops of water

FIGURE 14.5. Prevailing Winds

 **Activity**

1. Push the pencil through the hole in the cardboard disc. Position the disc just above the eraser.
2. Position the pencil so that the eraser is on the desk and the disc rests at a slight tilt.
3. Put a few drops of water on the disc near the center.
4. Holding the pencil, spin the disc to the right and observe what happens.

❓ Follow-Up Questions

1. What does each of the following items represent?

   ➲ The pencil   ➲ The disc   ➲ The water drops

2. What happened to the water drops when the disc was set in motion?
3. How are the water drops similar to winds?

➕ **Extension:** Carry out some research to learn more about the prevailing winds and the trade winds. Relate these winds to this activity.

SECTION FIFTEEN

The Universe

Since earliest times, scientists have studied the heavens. *Astronomy* is the science of the heavenly bodies, their behavior, and their characteristics. Discoveries in astronomy have occurred rapidly in the last fifty years due to the development of technology. Data-gathering telescopes and detailed spectral analysis have provided scientists with information that has helped develop models of the evolution and development of the universe. In this section students learn about telescopes, space shuttles, and satellites and how they work. They study the constellations and the positions of stars in the sky. Through modeling, students show how the stars are moving apart, and gain understanding as to what the universe might be like in the future.

15.1. TELESCOPES
An Eye on the Universe

The first telescope, a refracting instrument, was made of a combination of two lenses. The *objective lens* bends parallel light rays and focuses them at a point called the *focal point*. Before the rays can spread out again, the eyepiece lens bends the rays and focuses them on the eye. Galileo was one of the first astronomers to use this type of telescope to study the moon. In this activity you will use two magnifying lenses to simulate how the first telescope worked.

 **Materials**

Two magnifying glasses

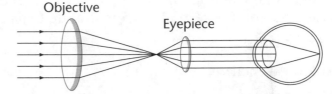

FIGURE 15.1. Telescope

1. Select a distant object to view (such as a tree or a building).
2. Close one eye and hold the magnifying glass lens near your open eye.
3. Look at the distant object through this lens. It may be blurry.
4. Hold the second magnifying lens in front of the lens held near your eye. Slowly move the second lens away from the first one until the distant object is no longer blurry.

❓ Follow-Up Questions

1. In this activity, which lens represented the objective lens and which one represented the eyepiece lens?
2. What was unusual about the orientation of the object you viewed through the two lenses?
3. Why is the unusual orientation of far-away objects not so big a problem when viewing stars as it might be when viewing a tree?

➕ Extension

Do some research and find the difference between a *refracting telescope* and a *reflecting telescope*. How are they alike? How are they different? What are the advantages of one over the other?

15.2. LIGHT-YEARS
Universal Time

Distances in space are often given in light-years. A light-year is the distance that light travels in one year. It is mind-boggling to consider that a light-year is about 9.7×10^{12} kilometers. The star Alpha Centauri, one of the closest stars to Earth, is about 4.3 light-years away. That means that the light we see coming from that star actually left the star 4.3 years ago. For closer objects to us, such as the Moon, we might use light-seconds instead of light-years. A light-second is about 300,000 kilometers. If you know the distance between Earth and another celestial body, you can determine how long it takes light to travel from that body to the Earth. In this activity you will calculate the number of seconds it takes light from the Sun to reach the Earth.

✅ Materials

Calculator; Pencil

1. Following is the formula you will use to determine how long it takes light to reach us from another celestial body:

$$\text{Time (seconds)} = \frac{\text{distance from Earth to the body (km)}}{\text{speed of light (300,000 km/sec)}}$$

Let's look at an example first. The Moon is about 385,000 km from the Earth. How long does it take the light coming from the moon to reach us on Earth? To find out, divide 385,000 km by 300,000 km per second. The answer is that light we see from the moon left the moon about 1.3 seconds ago.

2. The Sun is 150,000,000 km away from Earth. Calculate how long it takes light from the Sun to reach us.

❓ Follow-Up Questions

1. How many seconds ago did light striking the Earth leave the Sun?
2. Neptune is 4,496 million km away from Earth. How long does it take for light from Neptune to reach Earth?
3. When you think of light-years or light-seconds, it sounds like a measurement of time, but it is actually a measurement of distance. Explain why.

➕ Extension

Earlier you learned that Alpha Centauri was about 4.3 light-years from Earth. How far would that be in kilometers?

15.3. STAR CONSTELLATIONS
How Many Do You Know?

A glance at a cloudless night sky tells you that there are millions of stars in the heavens. If you take time to study them, some groups of stars seem to form shapes that resemble animals or people. Since ancient times, scientists have studied star patterns or constellations to help them mark time. Modern science recognizes eighty-eight star constellations. In this activity you will name some of the best-known constellations.

 **Materials**

None

 **Activity**

1. Take two or three minutes to list all the constellations you know.
2. Share your list with another student. If that student has a constellation that is not on your list, add it. Give your classmate the name of one constellation on your list that he or she did not already have.
3. Repeat step 2, giving one and getting one, with other students for 5 minutes.
4. Sit down and count your constellations. Find out who in your class wrote the most names.

Follow-Up Questions

1. Write your own definition for "constellation."
2. Ancient scientists named constellations for people or animals that were important in the stories of their times. If you could name a constellation, what title would you select?

Extension

Select one constellation that interests you and find out where it is located in the night sky. At what time of year might you see this constellation?

15.4. VIEWING CONSTELLATIONS
Moving Patterns in the Sky

The Earth both rotates on its axis and revolves around the Sun. Evidence of these movements can be seen in the motion of the constellations. A *constellation* is a group of stars that forms a recognizable pattern. There are eighty-eight identified constellations in the sky, but they do not always appear in the same place when you look up at the sky. As the Earth rotates on its axis, the positions of the constellations appear to shift from one night to the next. During certain seasons some constellations disappear from view because the revolution of the Earth around the Sun causes Earth to face a different region of the universe. In this activity you will select a constellation and make a viewer.

✅ Materials

Cardboard tube from an empty paper towel roll

Safety pin and tape

Black paper disc (cut to the same size as the cardboard tube opening)

White or tracing paper disc (same size as cardboard tube opening)

Reference book with constellation patterns

1. Look at the patterns of constellations in your reference book and find one that interests you. Some examples of constellations are Orion, Taurus, Gemini, and Canis Major.

2. Put the white paper over the top of the constellation you would like to view.

3. Trace the constellation on the white paper.

4. Place the white paper disc on top of the black disc. Use the safety pins to punch holes in the location of the stars in the constellation. Make sure the holes are punched through both the white and black discs. Dispose of the white disc.

5. Make the star viewer by taping the black disc on the end of the cardboard tube with the front of the paper facing the tube. The disc should completely cover one end of the tube.

6. While looking through the open end of the tube, hold the other end up toward a bright light source. You should see the constellation in your viewer.

15.4. VIEWING CONSTELLATIONS (continued)

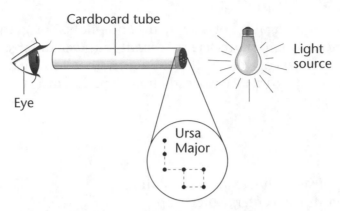

FIGURE 15.2. Constellation Viewer

❓ Follow-Up Questions

1. How do the constellations prove the Earth rotates and revolves?
2. Which constellation did you view in the activity? Describe its appearance in your viewer.

➕ Extension

During which season can your constellation be seen? How did the constellation get its name? Exchange viewers with some of your classmates. Can you identify their constellations?

15.5. THE GYROSCOPIC EFFECT
Spacecraft Navigation

Gyroscopes are used for navigation by astronauts and pilots. The gyroscope is pointed in the direction the astronaut wants the spacecraft to travel and it spins at a constant speed. If the spacecraft gets off course, the change in direction creates an outside force that signals the gyroscope to get the spacecraft back on its correct course. In this activity you will make a gyroscope.

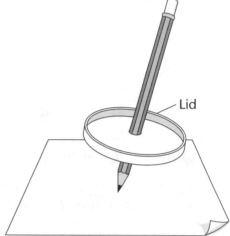

✅ Materials

Sharpened pencil; Plastic lid from a container with hole punched in the center; Ruler; Paper

1. Place a piece of paper on your desk top. Place the pencil point down on the paper and let go of it. What happens?

2. Insert the pencil through the hole in the plastic lid with the edges of the lid pointing upward. Position the lid so that it is about one inch from the pencil point.

FIGURE 15.3. The Gyroscopic Effect

3. Repeat step 1 with the pencil-lid combination. What happens?

4. Pick up the pencil-lid combination and hold it between your palms with the pencil point toward the paper. Quickly move your palms in opposite directions to create a spin as you release the pencil point on the paper. What happens?

❓ Follow-Up Questions

1. What happened when you tried to stand the pencil on its point in steps 1 and 3? What force do you think caused this to happen?

2. What happened in step 4 when you created a spinning motion?

3. Which do you think is more stable: a spinning object or one that does not spin?

➕ Extension

Attempt to make gyroscopes out of other items besides pencils and plastic lids. Find out if you have the same results with these objects as you did with the pencil and plastic lid. Explain your findings.

15.6. SPACE SHUTTLE ORBITS
Holding Onto Your Marbles

When objects such as rockets or the space shuttle go into space, they move in a straight line until something slows them. One of the first forces to act on a space vehicle is the gravity of the Earth. For example, the space shuttle orbits the Earth because Earth's gravity is pulling on it and constantly changing its direction. If there were no gravity from Earth, the shuttle would just fly out into space in a straight line. In this activity you will demonstrate why gravitational pull is needed to keep objects in orbit around the Earth.

 **Materials**

Paper plate
Marble
Scissors

1. Place a marble on a table and use your finger to set it in motion. Notice that it travels in a straight line.

2. Place the paper plate on the table. Position the marble on the edge of the plate (on the corrugated or ridged section of the plate). (See Figure 15.4.)

3. Use your finger to set the marble in motion around the plate. Notice what happens as the marble moves. Does it go out in a straight line or does it move in a circle?

4. Pick up the paper plate and cut it to remove a large pie-like slice of the plate (about one-third of the plate).

5. Repeat steps 2 and 3. Make sure you position the marble so it will eventually roll on the cutout section of the plate and onto the table. Watch what happens to the marble when it leaves the plate and goes onto the table. Does it still travel in a circular path?

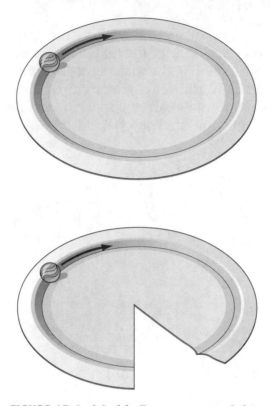

FIGURE 15.4. Marble Demonstrates Orbit

❓ Follow-Up Questions

1. How did the marble move on the plate when the whole paper plate was intact? Explain why you think this occurred.

2. What happened to the marble the second time, when it moved from the paper plate to the desk? Explain why you think this occurred.

3. What did the marble and the ridges on the rim of the plate represent in this activity?

➕ Extension

Do some research and see what must occur for the space shuttle to escape the orbit of the Earth and travel into outer space.

15.7. GRAVITY AND SPACE INSTRUMENTS
Writing in Space

Astronauts are asked to keep meticulous records during their space journey. Some of the writing utensils we take for granted on Earth do not function well in space. On Earth everything is affected by the force of gravity. In space the absence of gravity makes simple tasks more complex. Here on Earth the ink in a ballpoint pen runs down from the ink cartridge to the ballpoint end. The ink flows downward because gravity pulls it. Pencil lead, or graphite, does not flow, so writing with a pencil is not affected by gravity. In this activity you will see why pens are not very useful to astronauts.

 **Materials**

Sharpened pencil
Ballpoint pen
Notebook

 **Activity**

1. Turn to a blank piece of paper in your notebook.
2. Place the notebook on a table and write a couple of sentences in your notebook using a pencil. Then write the same sentences using a pen.
3. Turn to a separate sheet of paper in the notebook. Hold the notebook up in the air over your head. Write the same sentences with the pencil. Do the same with the pen.

Follow-Up Questions

1. Were you able to write in both pencil and pen in step 2?
2. Were you able to write in both pencil and pen in step 3? If not, explain what happened.
3. What force is required for some writing utensils in space? Which utensil is dependent on this force?

Extension

Try this same experiment with roller-ball pens, fountain pens, felt-tip markers, or other writing utensils. Which of these would you not advise astronauts to use when recording data in space?

15.8. VISIBLE LIGHT
A Blend of Colors

Stars emit many forms of *electromagnetic radiation*, energy that travels in waves. Electromagnetic radiation includes X-rays—*infrared energy*, which we feel as heat—and visible light. Visible light is a small but complex part of the spectrum that makes up electromagnetic radiation. Several colors make up visible light. Each color of light is transmitted on special *wavelengths*, energy waves of different sizes.

 **Materials**

Flashlight

Prism

Sheet of plain white paper

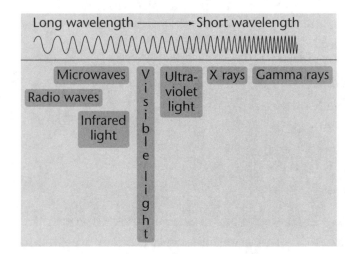

FIGURE 15.5. Electromagnetic Spectrum

Activity

1. In a darkened room, set the prism on a sheet of plain white paper.
2. Shine the flashlight through the prism.
3. Observe the colors produced on the white paper.

❓ Follow-Up Questions

1. What colors did you see on the white paper?
2. What do these colors tell you about the composition of white light?
3. Which color of light has the shortest wavelength? Which color has the longest wavelength?

➕ Extension

Visible light is the only type of electromagnetic radiation that we can see. Do some research on satellites that take images using visible light.

15.9. INFRARED LIGHT
Feel the Heat

Infrared energy is one of several types of radiation in the electromagnetic spectrum. Many living things, including people and animals, emit infrared energy. The Sun, Earth, and stars in distant galaxies also emit infrared energy. Infrared astronomy satellites pick up infrared signals from space, giving us a view of the cosmos that we cannot see with visible light. In this activity you will learn more about infrared light and compare the heat energy of infrared with the heat energy of visible light.

✔ Materials

Infrared light bulb suspended 30 cm above a thermometer (prepared by the teacher; see Teacher's Notes)

Flashlight

Thermometer

Ruler

1. Place the thermometer on a table. Hold the flashlight 30 cm above it.
2. When the teacher says "Go," turn on the flashlight. Your teacher will turn on the infrared bulb which is positioned above a second thermometer.
3. After two minutes, check the temperature on both thermometers.

❓ Follow-Up Questions

1. Describe the appearance of the infrared light.
2. What was the temperature under the flashlight bulb? What was the temperature under the infrared bulb?
3. Explain one way in which infrared and visible light differ.

➕ Extension

Do some research on the Landsat 7 satellite, which carries infrared sensors. What kinds of information does this satellite gather?

15.10. STAR MAGNITUDE
The Brightness of Stars

When you look at the stars, you see that some are brighter than others. The brightness of stars is measured as magnitude. The brighter the star, the lower its magnitude, so a bright star might have a magnitude of 1 and a dim star a magnitude of 5. In this activity you will see how distance affects magnitude.

 **Materials**

Large flashlight
Small flashlight
Sheet of plain white paper
Meter stick

 **Activity**

1. Work with a partner. In a darkened room, you and your partner hold the two flashlights about one meter above the paper. Turn on the flashlights.
2. Notice which flashlight is brighter and assign it a magnitude of 1.
3. Assign the dimmer flashlight a magnitude of 2.
4. Bring the magnitude 2 flashlight much closer to the paper. Notice how the brightness of the light changes.

Follow-Up Questions

1. In step 4, when you moved the magnitude 2 flashlight closer to the paper, was its light still dimmer?
2. Does distance affect magnitude? Explain your answer.

Extension

Carry out some research to determine the magnitude of Sirius, the brightest star, and Canopius, the second-brightest star.

15.11. INERTIA IN SPACE
Objects Keep Moving

The movement of objects in space can be explained by the *law of inertia*. According to this law, objects at rest remain at rest and those in motion remain in motion unless acted on by an outside force. On Earth that outside force is *friction*. However, friction does not affect objects in space. In this activity you will demonstrate the law of inertia.

 Materials

Length of foam (prepared by teacher; see Teacher's Notes); Marble; Four small pieces of tape; Ruler

Activity

1. Bend the length of foam into a **U** shape and position it with the base of the **U** on a table.
2. Hold a marble at the top of the foam on one side of the **U**. Measure and record the distance from the marble to the tabletop.
3. Release the marble. With a piece of tape, mark the highest point reached by the marble on the other side of the **U**. Measure and record the distance from the tape to the tabletop.

❓ Follow-Up Questions

1. How far up the foam did the marble move when you released it in step 3?
2. Why didn't the marble move farther?
3. If you sprayed the interior surface of the foam with lubricant, would the marble move farther? Explain your reasoning.

➕ Extension

Bend the piece of foam into different shapes and release the marble as before. For example, bend the foam into a **J** shape or a **W** shape. Does the shape of the foam affect how far the marble travels?

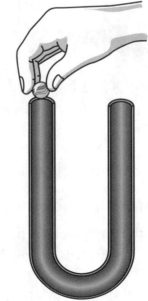

FIGURE 15.6. U-Shaped Foam Tube

15.12. THE PARALLAX EFFECT
A Different Perspective

To determine the distances to stars, astronomers use the parallax effect. First they note the position of a star in the night sky. In Figure 15.7 the star that astronomers observe is Star A. Six months later, when the Earth has revolved in its orbit to the other side of the Sun, they note the star's position again. Because the astronomers' position has changed, the position of Star A seems to have changed. The amount of change helps astronomers determine the distance to the stars. In this activity you will see how the parallax effect works.

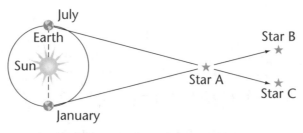

FIGURE 15.7. Parallax Effect

 Materials

Ruler

 Activity

1. Pick an object on the other side of the classroom.
2. Close your right eye. Facing the object, hold the ruler at arm's distance in front of you.
3. Position the ruler in front of the object.
4. Open your right eye and close your left. Observe the object again.

❓ Follow-Up Questions

1. How did the position of the ruler appear to change?
2. What caused this change?

➕ Extension

Try this activity outdoors and observe a distant building or tree.

SECTION SIXTEEN

The Solar System

O ur solar system—the Sun and its orbiting planets, moons, meteors, and asteroids—is an interrelated system. Every student of science knows that the movement of the Earth around the Sun affects our lives on this planet. The Sun provides the energy that supports life on Earth and drives weather. The Moon causes tides and provides us with a system of measuring time. The tilt of Earth on its axis is responsible for seasons, and the planet's spin causes day and night. In this section students carry out activities that help them understand the relationships of Earth to its immediate neighbors. Students also learn about gravity, the path of the Earth and the other planets in our solar system around the Sun, and the behavior of Earth on its axis. Students also study the Moon's formation, composition, and phases.

16.1. PLANETARY REVOLUTIONS
Birthdays on Mercury and Jupiter

The different planets in our solar system take different amounts of time to travel around the Sun. We know that Earth, the third closest planet to the Sun, makes one full trip or *revolution* around the Sun every 365 days. This is equivalent to what we call one year on Earth. Mercury, the planet closest to our Sun, makes one revolution every eighty-eight days, while Jupiter, the fifth closest planet to the Sun, completes a revolution approximately every twelve years. In this activity you will calculate how old you would be if you had lived your whole life on Mercury or Jupiter.

 **Materials**

Calculator

Pencil

1. Determine how old you would be on Mercury by doing the following:

   a. Convert your age in years to days by multiplying your number of years by 365 and then adding the number of days since your last birthday. This will give you your age in days.

   b. One year on Mercury is 88 days. Divide the number of days old you are here on Earth by 88. The answer will tell you how old you would be if you lived your whole life on Mercury.

2. Determine how old you would be if you had lived your whole life on Jupiter by simply dividing your age in Earth years by 12 (the number of years it takes Jupiter to revolve around the Sun). This will give you your answer in years.

❓ Follow-Up Questions

1. How old would you be on Mercury? On Jupiter?
2. Why do you think you were older on Mercury than on Jupiter?
3. Venus is the second closest planet to the Sun, and Mars is the fourth closest. On which planet do you think you would be older?

➕ Extension

Neptune revolves around the Sun approximately every 165 years. How old would you be if you lived your whole life on that planet?

16.2. JUPITER'S ATMOSPHERE

A Stormy Planet

Jupiter, the fifth planet from the Sun, has the distinction of being the largest planet in our galaxy. The gases helium and hydrogen compose about 92 percent of its atmosphere. One distinctive feature on Jupiter is the Great Red Spot. This area is an ongoing massive storm. This storm system is similar to a hurricane, but the Great Red Spot has been raging for several hundred years. Swirling storms on Jupiter are caused by vortex-like winds that spin around an area of relative calm. In this activity you will simulate the gas storms on Jupiter.

✅ Materials

Clear mason jar with tight-fitting lid; Teaspoon; Vinegar; Dishwashing liquid; Water; Glitter

Activity

1. Add water to the jar until it is about three-quarters full.
2. Place 2 teaspoons of vinegar into the jar.
3. Place 1 teaspoon of dishwashing liquid in the jar.
4. Sprinkle some glitter into the jar.
5. Screw the lid on the jar so it has a tight fit.
6. Hold the jar so your hand is around the middle but the jar is still facing up. Use a circular motion to swirl the contents around the jar.
7. Watch what happens to the contents of the jar as you swirl it.

❓ Follow-Up Questions

1. What happened to the contents of the jar as you swirled the jar around?
2. What feature on Jupiter might cause the movement you simulated with the movement of your hand in the activity?
3. What do the streams of liquids represent in this activity?

➕ Extension

Do some research and find out which other planets have violent storms. Find out what the atmospheres of those planets are like and what causes their storms.

16.3. ORBITING THE SUN
Earth's Trip Around the Sun

The planets in our solar system, including Earth, orbit the Sun. Many people believe that the Earth takes a circular orbit around the sun. However, the orbits made by Earth and the other planets of our solar system are not perfect circles. The pathway is called an *ellipse*. Perform this activity to see what an ellipse looks like.

✅ Materials

Pencil

Piece of cardboard (a little larger than a piece of notebook paper)

Clear tape

Ruler

Loop of yarn or string that is about 30 cm in circumference

Two thumbtacks

Piece of white computer paper

Activity

1. Place the cardboard on a table. Attach the white paper to the center of the cardboard with clear tape.

2. Using a ruler, locate the center of the paper. Draw a 7.5 cm horizontal line that it is centered at this point.

3. Place a thumbtack at each end of the horizontal line. The thumbtacks should penetrate the cardboard below.

4. Loop the yarn around the two thumbtacks.

5. Using your pencil, stretch the yarn toward the bottom of the paper so it is taut. Don't pull so hard that you dislodge the thumbtacks.

6. Keeping the yarn tight, use your pencil point to guide the pencil around the loop of yarn so it allows you to draw a shape.

16.3. ORBITING THE SUN (continued)

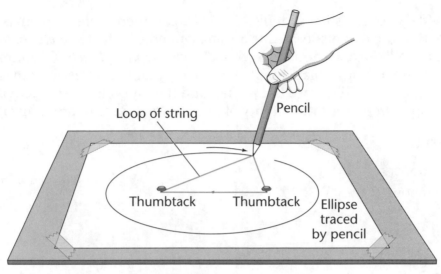

FIGURE 16.1. Elliptical Orbit

❓ Follow-Up Questions

1. What shape did you produce in your drawing?

2. What do you think would be a good definition for an ellipse?

➕ Extension

Do some research and determine why the Earth, as well as other planets, move more slowly the farther they are from the Sun.

16.4. PLANET FORMATIONS
How the Planets Were Made

In the early stages of the solar system's development, there were no planets. Scientists believe that the planets formed from smaller bodies called *planetesimals*. These planetesimals collided and formed larger bodies called *protoplanets*. Over time the high gravitational pull of a protoplanet pulled in smaller planetesimals. Eventually the protoplanets condensed and formed the planets and their moons. In this activity you will use water drops to represent the activity of planetesimals in the early universe.

✅ Materials

Medicine dropper
Wax paper (about 8″ × 5″)
Ruler

 Activity

1. Place a drop of water in the center of the piece of wax paper.
2. Place a second drop of water about two inches away from the first drop.
3. Lift one corner of the wax paper so that the second drop flows toward and into the original drop of water.
4. Add a third drop of water two inches from the original drop and repeat step 3.

❓ Follow-Up Questions

1. What happened when the first two drops collided?
2. What happened when the third drop collided with the original drop?
3. What process does this activity model?
4. What are the early stages of planet development?

➕ Extension

Straighten a paper clip into one long piece of metal. Repeat the drop experiment, but this time use the paper clip to pull the drops together. What does the paper clip represent in this activity?

16.5. SURVIVING ON THE MOON

Lunar Trek

Scientists must think critically to solve problems and sometimes to survive in the field. Some of the decisions made by an astronaut can mean the difference between life and death. Imagine that your spacecraft landed on the Moon in a location many miles from the target space station. You must journey across the Moon on foot to reach your destination. On the journey you can carry only a few items. In this activity you will decide what you would take with you on your journey.

 **Materials**

Pencil

 **Activity**

Listed below are items that you may want to take on your hike to the space station. Rank the following items in order of importance. Place the number 1 by the most important and 10 by the least important. Remember: time is of the essence.

_____Six liters of water

_____Packaged raisins

_____Two additional large cylinders of oxygen

_____Map of the stars and their location in relation to the moon

_____First-aid kit

_____Shot gun

_____Box of matches

_____Magnetic compass

_____Chemical flares

_____Radio

Follow-Up Questions

1. Which item do you think is most important?

2. What were your three least important items? Why did you select these?

Extension

Try this activity again, but imagine that you were lost in a desert on Earth. How would you alter the order of importance, and why? Why do you believe critical thinking is important for everyone?

16.6. SOLAR ECLIPSE
Blocking the Sun

Even though it is a much smaller celestial body, the Moon has the ability to totally block the Sun's light from our perspective on Earth. When the Moon passes between the Earth and the Sun, a solar eclipse occurs. In a total solar eclipse, the Moon appears as large as the Sun and blocks its light. This phenomenon only takes place about once every 350 years. This activity will demonstrate how a small Moon can totally block the light from the much larger Sun.

✅ Materials

3-inch ball of red clay
Grape-sized ball of blue clay
Two sharpened pencils of the same size

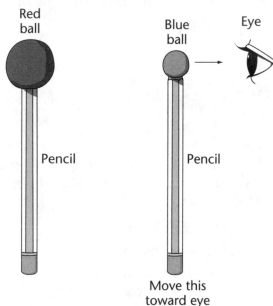

1. Place the blue clay ball on the sharpened tip of one pencil and the red clay ball on the tip of the other pencil.
2. Hold the pencil with the red clay ball in your left hand. Extend your arm so the ball of clay is as far from your face as possible.
3. Close one eye and hold the pencil with the blue clay in your right hand so it is between your open eye and the blue ball.
4. Slowly move the blue clay ball toward your eye.

FIGURE 16.2. Modeling an Eclipse

5. Continue moving the blue ball toward your eye until you find the point where the blue ball blocks the view of the red ball from your sight.

❓ Follow-Up Questions

1. Which celestial body does the red ball represent?
2. Which body does the blue ball represent?
3. What does your eye represent?

➕ Extension

Repeat this activity, but this time work with a partner. Find a way to use a penlight to serve as light from the Sun. See if you can find the point where the light from the Sun is totally blocked by the clay Moon.

16.7. ASTROLABE
Medieval Measurements

In ancient times astronomers used a very simple tool to measure the height of a star in the sky. This instrument, the *astrolabe*, enabled scientists to create the first star charts. People relied on the astrolabe to determine the altitude of objects above the horizon. Using measurements made with an astrolabe, navigators could calculate their latitude. Until recently the astrolabe has been pivotal in helping ships find their way through the seas. Today the Global Positioning System (GPS) has taken the place of the astrolabe. In this activity you will make and test an astrolabe.

✅ Materials

String (1 meter long)

Protractor with a tiny hole in the center of the flat side

Drinking straw

Metal washer

Tape

Activity

1. Tie the washer to one end of the string. Tie the other end of the string to the protractor by threading it through the hole in the center of the flat side.
2. Tape the drinking straw to the flat section of the protractor so the straw extends over both edges of the protractor.
3. Hold the astrolabe in one hand so that the curved side of the protractor is pointing downward. The string should be able to swing freely.
4. Point one end of the straw at an object near the top of your classroom, such as a wall clock or top of a screen. Look at the object through the straw. When you have it sighted, press the string against the protractor. Read the angle (degrees of the protractor) that the string falls across.
5. Subtract the angle you just measured (number of degrees) from 90 degrees. This is the altitude of the object you are sighting.

16.7. ASTROLABE (continued)

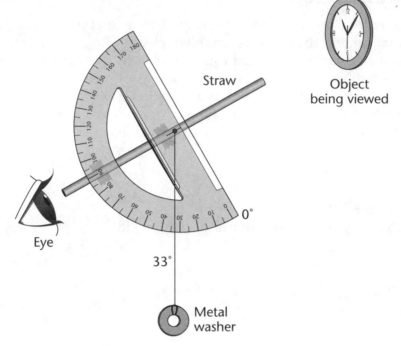

FIGURE 16.3. Sighting with an Astrolabe

❓ Follow-Up Questions

1. What is the purpose of an astrolabe? What was its primary purpose in medieval times?

2. What was the altitude of the object you observed today?

➕ Extension

Go outside and use the astrolabe to sight a tall object such as a treetop or a roof. Repeat the procedure in the activity to find the angle of altitude.

16.8. PRECESSION OF EARTH
Spinning on the Axis

Just like a toy top that wobbles before it falls, the Earth wobbles as it rotates on its *axis*, the imaginary line that extends through the poles. This wobbling motion is due to the slight bulge at the equator. If you traced the Earth's axis out into space, you would see the extension of the axis slowly tracing a cone shape. The wobble is very slow; it takes the Earth 26,000 years to trace one complete conical shape. This wobbling motion of Earth on its axis is called *precession*. Because of precession, Polaris and Vega alternate as the North Star every 13,000 years. In this activity you will use a toy top to represent the Earth and observe how precession occurs as the Earth moves on its axis.

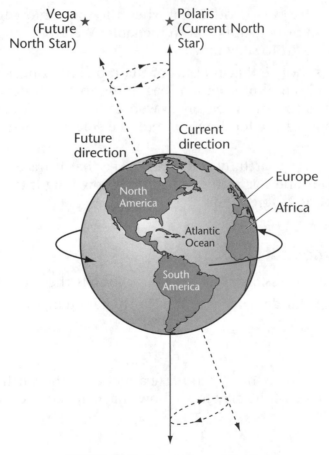

FIGURE 16.4. Precession of Earth

16.8. PRECESSION OF EARTH (continued)

✅ Materials

Toy top
Flat table
Watch with second hand

Activity

1. Spin the top on the table. Notice that when the top is moving quickly, its axis points straight up or perpendicular to the table. Watch the top continue to spin until you see it begin to slow down.

2. As the top slows, notice that the axis of the top is no longer perpendicular to the table. The weight of the top is beginning to pull it down. Notice that as the top continues to slow, it begins to wobble. If you look closely, you will see the upper axis of the top lean more to one side and then to the other side as the spin slows.

3. Observe the axis very carefully and you can see that it traces a cone shape as it goes around from one side to the other. Time how long it takes the axis to trace one complete cone before it falls.

❓ Follow-Up Questions

1. How long is the precession of the top? How long is the precession of Earth?
2. Explain why the star designated as the North Star changes over time.

➕ Extension

Use a toothpick and a piece of clay to make a model of the Earth that can spin on its axis. Vary the shape of the clay to see how shape affects precession.

16.9. LUNAR SURFACE REGOLITH

After the Meteorites Hit the Moon

Regolith—loose, fragmented material—can be found on Earth as well as on the Moon. Regolith is the result of weathering on Earth. However, on the Moon this material is a product of debris expelled from the surface when *meteorites*, the stony or metallic remains of meteoroids, strike. The composition and texture of lunar regolith varies depending on the location. A general rule of thumb is that the older the lunar surface, the thicker the regolith. In this activity you will simulate regolith formation on the Moon.

✅ Materials

Safety goggles; Two pieces of crisply toasted white bread; Four pieces of crisply toasted dark rye bread; Cardboard tray or some other large container to hold the bread; Heavy rock about the size of a tennis ball (should be fairly round in shape)

Activity

1. Stack the four toasted pieces of rye bread in the center of the cardboard tray. Place the two pieces of toasted white bread on top of the four rye pieces. The stack of bread represents the surface of the Moon.

2. Hold the rock two feet above the stack of bread, then release it so that the rock strikes the stack. Repeat this a second time. If the stack tips over, reposition it and try again. Once you have dropped the rock twice, observe the appearance of the bread stack and the crumbs that have formed.

3. Repeat step 2, but this time drop the rock twelve times. Observe the bread slices and the crumbs now.

❓ Follow-Up Questions

1. What did the rock and the crumbs represent in this activity?

2. How did the appearance of the bread and the amount of crumbs vary between step 2 and step 3?

3. Which crumbs were more abundant after you dropped the rock twelve times—rye or white?

➕ Extension

See how regolith formation is different on Earth from on the Moon. Take some toasted bread and rub a piece of sandpaper across the top of it. Look at the crumbs that fall from the bread. What does the sandpaper represent? How is this different from regolith formation on the Moon?

16.10. WEIGHT AND GRAVITY
Weighing In on the Earth, Moon, and Sun

Gravity is natural force that attracts one object to another. On Earth the force of gravity pulls all matter toward the surface. The amount of matter in each of us is our *mass*. Our *weight* is a measurement of the Earth's gravity on this mass. If we were on the Moon or the Sun, our mass would be the same, but the force of gravity would be different, so our weight would also be different. In this activity you will compare your weight on Earth with your weight on the Moon and the Sun.

✅ Materials

Calculator

A bathroom scale (optional; for students who do not know their weight)

1. Write down your weight in pounds on the Earth.

2. If it were possible for you to travel to the Moon and weigh yourself, how much would you weigh? Gravity on the Moon is about one-sixth of the gravity on the Earth. Calculate your weight on the Moon by dividing your weight on Earth by six. This is how many pounds you would weigh on the Moon.

3. If it were possible for you to travel to the Sun and weigh yourself (without burning up immediately), how much would you weigh? Gravity on the Sun is 28 times stronger than that of the Earth. Calculate your weight on the Sun by multiplying your Earth weight by 28. How many pounds would you weigh on the Sun?

❓ Follow-Up Questions

1. What do you weigh on Earth?
2. What would you weigh on the Moon? What would you weigh on the Sun?
3. Think about the size of the Earth, Moon, and Sun. Do you think their size and mass have anything to do with the pull of gravity? Explain your answer.

➕ Extension

Do some research and find how the other planets compare with Earth in their gravitational pull. Calculate how much you would weigh on each planet. On which planet do you think you would weigh the most? Why?

16.11. AURORAS
Party Lights in the Sky

The Sun is constantly emitting highly energized particles including electrons and positively charged ions. These particles make up the *solar wind*. Earth is protected from the solar wind by its magnetic field, the lines of which run from pole to pole. Surrounding each magnetic pole is a circular region called the *auroral oval*. When the solar wind reaches the magnetic field lines, the lines guide some of the particles toward the rings. Atmospheric gases around the rings become charged and glow. The brightness of these glowing gases, or *auroras*, depends on the activity of the Sun. In this activity you will build a model of Earth's magnetic field and the auroral rings.

✅ Materials

Styrofoam ball (about the size of a softball)

Two pipe cleaners of one color

Eight pipe cleaners of another color

Wooden skewer

Scissors

Glue

 Activity

1. Pierce the Styrofoam ball with the wooden skewer. The ball represents Earth, and the skewer emerging from each side of the ball represents the north and south magnetic poles.

2. Use the two pipe cleaners of one color to represent the auroral rings. Shape one pipe cleaner into a circle that will fit on top of the Styrofoam ball, like a cap. Place the ring on the ball, with one end of the skewer in the center of the ring, and glue it in place. Turn the ball over and glue the second pipe cleaner ring around the other end of the skewer.

3. Use the eight pipe cleaners of another color to represent the lines of Earth's magnetic field. Glue one end of each pipe cleaner to one of the auroral rings. Glue the other end of each pipe cleaner to the other auroral ring. The lines of magnetic field will form large C-shaped structures around the Styrofoam ball.

16.11. AURORAS (continued)

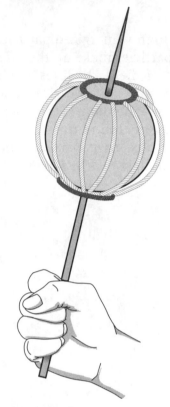

FIGURE 16.5. Pipe Cleaner Auroras

❓ Follow-Up Questions

1. Where on planet Earth do you think people are best able to view the auroras?

2. In the year 2012, the Sun is expected to be very active. How do you think this activity will affect the auroras?

3. If you were on a space ship over the North Pole, what would you expect to see when you looked down at Earth?

➕ Extension

Carry out some research on how the solar wind distorts Earth's magnetic field. Use your aurora model from the original activity to show these distortions.

16.12. MOON FACE
The Moon's Revolution and Rotation

Earth, like all other planets except Mercury and Venus, has a moon. Earth's Moon remains in orbit because of the pull of Earth's gravity. As the Moon travels around the planet , different amounts of its surface are lit, causing the Moon's phases. Any time you look at the Moon, you see the same surface because of the way the Moon rotates as it revolves in its orbit. In this activity you will discover why we never see the back side of the moon.

 **Materials**

Paper
Compass
Small ball of clay

1. Use the compass to draw a large circle on a piece of paper. This represents the Moon's orbit around Earth.
2. Draw a smaller circle inside the large one. Label the smaller circle "Earth."
3. Use the point of the compass to draw a face on one side of the small ball of clay. This represents the Moon.
4. Place the moon on the outer circle with its face toward the Earth.
5. Move the moon around the outer circle once, keeping its face toward Earth.

Follow-Up Questions

1. As the Moon traveled around Earth, how many times did it rotate on its axis?
2. A year is the time it takes a body to revolve around its entire orbit. A day is the time it takes a body to rotate on its axis. Compare the length of a lunar day and a lunar year.

Extension

Carry out some research to find out how long it takes for the Moon to rotate all of the way around the Earth. How does this period relate to our calendar?

TEACHER'S NOTES

Section 1. Organization of Matter

1.4. Identifying and Naming Isotopes: "EggCeptional" Isotopes

Prior to making the egg isotopes, decide what items you will use to represent protons, neutrons, and electrons. Suggestions include craft red buttons for protons, blue buttons for neutrons, and yellow beads for electrons. You can give all students the same isotope, or you can vary it. For instance, for sodium-23, you would put in eleven red buttons, eleven yellow beans, and twelve blue buttons. If you use different isotopes for different students, they could later switch eggs and practice figuring out isotope numbers.

1.5. Chemical and Physical Changes: Examining Paper for Change

Place the following items in envelopes for each lab group. Prior to the changes, each piece of paper should be of equal size.

Burned paper

Paper that has a circle cut out of the middle

Paper folded over three times into a square

Paper that has been soaked in water and dried

1.11. Mendeleev's Periodic Table: It Was All in the Cards

Make a photocopy of the following page for each student. Students will cut out the cards themselves.

Element A9
Atomic Mass: 9
(Solid)

Element A8
Atomic Mass: 8
(Liquid)

Element A7
Atomic Mass: 7
(Gas)

Element A1
Atomic Mass: 1
(Gas)

Element A2
Atomic Mass: 2
(Liquid)

Element A4
Atomic Mass: 4
(Gas)

Element A5
Atomic Mass: 5
(Liquid)

Element A6
Atomic Mass: 6
(Solid)

Element A3
Atomic Mass: 3
(Solid)

Section 2. Interactions of Matter

2.1. Acids and Bases: Cabbage Juice Indicators

Before the activity, prepare cabbage juice by chopping a red cabbage into large chunks and boiling for about 15 minutes. Strain the juice from the cabbage and store in the refrigerator until needed. For each lab group, prepare a well plate or 5 shallow dishes of solutions. Label 5 wells (or 5 dishes) as A1, A2, A3, A4, and A5. Half-fill as follows:

A1: vinegar

A2: ammonia solution

A3: lemon juice

A4: baking soda solution

A5: Alka-Seltzer solution

To prepare the baking soda solution, stir about 1 teaspoon of baking soda in a cup of water. For the Alka-Seltzer solution, mix one Alka-Seltzer tablet in a cup of water.

2.4. Exothermic and Endothermic Reactions: Hot Packs and Cold Packs

Prior to the activity, prepare a bag of calcium chloride for each student by placing 3 tablespoons of calcium chloride powder in a small plastic bag and sealing it. Label the bag as calcium chloride. Also prepare a bag of ammonium nitrate for each student by placing 3 tablespoons of ammonium nitrate in a small plastic bag, sealing it, and labeling each of these bags as ammonium nitrate.

2.5. Chemical Reactions: Alka-Seltzer and Water Temperature

To save on the amount of Alka-Seltzer you need for the activity, break each tablet in half and give students half-size pieces rather than whole pieces.

2.9. Single Replacement Reactions: Turning Iron into Copper

Place 2 teaspoons of copper sulfate in a resealable plastic bag for each student. Put 2 tablespoons of water into a small cup for each student.

Section 3. Energy of Motion

3.12. The Three Classes of Levers: Lots of Levers and Lots of Class

Prior to the activity, photocopy ten or more pictures of levers in action for your students. Cut these pictures apart and place them in envelopes so that each student has ten pictures representing different types of levers. Suggestions include a wheelbarrow, a screwdriver prying off the lid of a paint can, a batter hitting a baseball, a person sweeping, a hinged nutcracker, a claw hammer pulling out a nail, scissors, tweezers, a hinged door, and a teeter-totter or seesaw. Be sure to include a picture of a wheelbarrow with a mound of dirt or sand in it, because you will use this image in the activity.

Section 4. Heat, Light, and Sound Waves

4.12. Energy Conductors and Insulators: The Cook's Choice

Prepare a large container of hot water for each student prior to class. The container should be large enough to fit a plastic, metal, and wooden cooking spoon in it. Water should be hot, but not scalding, so that students do not get burned.

Section 5. Magnetism and Electricity

5.2. Closed Circuits: A Battery, a Bulb, and a Paper Clip

You may want to give the students the bulb with a wooden clothespin around it, so they can hold onto the clothespin rather than the bulb when attempting to light it.

5.3. Electrochemical Cell: Nine-Volt Battery Electrolysis

Prior to the activity, sharpen some pencils enough to provide graphite. When preparing the water dish, dissolve some sodium sulfate to provide the electrolytes that will enable the water to conduct electricity. You can place alligator clips on the ends of the copper wire if you wish, so that students do not have to wind the bare copper wire around the ends of the pencils.

5.6. Schematic Circuit Diagrams: Seeing the Circuit

Prepare the envelopes ahead of time for each student by placing a one-meter length of string, three resistor symbols, a battery symbol, and four arrows in each envelope.

Section 6. The Cell

6.6. Cell Transport: When It Come to Cells, Small Is Good

Before class, prepare 2 potato cubes for each student or lab group. Cubes do not have to be exactly 1 cm^3 and 3 cm^3.

6.11. Photosynthesis and Respiration: Formula Scramble

Type or write the following words and symbols on individual pieces of paper, and place a complete set in each student's envelope:

oxygen	energy
carbon dioxide	oxygen
glucose	carbon dioxide
water	glucose
+	water
+	+
⟶	+
sunlight	+
chlorophyll	⟶

If you do not mind the activity taking more than five minutes, you can ask students to write these words on slips of paper and cut them out so that you need not prepare the envelopes beforehand.

Section 7. Genetics

7.10. Protein Synthesis: Modeling Transcription

Prepare the envelope of red bases by writing the following letters on individual pieces of red construction paper and cutting them out. Label this envelope "DNA bases."

A C G C T T C C A

Prepare the envelope of blue bases by writing the following letters on individual pieces of blue construction paper and cutting them out. Label this envelope "RNA bases."

U G C G A A G G U

If you prefer, you can have students write the letters on different colored construction paper and then cut them out for themselves.

Section 8. Evolution

8.6. Adaptive Radiation: The Beaks of Darwin's Finches

Prior to this activity, cut pieces of yarn into three-inch lengths. Place about fifty pieces of yarn in a cup. Each student will need a cup of this yarn, which will represent bird food.

Section 10. Ecology

10.3. Food Web: Piecing Together a Food Web Puzzle

Prior to this activity, find and photocopy several pictures of food webs. Cut the food webs into puzzle pieces and place the pieces of one food web into an envelope. Repeat this process for each student in the class. You may consider laminating the pieces so you can reuse them each year.

10.5. The Importance of Niches: Extinction and the Paper Clip Niche

Prior to doing the activity for the first time, prepare two envelopes (envelope A and B) for each student. Place ten regular paper clips in each A envelope. In each B envelope, place ten paper clips that have been elongated or straightened so there is no longer a curved section.

10.7. Human Pollution: Plastic Killers

Prior to starting the activity, collect the plastic rings that hold together six-packs of cans. Cut the rings apart so that you have six complete rings from each six-pack set. Each student will need one ring.

Section 12. Structure of Earth Systems

12.6. Mineral Hardness: Mineral Ranks

Prior to doing this activity, prepare a cup of five minerals for each student or pair of students. Label each mineral as A, B, C, D, or E. Minerals that could be used in this experiment include talc, gypsum, fluorite, calcite, and quartz.

Section 13. Earth's History

13.1. Inferences from Fossils: Who Was Here?

Before class, fill a reusable or paper bag with some baby items. Suggestions include a diaper, a pacifier, a bootie, a jar of baby food, ribbons, and a baby spoon. If these items are not available, fill the bag with items that are typical of a specific type of individual. Other ideas include a teenager, a plumber, an accountant, or a teacher.

13.4. Continental Drift: Puzzling Over the Continents

Make enlarged copies of the following figure for each student. Cut out the continents and put them in an envelope. The figure on the next page shows how the pieces should look after students have assembled them.

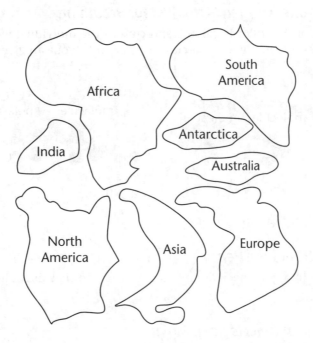

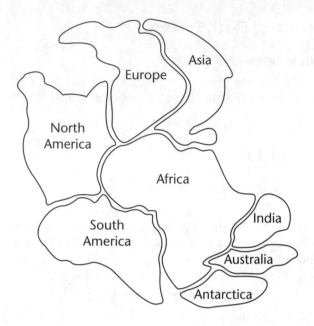

Section 14. Meteorology

14.6. The Loss of Ozone: Oxygen Is Not Just for Breathing

Make enlarged copies of the following figure and cut out the individual molecules. Place the molecules in envelopes for the students. If class time permits, you can gives students copies of the figure to cut out.

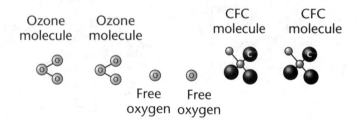

Section 15. The Universe

15.9. Infrared Light: Feel the Heat

Place an infrared bulb in a gooseneck lamp and position it so that the bulb is 30 cm above the tabletop.

15.11. Inertia in Space: Objects Keep Moving

For each group of students, provide one piece of foam. Prepare the foam by cutting lengths of tubular foam pipe insulation into sections that are about four feet long. Cut each tubular section of foam in half lengthwise.

ANSWER KEY

Section 1. Organization of Matter

1.1. Boyle's Gas Law: Marshmallow Under Pressure

1. When you pushed in the plunger, the air pressure increased, pushing the bubbles out of the marshmallow and decreasing its size. When the plunger was pulled out, the pressure decreased so the marshmallow expanded in size.

2. Boyle's law says that when temperature is constant, the pressure and volume are inversely related. This means that when pressure is low, volume is high, and vice versa. This is what you saw happen in the activity.

1.2. Buoyancy: Ketchup Packet Cartesian Diver

1. When you squeezed the bottle, the packet sank to the bottom of the bottle.

2. When you released the bottle, the packet rose back toward the top.

3. When you squeezed the bottle, you increased the pressure on the air bubbles in the packet, reducing their size and making the density of the packet greater than the density of the water. That caused the packet to sink. When you decreased the pressure, the density of the packet was reduced and it floated upward.

1.3. Counting Molecules and Atoms: Number of Molecules of Chalk in Your Signature

1. Answers will vary.

2. Answers will vary.

1.4. Identifying and Naming Isotopes: "EggCeptional" Isotopes

1. Answers will vary.

2. Answers will vary.

3. Answers will vary.

1.5. Chemical and Physical Changes: Examining Paper for Change

1. The burned paper was the only one that experienced a chemical change. In this type of change a new substance was formed.

2. The cut, folded, and soaked paper experienced physical changes. The appearance of the paper changed, but no new substance was formed.

3. Answers will vary, but students need to indicate that a new substance forms as a result of a chemical change.

1.6. Physical Properties of Matter: Tootsie Roll Properties

1. Answers will vary, but the density of the Tootsie Roll should be less than 1 g/ml.

2. Answers will vary.

1.7. Density: Can't Hold a Good Ping-Pong Ball Down

1. The Ping-Pong ball rose to the top of the container, while the metal ball sank.

2. The beans have a density greater than that of the Ping-Pong ball, but less than that of the metal ball.

1.8. Atomic Size in Picometers: Cutting Paper to Atom Size

1. Answers will vary.

2. Answers will vary.

3. No.

1.9. Surface Tension: Why Some Insects Can Walk on Water

1. Answers will vary, but the number of drops will most likely be greater than students expect.

2. Water forms a dome on top of the penny.

3. The weight of the water overcame the pull of attraction holding the water molecules together.

1.10. Birds in Flight: How Birds' Wings Enable Them to Fly

1. Answers will vary, but most students predict that the cans will separate.

2. The cans moved together.

3. An increase in velocity between the cans reduces air pressure and the cans come together, rather than fly apart. The upper curve of the wing makes air travel faster around the top surface than it does around the lower surface. This reduces the air pressure on top of the wing. The greater air pressure below the wing lifts the bird upward in flight. The differences in air pressure above and below a wing are explained by Bernoulli's Principle, which states that as air speed increases, air pressure decreases.

4. Both are successful based on Bernoulli's Principle.

1.11. Mendeleev's Periodic Table: It Was All in the Cards

1. Answers will vary, but most students will arrange the cards according to solids, liquids, or gases.

2. In the liquid category with an atomic mass of 11.

1.12. Volume of a Cylinder: The Long and Short of Volume

1. Answers will vary.

2. The shorter cylinder with the greater diameter or width has more volume, because in the formula the radius is squared.

Section 2. Interactions of Matter

2.1. Acids and Bases: Cabbage Juice Indicators

1. Vinegar (A1) and lemon juice (A3) are the acids.

2. The bases are ammonia (A2), baking soda (A4), and Alka-Seltzer (A5).

2.2. Polymers: Water-Loving Chemicals in Diapers

1. White

2. It formed a gel-like material.

3. The water from the pool could combine with the diaper, causing the polymer to form a gel-like solid. The diaper would become very heavy and would no longer function properly.

2.3. Freezing Point: Why We Sprinkle Salt on Icy Roads

1. The string stuck to the ice cube.

2. The salt lowered the freezing point of the ice, causing it to melt and refreeze around the string.

3. The salt lowers the freezing point of the ice, so that you can make ice cream quickly. The salt causes the ice around the canister of an ice cream churn to melt. The lower freezing point of the melted ice draws heat from the ice cream mixture and results in the rapid cooling and freezing that causes the ice cream to solidify.

2.4. Exothermic and Endothermic Reactions: Hot Packs and Cold Packs

1. Calcium chloride makes a good hot pack, and ammonium nitrate makes a good cold pack.

2. Calcium chloride produced an exothermic reaction, and ammonium nitrate produced an endothermic reaction.

3. You can't tell just from the results of this experiment, because all physical and chemical reactions involve energy.

2.5. Chemical Reactions: Alka-Seltzer and Water Temperature

1. The warmest cup.

2. As temperature increases, the speed of the reaction will increase.

2.6. Balancing Chemical Equations: Rearranging Atomic Dots

1. $4Al + 3O_2 \rightarrow 2Al_2O_3$.

2. You do have the same kinds of atoms on both sides of the equation, but the arrangement of the atoms may be different.

2.7. Limiting Reactants: Putting a Halt to the Reaction

1. Five.

2. The centers.

3. There were four guards left over, and there were seven forwards left over.

2.8. Writing Ionic Formulas: Equaling the Ions

1. $CaCl_2$

2. Al_2O_3

2.9. Single Replacement Reactions: Turning Iron into Copper

1. The copper sulfate solution was originally blue. After the reaction occurred, the solution turned a yellow-green color. The steel wool was originally gray. After the reaction, the steel wool took on a copper color.

2. Iron sulfate and copper.

2.10. Double Replacement Reactions: Trading Partners

1. AB (pink) + (pink) CD (pink) $\rightarrow$ (white) AD (green) + (green) CB (green)

2. The positive ions were represented by pink A, pink C, green A, green C. The negative ions were pink B, pink D, green B, and green D.

2.11. Polarity and Solubility: Breaking Bonds of Packing Peanuts

1. The water dissolved the cornstarch peanuts, but not the Styrofoam peanuts. The nail polish dissolved the Styrofoam, but not the cornstarch peanuts.

2. Water is polar, as is the cornstarch. Styrofoam is nonpolar, as is acetone.

Answer Key

2.12. Surface Area and Solubility: Sweet Solutions

1. Answers will vary, but the mint that was chewed should have dissolved faster than the mint moved around with the tongue. The mint moved with the tongue should have dissolved faster than the mint just held in the mouth.

2. Answers will vary, but students should indicate that agitation and chewing increase surface area of the mints. The solute was the mint, and the solvent was saliva in the mouth. The combination of the two formed a solution.

Section 3. Energy of Motion

3.1. Potential Energy and Kinetic Energy: Bouncing Golf Balls

1. No.
2. The bounce height was lower.

3.2. Potential Energy: The Energy of Falling Objects

1. The steel ball made the deepest indentation because it had the greatest mass.
2. The Ping-Pong ball had the least potential energy because of its smaller mass. The steel ball had the greatest potential energy because of its larger mass.

3.3. Friction Through a Fluid: Fluids and Falling

1. The flattened piece.
2. The flattened piece had much more surface area, and this increased the friction.

3.4. Newton's First Law of Motion: Inertia—the Magician's Friend

1. The penny was at rest, and when you thumped the card from under it quickly, the penny remained at rest. It simply fell into the cup, rather than flying away with the card.
2. Both demonstrated the law of inertia.
3. The rougher the texture of the cloth, the less likely the trick will work. The friction of the tablecloth could place a horizontal force on the dishes, causing them to move with the cloth rather than stay put on the table.

3.5. Law of Conservation of Momentum: Marble Collisions

1. It moved forward. The marble that was flicked with your finger came to a stop once it set the other marble into motion.
2. Answers will vary. When two marbles are moved forward together and they strike two resting marbles, the two resting marbles roll off together and the two you flicked with your finger stop. The law of conservation of momentum says that momentum before a collision equals momentum after the collision, so the marbles set into motion by your finger transferred their momentum to the marbles being struck farther down the ruler.

3.6. Static Friction: Going Against the Grain

1. Answers will vary depending on the objects used. If the suggested objects were used, the washer has the least static friction and the eraser has the most static friction. The surfaces of the substances influence the amount of friction created.

2. Answers will vary, but you can increase static friction by putting sandpaper on the bottom of the objects, or you can decrease it by putting oil on the bottom of the objects.

3.7. Newton's Second Law of Motion: Acceleration of the Coffee Mug

1. Yes, they are directly proportional.

2. Yes, they are inversely proportional.

3.8. Using the Speed Formula: Speedy Manipulations

1. Time = distance/speed

2. T = 180 miles/60 mph = 3 hours

3.9. Newton's Third Law of Motion: What Is a Reaction?

1. When you pushed forward with the left hand, the right hand exerted a force back on the left. The action had an equal and opposite reaction.

2. Five Newtons. Yes, the same force was being exerted on both scales in the activity due to the third law of motion.

3.10. Inclined Planes: Making Lifting Easier

1. Less force was needed to pull the block up the ramp.

2. Increasing the length of the ramp reduces the force needed.

3.11. Levers: First-Class Machines

1. Effort force is applied to the lever to move an object. Resistance force is due to the weight of the object.

2. The greater the distance, the less force needed to move the object.

3.12. The Three Classes of Levers: Lots of Levers and Lots of Class

1. Answers will vary depending on the pictures the teacher chooses. In the examples given in the Teacher's Notes, the first-class levers are the screwdriver prying up the lid, the claw hammer removing a nail, the scissors, and the teeter-totter. The second-class levers are the wheelbarrow, the nutcracker, and the hinged door. The third-class levers are the baseball batter, the person sweeping, and the tweezers.

2. Answers will vary, but most students will say first-class levers are easier to identify.

Answer Key

Section 4. Heat, Light, and Sound Waves

4.1. Thermal Energy: What Does Temperature Really Measure?

1. Yes. Answers will vary as to amount of increase.

2. Yes. The movement of the particles increased and the particles of sand bounced off of one another, resulting in an increase in kinetic energy and thus an increase in temperature.

4.2. Measuring Temperature: Human Thermometers

1. Cool.

2. Warm.

3. No. Answers will vary, but students should note that their sense of temperature changed with the circumstances in the experiment.

4.3. Refraction: A Real Light Bender

1. The line appeared to move to one side as you poured water into the glass.

2. Light slows when it moves from air into water, a denser medium. The slowing causes the light waves to change direction, or bend, causing a change in the appearance of the line.

3. Answers will vary, but students should indicate that the refraction of light from air into denser water creates an illusion.

4.4. Concave and Convex Mirrors: An Up-Close Look at the Spoon

1. Answers will vary, but most students will indicate their image was upside down in the concave side and right side up in the convex side.

2. As you moved the pencil toward the concave side of the spoon, the image started out upside down, but eventually flipped right side up and was enlarged. In the convex side of the spoon, the image of the pencil point remained right side up as you moved forward, but it did not enlarge as you got closer to the spoon.

4.5. Magnifying Lens: Water Drop Microscopes

1. Answers will vary, but students should indicate that the leaf was magnified.

2. Answers will vary.

4.6. Mechanical Waves: The Stadium Wave

1. Transverse; forward across the row and back again.

2. The medium was the students; the direction was up and down (perpendicular to the wave itself).

4.7. Transverse Waves: Anatomy of a String Wave

1. A crest is the high point on a transverse wave, and a trough is the low point on a transverse wave.

2. Reducing wavelength increases frequency.

4.8. Compressional Waves: Making Waves with a Slinky

1. Answers will vary, but students should indicate that at some places on the Slinky the coils are compressed together and at other locations they are stretched out.

2. The ribbon moves back and forth with the coils. The matter in the medium does not move forward with the wave. The wave carries only the energy forward.

4.9. Sound and Its Mediums: Sound Matters

1. After.

2. String.

3. The closer the molecules are together, the easier it is for one molecule to bump into the next one and the louder we hear sound.

4.10. Sound Vibrations: Rubber Band Music

1. Increase.

2. The thinnest rubber band had the highest pitch.

4.11. Sound and Water: Tuning Forks and Water

1. No.

2. Tiny water waves were created.

3. Vibrations produced in water are visible and mimic the invisible vibrations of air molecules.

4.12. Energy Conductors and Insulators: The Cook's Choice

1. The metal spoon is warmest.

2. The metal spoon.

3. Denser materials generally conduct heat better than less dense materials. The densest of the utensils used in this activity was the metal spoon.

Section 5. Magnetism and Electricity

5.1. Charging by Friction: Balloons and Dancing Salt Grains

1. Hair stood out from your head because of static friction. Many of the salt particles were attracted to the charged balloon.

2. The balloon had a negative charge after being rubbed on the hair, so the positive sodium ions in the petri dish were attracted to the balloon.

5.2. Closed Circuits: A Battery, a Bulb, and a Paper Clip

1. The paper clip conducted electricity.

2. Yes.

3. Yes. The circuit must be closed for the current to complete the trip from one terminal to the other.

5.3. Electrochemical Cell: Nine-Volt Battery Electrolysis

1. The power source provides electrical energy to support the chemical reaction.

2. Water and energy yield oxygen and hydrogen.

3. Answers will vary. The sodium sulfate made the water a better conductor.

5.4. Resistance: Series and Parallel Circuits

1. The straws taped side by side.

2. Series.

5.5. Making Electricity: A Shocking Activity

1. A tingle.

2. The coins were the metal electrodes, and the lemon juice was the chemical that conducted the current.

3. Yes. Answers will vary. (The metals have opposite charges.)

5.6. Schematic Circuit Diagrams: Seeing the Circuit

1. The flow of current would stop at that point.

2. The schematic diagram should look something like the image shown here.

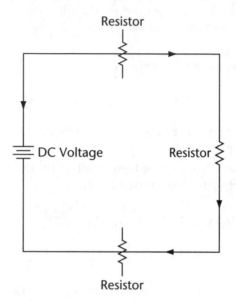

5.7. Electromagnets: The Art of Magnetizing a Nail

1. Answers will vary.

2. Answers will vary, but students should be able to pick up more paper clips this time than the first time.

3. As the number of loops increase, the strength of the magnet also increases.

5.8. Magnetic Field: Long-Distance Attraction

1. Answers will vary.

2. No; answers will vary.

5.9. Magnets: What's in a Refrigerator Magnet?

1. Yes. How you held the magnets determined whether you were putting two like or two different charges together. Like charges would cause the magnets to repel each other, and unlike charges would cause them to attract.

2. Answers will vary, but students should see a bar pattern.

5.10. Magnetizing Metals: The Magnetic Nail

1. No. The nail is not magnetized at this point.

2. Yes. The nail had been magnetized with the bar magnet.

3. No. Dropping the nail on the floor caused the orientation of the magnetic domains to be altered. When dropped on the floor, the iron atoms no longer all pointed in the same direction and the magnetic effect was lost.

5.11. Magnets and Compasses: Which Way Is North?

1. The needle.

2. The paper clip swung toward north.

3. Answers will vary, but the paper clip and the compass should be very close in agreement.

5.12. Magnetic Forces: Force Blockers

1. Answers will vary.

2. Answers will vary. The ruler showed the distance between the two magnets. The shorter the distance, the more effective the force blocker.

Section 6. The Cell

6.1. Characteristics of Life: Is It Alive?

1. Answers will vary. Some possibilities include the need for energy and the ability to move.

2. Answers will vary. One possible answer is that rocks are not made of cells.

6.2. Energy Molecules: ATP and ADP

1. ATP contains three phosphates. ATP molecules are full of energy.

2. ADP contains two phosphates. ADP gains energy.

6.3. ATP and Lactic Acid: Muscle Fatigue

1. Answers will vary, but most will say that their biceps are tired.

2. Lactic acid built up in the bicep muscle as the muscle became fatigued.

3. Yes. Some people in class may be used to doing bicep curls when weight lifting, so it is harder to fatigue their muscles.

6.4. The Cell Cycle, Part One: Getting Started

1. Two.

2. The chromosomes replicated.

3. Centromere.

6.5. The Cell Cycle, Part Two: The Process

1. Two.

2. A cell must make a copy of its chromosomes so that each new cell will have a complete set of DNA.

6.6. Cell Transport: When It Come to Cells, Small Is Good

1. Potato cube with a 1 cm^3 volume.

2. Small cell.

3. No.

6.7. Proteins as Enzymes: Saltine Crackers and Amylase

1. Answers will vary, but students should not indicate there was any sweet flavor to the cracker.

2. Yes. The cracker took on a sweet taste.

3. Enzymes were converting starch into sugar.

6.8. Plant Cell or Animal Cell: Shoestring Venn Diagram

1. Centrioles and flagella.

2. Chloroplasts, cell wall, and large vacuoles.

3. Cell membrane, ribosomes, mitochondria, and cytokinesis.

6.9. Enzymes: Temperature and Paperase

1. Answers will vary, but paperase should have produced more pieces of paper on the first trial.

2. Application of ice slowed down paperase.

3. Temperature differences can affect the activity of enzymes.

6.10. The Mitochondria: Surface Area and the Folded Membrane

1. Answers will vary depending on the size of the box used. Answers will vary depending on the contents of the box.

2. The envelopes increase the surface area of the box, just as the folds of the mitochondria increase its surface area.

Answer Key

6.11. Photosynthesis and Respiration: Formula Scramble

1.

$$\textit{Photosynthesis: } \text{carbon dioxide} + \text{water} \xrightarrow[\text{Sunlight}]{\text{Chlorophyll}} \text{glucose} + \text{oxygen}$$

$$\textit{Respiration: } \text{oxygen} + \text{glucose} \longrightarrow \text{carbon dioxide} + \text{water} + \text{energy}$$

2. They both produce products that the other needs for survival.

Section 7. Genetics

7.1. DNA: Candy Nucleotides

1. They are alike in that each nucleotide consists of a sugar, a phosphate, and a base. They differ in the type of base used in each one.
2. Sugar, phosphate, and base.

7.2. Chromosomes: Learning to Speak "Chromosome"

1. Two.
2. Replication occurs so each new cell can receive a copy of the chromosome.

7.3. Genetic Diversity: Crossing Over During Meiosis

1. Homologous chromosomes are matching chromosomes from each parent.
2. Three.
3. One.

7.4. Genetic Combinations: Tall and Short Pea Plants

1. 25 percent.
2. 0 percent.
3. A Punnett square can be used to predict the likelihood that offspring will inherit certain traits.

7.5. Mendel's Law of Segregation: Cystic Fibrosis

1. Answers will vary depending on the result of the first flip. CC and Cc represent normal lung function, while cc indicates cystic fibrosis.
2. Answers will vary, but most students' flips will show more children with normal lung function than children with cystic fibrosis.

7.6. Dominant and Recessive Genes in Cat Breeding: Curly-Eared Cats

1. Both parents had curly ears.

2. Answers will vary, but the data of many students will show more curly-eared kittens than straight-eared kittens.

3. Kittens with white-white pipe cleaner combinations.

7.7. Pedigrees: The Higgenbothum Hairline

1. Three.

2. Two.

3. Dominant. Answers will vary, but should reference the pedigree.

7.8. Sex-Linked Traits: Flipping Over Color Blindness

1. Answers will vary. Usually the boy-girl ratio is close, but not always.

2. Answers will vary. For a girl to be color-blind, she has to have $X^c X^c$. For a boy to be color-blind, he would have $X^c Y$.

3. It is more common in boys. They have to inherit only one recessive gene, but girls have to inherit two recessive genes.

7.9. Gene Splicing: Human Growth Hormone and Recombinant DNA

1. Gene splicing is the process of putting the desired gene in the plasmid to produce recombinant DNA.

2. Restriction enzymes cut open the plasmid at specific sites on the plasmid so the new gene can be inserted. The ligase is responsible for affixing the new gene into the opened plasmid at that specific location.

7.10. Protein Synthesis: Modeling Transcription

1. UGCGAAGGU.

2. The base thymine is found in DNA, but not RNA. (The base uracil is never found in DNA.)

Section 8. Evolution

8.1. Natural Selection: Life as a Peppered Moth

1. Answers will vary, but students usually pick up more dark beans on light paper and more light beans on dark paper.

2. When the tree was light gray in color, the dark moths were easily seen and eaten by predators. Once the bark color changed to dark gray, the dark moths were harder to see. They survived and began to reproduce in greater numbers than the light-colored moths, who now were clearly seen and eaten by the predators.

Answer Key

8.2. Advantageous Traits: Which Creature Is the Fittest?

1. Answers will vary depending on the count, but most students will find that the rice and the black-eyed peas were more likely to fall through the hole than the pinto beans.

2. In this activity it is advantageous to have a large size so you avoid falling through the hole in the cup. Natural selection says that individuals with variations that increase their chance of survival will live to produce more offspring like themselves.

3. The pinto beans were more likely to survive the earthquakes because their larger size prevented them from falling easily through the gaps created by the earthquake.

8.3. Primate Adaptations: The Importance of the Opposable Thumb

1. Answers will vary, but it should have taken much longer to tie the bow when the thumbs were taped to the hand.

2. Answers will vary and can include writing, throwing a ball, swinging a bat, sweeping the floor, typing, or texting.

8.4. Steps of Natural Selection: Natural Selection Sequencing

1. The following sequence is correct:

   a. Difference or variations occur among individuals of a species.

   b. Some variations are helpful, and individuals with helpful variations survive and reproduce.

   c. Organisms produce more offspring that can survive.

   d. Over time offspring with helpful variations make more of a population and can become a separate species.

   e. Variations among parents are passed to offspring.

2. No. Answers will vary as to the reason all steps are essential.

8.5. Plant Adaptation: Features for Survival in the Rain Forest

1. The leaf with the pointed tip.

2. The leaf with the pointed tip represents the "drip tip" leaf, since it allows water to run off the surface of the leaf sooner than the round tip leaf. Quickly dispelling moisture helps prevent growth of mold and mildew.

8.6. Adaptive Radiation: The Beaks of Darwin's Finches

1. Answers may vary, but most students will collect more worms with the tweezers. The tweezer-beak allows the finch to grasp the worm on both sides of the body when lifting it.

2. Answers will vary, but should note that it is possible they might not survive unless they leave the island and go elsewhere in search of food.

8.7. Variations and Survival: Pine Needle Variation

1. Answers will vary.
2. Longer leaf lengths might allow more food storage and enable the tree to gather more sunlight for photosynthesis.

8.8. Horse Evolution: Horse Height Over Time

1. Answers will vary, but many students might indicate it was about the size of a dog.
2. It could hide under the large branches of a tree to escape predators.

8.9. Fossil Dating: Stacking Up Rock Layers

1. Bacteria.
2. 2,900 million years.
3. Fossils in the bottom of the stack are the oldest, because over time newer rock layers with more recent fossils are deposited on top of the older layers.

8.10. Antibiotic Resistance: Present-Day Evolution

1. Some bacteria carry the gene for antibiotic resistance.
2. They would survive and continue to reproduce.

Section 9. Diversity of Life

9.1. The Six Kingdoms: Kingdom Match Game

In the main activity, the characteristics should be organized as follows:

Animalia: humans, tick, all are multicelled heterotrophs

Plantae: all have cell walls and chloroplasts, fern

Fungi: mildew, cell wall of chitin, mushroom

Protista: algae; Euglena; most, but not all, are unicellular

Eubacteria: *E. coli,* has no nucleus

Archaebacteria: first organisms on Earth, likes extreme environments, has no nucleus

1. Answers will vary, but students should indicate that plants are all multicellular organisms that possess chloroplast. They may also say that plants are autotrophs (using photosynthesis).
2. Eubacteria, Archaebacteria, Protista, and Fungi.

9.2. Vascular Plants: Checking Out a Fern Frond

1. Vascular tissues carry water and dissolved nutrients throughout the plant much as blood vessels carry blood and dissolved nutrients throughout animals.

2. One large vessel.

3. Sori are small brown structures that look like little bumps.

9.3. Flower Parts: Dissecting the Flower

1. Answers will vary depending on the types of flowers used.

2. Answers will vary, but there will be only one pistil and multiple stamens. The ovule, which will later become the seed, needs to become fertilized. Multiple stamens increase the possibility of fertilization.

3. Wind, water, insects.

9.4. Food Storage in Seeds: Dissecting a Dicot

1. The drawing should look something like the image shown here.

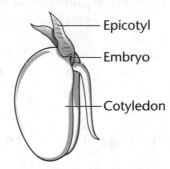

2. The cotyledon is the food storage area, so those areas should be shaded.

9.5. Seed Dispersal: Where the Plants Come From

1. Answers will vary.

2. Answers will vary.

9.6. Animal Symmetry: What Symmetry Is This?

1. Answers will vary, but students might list letters such as K, L, or E.

2. Answers will vary, but students should list three animals that have bilateral symmetry, such as humans, apes, or dogs.

9.7. Viruses: Nuts and Bolts of a Bacteriophage

1. Answers will vary. The capsid should be the top of the virus. It is a protein coat.

2. The genetic material would be inside the capsid.

3. Protein coat and genetic material.

9.8. Bird Digestion: Why Birds Don't Need Teeth

1. They were crushed into small pieces or powder.

2. The gizzard is rough so it can pulverize material and do the job that teeth usually do in animals.

9.9. Examining a Fungus: Close-Up Look at a Mushroom

1. Answers will vary.

2. Answers may vary, but students should indicate that the hyphae are stringlike structures whose major role is to obtain nutrients for the mushroom.

9.10. Taxonomic Categories: Addressing Classification

1. When addressing a letter, the more specific information is at the top, where you write the name of the recipient. As you move down the address, you become more general and include a broader area.

2. The ZIP Code generally indicates a specific city, so it would be highlighted in blue. (For cities that have several ZIP Codes, this would be more specific than just the city.)

Section 10. Ecology

10.1. Energy Flow Through the Food Chain: The 10 Percent Rule of Energy Flow

1. The fourth-level consumer would have received 10 percent of the energy from the third-level consumer. You would have put 0.01 ml of water into the fourth-level consumer's cup.

2. There is not enough energy available to continue the food chain after the second-level or third-level consumers.

10.2. Population Growth Rate: Growing Exponentially

1. Offer A would pay $150 a week. Offer B would pay $163.84 a week.

2. Job B is more like exponential growth, because the amount continues to double each time. If there were no limit to your hours, your pay would continue to increase exponentially.

3. Employer B pays out more to employees than Employer A as soon as fifteen hours have been worked in a given week. The figure would become astronomical if employees could work unlimited hours. Employer A would never pay more than $10 an hour.

10.3. Food Web: Piecing Together a Food Web Puzzle

1. Answers will vary depending on the food web selected.

2. Answers will vary.

3. The highest level consumer in the food web will receive the least energy.

10.4. Population Estimations: Mark and Recapture of Wildlife

1. Answers will vary.

2. Answers will vary.

10.5. The Importance of Niches: Extinction and the Paper Clip Niche

1. Making chains of paper clips.

2. When the species that shaped the clips to a rounded form became extinct, it increased the time required for me to do my job. Now, instead of just making a chain, I had to also shape the clips before filling my niche.

10.6. Symbiosis: Want Ads for Mutualism

1. The Egyptian plover gets food by eating the parasites in the crocodiles.

2. The crocodile is freed from blood-sucking parasites.

3. The relationship is mutualistic, because both organisms benefit.

10.7. Human Pollution: Plastic Killers

1. Plastic rings can find their way into the water. They can get tangled around the mouths or necks of animals. They take hundreds of years to break down after they have entered waterways.

2. The seal would have died of starvation.

10.8. Plant Growth Requirements: When Seeds Get Too Crowded

1. Answers will vary depending on the size of the class.

2. Overcrowding would result, and all the available nutrients would be used up.

3. This activity shows that populations that reproduce quickly can become overcrowded. When overcrowding occurs, the available resources will be consumed. Some members of the population will not be able to survive, and some will become sickly.

10.9. Packaging and the Environment: Convenience or Conservation?

1. Answers will vary.

2. The four half-pints of milk used more natural resources.

10.10. Arthropod Behavior: Response of the Pill Bugs

1. Pill bugs prefer moist environments. They need moisture to survive, since they have gills for respiration.

2. Yes. When hunting for pill bugs, it is best to look in dark areas with lots of moisture, such as under rocks.

Section 11. Body Systems

11.1. The Role of Bile in Digestion: Emulsifying Fat

1. The oil spread out and floated on top of the water.

2. The oil broke up into little droplets.

3. The cooking oil represents fats or lipids. The detergent represents bile.

11.2. Tendons: Visualizing How the Fingers Work

1. The tendons look like little cords or ropes under the skin.

2. Answers will vary, but students should indicate the action of the tendons can be traced back up the forearm.

11.3. The Heart: The Strongest Muscle of the Body

1. Answers will vary, but most students will get far fewer than seventy squeezes in sixty seconds.

2. Answers will vary, but most students will indicate fatigue in the hand.

3. It would be impossible to squeeze the tennis ball at this rate for twenty-four hours. The heart is a much stronger muscle.

11.4. Partnering of the Brain and Eyes: Putting the Fish in the Bowl

1. The fish looked like it was inside the fishbowl.

2. Answers will vary, but students should relate this to persistence of vision.

11.5. Lung Capacity During Exercise: Balloons and Vital Capacity

1. Answers will vary.

2. Vital capacity is the amount of air you breathe out after taking a deep breath.

11.6. Blood Vessels: Arteries or Veins?

1. The vessel seemed to enlarge in size.

2. Toward the heart.

3. You were pressing on a vein.

11.7. Muscle Interactions: Pairing of the Biceps and Triceps

1. The biceps muscle was harder when you were attempting to lift up on the desk. The triceps was harder when you pushed down on the top of the desk.

Answer Key

2. Answers will vary, but students should point out that when the biceps are contracted, the triceps are elongated and vice versa.

11.8. Mechanical Digestion: The Initial Breakdown of Digestion

1. Mechanical digestion due to the action of the teeth and tongue.
2. More sugar will be dissolved in the cup of water with crushed sugar.
3. Before food is swallowed, the teeth and tongue begin the process of mechanical digestion.

11.9. Peristalsis During Digestion: Moving Food Through the Esophagus

1. Answers will vary, but students should mention they had to squeeze and push on the tennis ball.
2. **a.** Mouth
   b. Esophagus
   c. Food particles
   d. Peristalsis due to contractions
   e. Stomach

11.10. Why We Sweat: Staying Cool with the Sweat Glands

1. The temperature decreased from the first reading to the second reading.
2. When sweat evaporates from your skin, the body is cooled.
3. Rubbing alcohol has a higher rate of evaporation than water and enables you to see temperature change quickly.

Section 12. Structure of Earth Systems

12.1. Core Sampling: Seeing Inside the Cupcake

1. Like a cupcake, the Earth is made of several layers and contains various components.
2. Yes. Core sampling might help you locate oil or types of rock that hold oil.

12.2. Metamorphic Rocks: Pressure and the Candy Bar

1. Answers will vary.
2. Answers will vary, but students may not be able to see any layers.
3. When rock is exposed to extreme pressure, it changes in appearance.

12.3. Sedimentation: Making Sedimentary Rocks

1. Processes that break up the Earth's crust.
2. Small pieces of sediment from broken rock.

3. The sediment slowly dropped to the bottom of the jar.

4. 66.6 years.

12.4. Soil Conservation: How Much of the Earth Is Usable Soil?

1. Answers will vary and could include farming and sites for building.

2. Answers will vary and could include bulldozing soil for construction and removing vegetation from soil, which increases the rate of erosion.

12.5. Physical Weathering of Rocks: Sugar Cube Breakdown

1. The sugar cubes were smaller and more irregular.

2. Shaking represents erosion. The sugar cubes represent rocks.

3. The sugar cubes did not change in composition—only in appearance.

12.6. Mineral Hardness: Mineral Ranks

1. Answers will vary.

2. Answers will vary.

3. Talc.

12.7. Cross Section of the Earth: Egg Modeling

1. The eggshell represents the Earth's crust, the egg white is the mantle, the yolk represents the core, and the pinprick inside the yolk represents the inner core.

2. Answers will vary and could include the fact that the egg and the Earth have similar layers, but the egg and the Earth are not exactly the same shape.

12.8. Porosity of Soil Samples: Soil's Holding Power

1. Answers will vary.

2. Answers will vary.

12.9. Groundwater and Permeability: Just Passing Through

1. Water in the cup of clay remained on top of the clay. In the other cup, some water permeated the soil.

2. The cup of soil represented the permeable substance; the cup of clay represented the impermeable substance.

3. Answers will vary. The activity demonstrates that water accumulates on top of impermeable surfaces.

12.10. Water in the Ocean: Sink or Float?

1. Float.
2. Sink.
3. Salt water is denser than freshwater. When the two are mixed, salt water sinks beneath freshwater.

12.11. Ocean Currents: Temperatures Start the Motion

1. It sinks.
2. The meltwater and the water in the beaker would eventually mix together (diffuse).

12.12. Bottle Eruption: Volcanic Activity

1. The bottle represents the volcano.
2. Red foam represents lava.
3. The chemicals inside the bottle represent magma.

Section 13. Earth's History

13.1. Inferences from Fossils: Who Was Here?

1. Evidence is information one gathers directly. An inference is a conclusion drawn from evidence.
2. Answers will vary, but the evidence might suggest that the animal was a meat eater that flew, used claws to kill prey, stood on its back legs, and used its tail for balance.

13.2. Magnetic Rocks: Lodestones

1. No.
2. Yes.
3. Yes. The rock that was temporarily magnetized can also magnetize another magnet.

13.3. Radioactive Rocks: The Age of Rocks

1. One-fourth; one-eighth; one-sixteenth.
2. Three thousand years old.

13.4. Continental Drift: Puzzling Over the Continents

1. Answers will vary.
2. Answers will vary.

13.5. Strength of Earthquakes: It's the Cracker's Fault

1. Fault lines.

2. The cracker used in step 5; the cracker used in step 5.

3. When fault lines are rough and uneven, rock movement creates strong earthquakes.

13.6. Fossil Molds and Casts: Making Fossils

1. The coin—it is easier to press the clay around a firm object.

2. When an organism dies, it makes a mold in soft sediment. The mold gets filled with material that forms a cast.

3. Cast.

13.7. Glaciers: Ice in Motion

1. Soil. The card rearranged particles and disturbed the surface of the sand-salt mixture.

2. Glacier.

3. Glaciers disturb the Earth's surface, pushing aside or picking up objects as they move along.

13.8. Deformation of Rocks: Rocks Under Stress

1. Tension stress.

2. Shear stress pulls the marshmallow in more than one direction.

3. Compression stress squeezes and shortens rocks, tension stress pulls rocks apart, and shear stress distorts the shapes of rocks.

13.9. Geologic Time Scale Model: Earth's History on a Football Field

1. Oldest evidence of life: 3,800,000,000 years ago (82 yards)

2. Oldest fish fossils: 510,000,000 years ago (11 yards)

3. Homo sapiens appear in fossil record: 100,000 years ago—(0.002 yards)

4. Just over 80 yards

13.10. Graded Bedding: Breaking the Law

1. This activity demonstrates that large particles of sediment settle before small particles. Finding rocks with large particles can help identify the oldest layer.

2. The arrangement of layers of heavy and coarse particles at the bottom is called *graded bedding*. Large particles settle before small ones.

13.11. Seismic Waves: Human Wave Form

1. A P-wave began at one end of the line when the teacher pushed one student. Each student in turn felt the compression.

2. An S-wave began at one end of the line when a student bent at the waist. This pulled down the next student, which pulled the next student, continuing the motion down the line.

13.12. Mountain Building: Paper Peaks

1. Your hands represent the forces causing plates to collide. The newspaper represents the colliding plates and the resulting mountains.

2. The paper crumples and bends, forming folds.

3. When two plates collide, the crust between them is crumpled and folded like the newspaper.

Section 14. Meteorology

14.1. Temperature Inversions: Weather Patterns and Pollution

1. The cold water represents cold dense air, and the hot water represents warm, less dense air.

2. The hot water floated on top of the cold water.

3. The hot water sat on top of the cold water, just as warm air sits on top of cool air.

14.2. Cloud Formation: The Cloudy Bottle

1. Adding the alcohol created high humidity.

2. Squeezing the bottle increased the pressure.

3. Decreased.

14.3. Warm Air Rises: Refrigerated Balloons

1. The room-temperature balloon.

2. The refrigerated balloon.

3. Refrigerating a balloon cools the air inside it, slowing the air molecules and enabling them to get closer together.

14.4. Water Vapor: Dew on the Beaker

1. Answers will vary depending on relative humidity.

2. Answers will vary depending on relative humidity.

3. At night, when the Sun is no longer warming Earth, the surface cools. Water will condense as it cools.

14.5. Rain Gauge: Let It Pour

1. Answers will vary and can include planning daily activities, knowing whether or not to work in the soil, and understanding the availability of water in the ground.

2. Snow cannot be measured with this device. Snow can be measured in inches from a flat surface. The snow can be transferred to a rain gauge; after it melts, you can find the liquid equivalent.

14.6. The Loss of Ozone: Oxygen Is Not Just for Breathing

1. A free chlorine atom can remove one oxygen atom from an ozone molecule.
2. CFC molecules.
3. They can avoid the use of CFCs.

14.7. Temperature: Do You Want That in Celsius or Fahrenheit?

1. To determine temperature.
2. Celsius.
3. Answers will vary.

14.8. Heat Transfer: Spiraling Upward

1. The spiral slowly rotated.
2. The spiral moved because warm air from the candle moved upward by convection.

14.9. Read a Climatogram: Quick Take on Climate

1. December; August.
2. July; February.
3. Answers will vary.

14.10. Air Has Weight: Living Under Pressure

1. The free end of the stick flew upward.
2. The stick did not move.
3. The air's weight held down the newspapers covering the meter stick.

Answer Key

14.11. Make It Rain: Bottle Rainstorm

1. Water condensed on the plate.
2. a. Hot water in the jar.
   b. Ice in the plate.
   c. Water drops falling from the plate.

14.12. Winds: Air Masses in Motion

1. Earth's axis; Earth; winds.
2. The water drops moved toward the right and formed curved paths.
3. The water drops were moved in a curving path in the same way that winds are moved by the Earth's rotation.

Section 15. The Universe

15.1. Telescopes: An Eye on the Universe

1. The lens near the eye is the eyepiece lens; the other is the objective lens.
2. The object was upside down.
3. A star's orientation is not important, since there is really no "up" or "down" in space.

15.2. Light Years: Universal Time

1. 500 seconds.
2. 14,986.66 seconds.
3. The distance light travels in a given amount of time is the basis of the measurement.

15.3. Star Constellations: How Many Do You Know?

1. Answers will vary. Constellations are patterns created by stars.
2. Answers will vary.

15.4. Viewing Constellations: Moving Patterns in the Sky

1. Constellations appear to be in different regions of the sky on different nights.
2. Answers will vary.

15.5. The Gyroscopic Effect: Spacecraft Navigation

1. The pencil fell over because of gravity.

2. The pencil stood for a few seconds.

3. A spinning object.

15.6. Space Shuttle Orbits: Holding Onto Your Marbles

1. In a circular path; the plate provided a circular path for the marble.

2. When the marble moved from the plate to the desktop, it moved in a straight line. The plate was no longer present to provide the circular path.

3. The marble represents a space rocket or shuttle, and the ridges on the rim of the plate represent gravity.

15.7. Gravity and Space Instruments: Writing in Space

1. Yes.

2. No. The pen did not work well in the upside-down position.

3. Gravity; pen.

15.8. Visible Light: A Blend of Colors

1. The colors of the rainbow.

2. White light is made up of several colors.

3. Violet has the shortest wavelength; red has the longest.

15.9. Infrared Light: Feel the Heat

1. Answers will vary depending on the type of infrared bulb used. The light may be red.

2. Answers will vary.

3. Answers will vary. Students may say the infrared light is warmer than visible light.

15.10. Star Magnitude: The Brightness of Stars

1. No.

2. Distance can reduce the magnitude. As distance increases, the amount of light that reaches Earth decreases.

15.11. Inertia in Space: Objects Keep Moving

1. Answers will vary.

2. Friction inferred with movement of the marble.

3. Yes. A lubricant reduces friction.

15.12. The Parallax Effect: A Different Perspective

1. The ruler seemed to shift.
2. Observing the ruler through the right eye changed your perspective.

Section 16. The Solar System

16.1. Planetary Revolutions: Birthdays on Mercury and Jupiter

1. Answers will vary depending on students' ages.
2. Mercury moves around the Sun relatively quickly, so a year is short.
3. Venus.

16.2. Jupiter's Atmosphere: A Stormy Planet

1. The contents swirled.
2. The great swirling storms.
3. Gases.

16.3. Orbiting the Sun: Earth's Trip Around the Sun

1. Ellipse.
2. Answers will vary. Students might define an ellipse as an oval shape.

16.4. Planet Formations: How the Planets Were Made

1. The two drops formed one large drop.
2. The third drop became part of the large drop.
3. Formation of a planet.
4. Small masses collided and formed larger masses that eventually became the planets.

16.5. Surviving on the Moon: Lunar Trek

1. Answers will vary. Students might have selected oxygen, the compass, or the radio.
2. Answers will vary. Students might have selected matches, which would not light on the Moon; the shotgun, which they would not have to use since there's no life on the Moon; or raisins, which they would not be able to eat while wearing space suits.

16.6. Solar Eclipse: Blocking the Sun

1. The Sun.
2. The Moon.
3. Earth.

16.7. Astrolabe: Medieval Measurements

1. The purpose of the astrolabe is to find the altitude of an object above the horizon. In medieval times, it was used to determine latitude.

2. Answers will vary.

16.8. Precession of Earth: Spinning on the Axis

1. Answers will vary; 26,000 years.

2. Due to precession, the northern axis of Earth does not always point to the same star. During part of precession, the axis points toward Polaris. During another part, it points toward Vega.

16.9. Lunar Surface Regolith: After the Meteorites Hit the Moon

1. The rock represents a meteor, and the crumbs are regolith.

2. The bread was more cratered and the crumbs more abundant after step 3.

3. Rye.

16.10. Weight and Gravity: Weighing In on the Earth, Moon, and Sun

1. Answers will vary.

2. Answers will vary; answers will vary.

3. Yes. The Sun is larger than Earth and has a greater gravity. The Moon is smaller than Earth and has less gravity.

16.11. Auroras: Party Lights in the Sky

1. Auroras are best viewed near the poles.

2. The auroras will be brighter.

3. Answers will vary. A glowing oval caused by ionized gases around the pole will be visible.

16.12. Moon Face: The Moon's Revolution and Rotation

1. Once.

2. They are the same.